WOOD
WOOD
WOOD
WOOD

MY PRIME TIME
MIDDLE AGE IS ONLY THE BEGINNING!

Nelson Aspen

NEW HOLLAND

First published in 2014 by New Holland Publishers Pty Ltd

London • Sydney • Cape Town • Auckland

The Chandlery Unit 114 50 Westminster Bridge Road London SE1 7QY United Kingdom

1/66 Gibbes Street Chatswood NSW 2067 Australia

Wembley Square First Floor Solan Road Gardens Cape Town 8001 South Africa

218 Lake Road Northcote Auckland New Zealand

www.newhollandpublishers.com

A record of this book is held at the British Library and the National Library of Australia.

ISBN 9781742574646

Managing Director: Fiona Schultz

Publisher: Linda Williams

Project Editor: Simona Hill

Designer: Keisha Galbraith

Production Director: Olga Dementiev

Printer: Toppan Leefung Printing Ltd

10 9 8 7 6 5 4 3 2 1

Keep up with New Holland Publishers on Facebook

www.facebook.com/NewHollandPublishers

CONTENTS

DEDICATION

To the greatest examples of ageing well—Mother and Dad. And to my best friend: there's no one else I'd rather grow old with than Glenn. Our friendship is the touchstone of my adult life and makes every birthday worth celebrating.

FOREWORD

In television, 'prime time' is designated as the most-watched, and therefore most lucrative block of hours in the viewing schedule. Fortunately for us, 'prime time' in life is considerably longer than the four hours it lasts in the world of television and can be stretched over the course of 20 or 30 years, depending on how much luck you have, and the level of liveliness that you put into that life. When the indulged kids of the Post-War population (a.k.a. The 'Me' Generation) came of age in the late twentieth century, society seemed to become more focused on the pleasures of the youth culture than at any other time in history. Life expectancy increased and the world's communities grew. Prime time changed, too. For people considered middle aged (a vague time span, but for the sake of argument let's broadly estimate that as early 40s through late 50s), they are experiencing 'prime time'.

If they're not, they SHOULD BE! During these years we are at the peak of our powers... our personal bests. It's our time. We're the stars of the show. If the future belongs to the young, then that means that the here and now are all about us. I believe that wholeheartedly… and I'm here to make sure you do, as well.

After some very positive publishing experiences I had been thinking about my next literary endeavor. I didn't want to pursue/pitch something merely for the sake of churning out fodder. Even in a world full of e-books, we still have to consider the trees. Having conducted thousands of celebrity interviews, I thought perhaps a volume of 'conversations' that ended up on the cutting room floor might make interesting reading, until I realized that there's a REASON why film and video editors pick out the best bits and splice out the rest.

Travel was another subject I was keen to tackle. Having been fortunate enough to visit many of the world's most spectacular destinations, both as a tourist and as a journalist on assignment, I knew it would be fun to revisit some of my globe-trotting adventures, as well as offer some guidance and perspective on the pleasure and pain of travel. No doubt I'll write that one day… but I think my passport needs a few more stamps in it first.

As you'll later read, I had big plans for my half-century birthday celebration. Linda Williams, my publisher, was on the guest list for the party (and wound up being the winner of the 'guest who travelled farthest' honours). So was my beloved colleague, Melissa Doyle, for ten years my daily broadcast partner on the Australian morning show, *Sunrise*. I knew that 50 was too major a milestone to go unannounced, so why not write about THAT? Excitedly I called Linda with my ideas and she immediately 'got it'.

So, here we are. Once I hit 50, I would always be 'over fifty'… so why not hone my expertise on living well in middle age and share it with folks who are interested? Heck, I'll only keep getting wiser about it, right?

I set out to encompass all the aspects of what I think are important issues for people close in age to me. Health and fitness, of course… before my TV career took off, they were my 'bread-and-butter' and still the love of my life. Diet and nutrition—you are what you eat—and this becomes especially noticeable with time. Fiscal responsibility—the fact is, money makes the world go around and it's as necessary a component to quality of life as a sound mind and body. Attitude—so much of happiness is mental, emotional and spiritual. It needs to be worked out like any other body part. Of course, my professional (and a big chunk of my personal) life is celebrity-oriented, so you'll find a collection of humorous and helpful observations, anecdotes and interactions with some famous people I know, whom you may already feel like you know, too.

I think you'll find more than a few helpful suggestions to help you make life less enervating and more interesting. Don't feel compelled to read the chapters in any particular order. I want this to be the kind of book you can pick up and put down intermittently, referring back to when you have a certain subject matter that is on your mind. Don't be afraid to pull out the highlight pen and mark it up. I'd be only too pleased to know that you are making notes that apply to your own life.

Most of all, I want to share the joyful experiences I find that life has to offer as we get older. 'You're not getting older, you're getting better,' may have become a cliché, but only because it's true.

My Prime Time: Middle Age is Only the Beginning!

HOW DO YOU DO!

MONDAY, JULY 1, 1963

The US post office was introducing the new zip code, President John F Kennedy was in the White House and Alfred Hitchcock's *The Birds* was big business at the cinema box office. A new soap opera called *General Hospital* had housewives hooked on television (although *The Beverly Hillbillies* still ruled in prime time)… yellow 'smiley faces' were springing up on bumper stickers, T-shirts and posters everywhere. A new comic book character named *Spider-Man* was giving *Batman & Robin* a run for their money. Weird contraptions called lava lamps were lighting up the hippest homes. In spite of the new Beatlemania craze, *The Lion Sleeps Tonight* was topping the music charts and blaring out of transistor radios all across America as the lazy, hazy days of summer rolled on.

On the Aspen farm outside Philadelphia, excitement was mounting over the arrival of Joyce Ann and Nelson's first child together. They had married the summer before, each bringing two children from previous marriages, and their newly blended family was soon to be 'The Brady Bunch-Plus-One'. Plans were already underway to welcome the child whom Doc Aspen had already nicknamed 'The Prince of Pennsylvania'. Consequently, as Joyce Ann floated in the pool, her swollen belly soaking up the sun, she kept repeating to her mother, Anna, "It's gotta be a boy, it's gotta be a boy".

Even at 34 (practically middle aged by the standards of the day), Joyce Ann was relaxed about childbirth especially since everything had been arranged with her characteristic fastidious planning. The nursery was painted, the bassinet readied, the rocking chair polished and a nanny on standby. Because of her unusual blood type, O negative, the baby would be induced after Doc finished his medical rounds and they could wait for the obstetrician to finish dinner before joining them to deliver their child. Of course, her official due date wasn't until July 15, but Joyce Ann had made a life-long habit of always being early… compulsively so (one of many traits she would pass down to her youngest child). The sooner their bundle of joy arrived, the sooner the five kids could all begin enjoying the summer holidays.

So, Joyce Ann relaxed and applied another coat of baby oil to enrich her already bronzed body, still Ursula Andress-statuesque in spite of the protuberance of pregnancy. She lighted a cigarette and sipped a martini… Doc would be home soon and they'd head to the hospital.

Memorial Hospital occupied most of the block at the intersection of High and Biddle Streets. Doc's practice was across the street, where the couple had first lived as newlyweds and where now his mother, Katharine, resided. On the opposite corner was the Quaker Elementary School where the younger Aspen kids would be starting classes in September. West Chester, Pennsylvania, was a quiet and historic town dominated by lush farms, Greek revival architecture and green, rolling hills. It was in this part of the country that the Wyeth family of artists achieved prominence and George Washington led his troops during the Revolutionary War.

Joyce Ann and Doc met with Dr Abbott for the inducement, after which he cheerily told them, "I'll be back after dinner and we'll deliver that baby". Less than an hour later, Joyce Ann was having contractions and it was clear that the obstetrician's dining schedule was not going to accommodate the infant's early arrival.

As a nurse helped Joyce Ann onto a gurney and began to wheel her toward the delivery room, Doc found himself giggling nervously. A tough-as-nails and very macho 38-year-old orthopedic surgeon and Navy veteran, the prospect of unexpectedly having to deliver his own child filled him with anxiety, which manifested itself in fits of giggles. In full-blown labour and careening down the corridor flat on her back, Joyce Ann's usual poised demeanour had evaporated and ceded to her fiery Germanic and Cherokee Indian roots as she cursed skyward, "Jesus Christ, let me remember that this son-of-a-bitch is LAUGHING while this is happening to me!"

This continued throughout the process of Doc and the nurses scrubbing up to enter the delivery room (it was highly unusual for expectant fathers to accompany their wives at this stage of the process). He giggled. She cursed. Dr Abbot's answering service was alerted and there was no stopping Mother Nature at this point. As Joyce Ann hungrily grabbed at the ether mask, Doc could see the baby's head appear. The giggling stopped and his expertise kicked in. He'd delivered more than 400 babies during the war overseas, but never one of his own. Well… if you want something done right, he reasoned, do it yourself.

Nelson Page Aspen, Jr. was brought into the world at 6:59 pm as Dr Abbott bolted into the room. Doc proudly handed over his new son for the requisite cord-cutting and clean up. The kid was just in time for dinner. Not surprisingly, a life-long love affair with food was in store for him… along with many amazing adventures!

NATURE AND NURTURE: IS THERE A LONGEVITY GENE?

O f all the perks of my job as an American Entertainment Correspondent and Presenter for a host of international media outlets, the most marvelous for me is the fact that I can enjoy 'dipping my toe' into the pool of notoriety on occasion, but live my routine day-to-day existence in relative anonymity. While many of you may be familiar with my career in front of the camera and on the microphone, I'm excited to be introduced to an even wider audience who have flattered me with the purchase of this book.

As you see by the chapter headings, you're in store for some fun facts… insights, anecdotes and more than a few celebrity encounters. First, I want you to find out a little about me and what led me to where I am today as I write this at age 50+… and what forces and incidents shaped and influenced me along the way. I have frequently been described as "Hollywood's happiest TV personality" and I find that a high honor and a bit of a responsibility. This book will relate, chapter by chapter, the elements that contribute to making me wholly happy… and my desire is that it will help you achieve similar results not only regardless of your age, but because of it.

Where will you be in your 50s? If you'd asked me that in my child-hood, I'd have probably answered that I would be a married grandfather who worked as a school teacher (I loved playing 'school'... especially giving tests). Father figures on our TV screens at that time, such as Mike Brady and Pa Ingalls, were warm and wise... imagine how messed up I'd be if all I had to nurture me was Don Draper, Charlie Harper and the real househusbands of Beverly Hills!

As the world began to open up to me, I knew 'performance' was in my destiny, so by 50 I thought I was certain to be a movie star or at least the patriarch on one of my favorite soap operas. In my salad days, I foresaw 50 as very much the height of my career as a talk-show host *à la* Regis Philbin. Interestingly, the professional aspects of all those dreams were somewhat recognized. It's with hindsight that I can determine how I ended up on such a twisting, turning and terrific life path... and am still excited about where the journey will lead me next.

I came of age working on a now-defunct daytime serial called *Search for Tomorrow*. In its final episode, after an amazing 35-year television run, the two lead characters looked at each other reflectively and 'Stu' asked the always hopeful 'Joanne' what she was searching for in life. "Tomor-row," she answered plainly, with a slight grin. "And I can't wait!"

In the early 1970s, long before most people could even define 'obesity', I kept growing bigger and bigger... perpetuated by Mom's misguided attempts at satisfying me with so-called diet food. If cookies were advertised as 'lite' or 'lo-cal', she figured it would be okay for me to eat the entire box of them. By the time I got to high school, I was the finest actor/writer/artist in school... and certainly the widest. Bursting out of my husky-sized clothes, and suffering the cruel taunts of my peers, I was miserable. Bullying may be discussed on every talk show these days (certainly social media has exacerbated and metastasized the problem), but back then it was merely an unfortunate part of adolescence many of us had to live with. Too fat to participate in athletic activities, I was eventually excused from gym class altogether, so the vicious cycle continued. It would take something pretty significant to snap me out of it as I closed in on 200 pounds of stretch marks and flab.

That significant something was losing out on the lead in the school musical, *The Boy Friend* (notable as the musical that launched the Broadway career of Julie Andrews). There was no doubt I was the better actor and singer than the student who was cast in the title role, but with my appearance, all I could reasonably portray was a character part: the old geezer. Incidentally, I've been fortunate to interview the divine Dame Julie so many times that we've become 'professional friends' over the years, but we really bonded when I told her my first musical production was *The Boy Friend*. She assumed I'd played Tony the lead, but when I said I'd actually been 'Percival', she threw her head back with a hearty laugh and exclaimed, "Oh! The old man!" Harumph!

Passing as 'Percival' wouldn't be too hard. With my corpulent body, all that was needed was some gray spray paint in my hair and a few drawn-on wrinkles. I was gutted by the injustice (and, oddly enough, surprised: even though my first professional job had been at age 8 playing Piglet in a production of *The House at Pooh Corner*). With eight weeks of rehearsal, I decided to wreak vengeance by fasting off the fat. Not a healthy decision and one I'd never recommend or try again… but it was the drastic action I needed to kick-start a weight loss. By opening night, I was downright skinny and my now-baggy costume hung off my newly bony frame. In the next production, *Once Upon a Mattress*, the romantic leading role of Sir Harry was mine. Vengeance, finally, ha ha!

I remember those days with almost no objectivity whatsoever… all the memories are skewed by my perception of being a picked-on, pimply and pudgy teenager. It seemed like most of Bishop Shanahan's graduating class of 1980 stayed in the Chester County environs, while I fled as quickly as possible to New York. Where else would the student voted 'class actor' go?

I divorced myself not only from the adolescent angst of those years, but from the people I subconsciously held responsible for the torment: my peers. New York meant new friends… a reinvented and independent me… as well as the confidence to develop into my own semi-adult person. In the pre-internet days of the early '80s, keeping in touch required more effort than nowadays, so I let go of all those relationships; even the good ones. The only return I made was the five-year reunion, which was more of a chance to salve my still-sore wounds of puberty: showing up rail-thin in a flashy suit and with a pretty blonde girl from Manhattan as my date. I was determined to show that 'living well was the best revenge' and I made a quick night of it before hurrying off again early the next morning.

Fast-forward another quarter century and I was tracked down by a classmate who wanted to plan a 30-year reunion and was willing to accommodate my travel schedule from Hollywood, since I'd been the most conspicuously absent grad in the intervening years. Through email, Karen and I caught up and cultivated a new friendship beyond anything we knew as teenagers. She remembered things that had long been deleted from my memory bank and also delighted me with all the news and gossip about 'whatever happened to… so and so' from those bygone years. I had to check the yearbooks again just to recall who some of those people were! There were the requisite marriages, divorces, deaths and disabilities that come with life… my own existence so blessedly untouched by any real disasters that I somehow managed to remain a perpetual youngster in my own mind. Meanwhile, everybody else was becoming a grandparent!

The reunion date was set for May 2010, and would be an outdoor affair, graciously hosted by Karen and her husband—her high-school boyfriend. Of course, I couldn't resist buying a new suit for the occasion and was excited to make an entrance, yearbook in hand (no one else thought to bring one). After all, I was flying in from LA, baby! The first person to greet me was a smiling, matronly woman with arms spread wide open for a bear hug. I had absolutely no idea who she was. She certainly didn't look like anyone in that yearbook—well, maybe one of the teachers. As expected, everyone had changed with the decades… grayer hair… less hair… bigger hair… wider hips… walking limps… none of it mattered after a few minutes. Our shared history made us all friends… some of those friendships rekindled and ripened, others brand new. When we all huddled together in Karen's backyard so that one of her (teenage) sons could take a group photo, I realized that I had finally let go of all those post-puberty resentments that had not only shaped my adult life, but still managed to hold a negative grip on it. Lots of people look back on high school years as the best days of their lives. Not me! The torture of the teens wasn't anyone's fault or responsibility… my misery was my own. And it was permissible for me to let it go and like these people in spite of (or perhaps BECAUSE of) the era in which we all met. I was moved and forever changed by that backyard barbecue. The 'poor little fat kid' only existed in old photo albums. Thank you, sweet Karen.

Some older folks not only live in the past, but they hold on to grudges, slights, rivalries or other bitter entities. My class reunion proved to me that the real wisdom of age comes from living in the here and now, honouring but not clinging to, the past.

In 2013, one of those school chums emailed to notify me that our one-time student council president, pretty Sharon, had passed away after a long and ugly battle with cancer. She and I had been in all the same classes and clubs, having a friendly competition over the course of our shared time at Shanahan. She beat me for class president, but I was Valedictorian. If memory serves me correctly, we were co-editors at the newspaper, yearbook and literary magazine. She was a smart cookie, devout citizen and team player. I found out, through her obituary, that she was also a beloved mother and daughter who went through a horrific and painful journey's end. And I realized too that she was the smiling woman who first greeted me with a hug at the reunion. I'd known about the passing of other classmates… but for Sharon, I cried.

I watched my grandparents go through the loss of friends and siblings… and now I see my parents attending many more funerals than weddings. Being 'the last man standing' isn't easy… but it gets easier with the recognition that it's inevitable. Maybe the Irish have the right idea with big, boisterous wakes for their departed loved ones. If I can be remembered fondly and with gusto at a gathering as filled with kindness as that 30th reunion, I will certainly smile down.

"The time to be happy is now. The place to be happy is here. The way to be happy is to make others so." Elbert Hubbard

Time *magazine quoted a study that revealed that, "About 80 per cent of young people who say they have a good relationship with their parents are also happier with life in general."*

As of now, my parents are amazingly independent, vital and active octogenarians who look poised to live well into their 90s just as three of my four grandparents did. For all the advances in medical science, diet and exercise, I believe that the best asset you can have in your quest for a long, quality life is a good gene pool. While I admittedly wish I were a few inches taller and could pick and choose exactly where I do and don't have hair on my body, I have no real complaints.

In 1995, at age 66, my mother (born 1929; they still blame the Great Depression on her!) had a heart attack and subsequently required emergency triple bypass surgery. That was followed the next day by a small stroke (with no lasting effects, mercifully, except for a propensity for mood swings… something she denies. "I'm not angry, I'm honest.") but the doctors told her it would buy her another five years. "Two weeks later, two of the three bypasses failed, so the surgeons put stents in to compensate. Eighteen years later, here I am! I was supposed to be gone but I'm too ferocious! I don't even remember who the doctor was, but if I saw him now I'd punch him! I'm sure he didn't do anything wrong, but he didn't do anything right, either. It's like having a cake collapse in the oven: Sometimes, that's just the way it goes."

Mom will often remark on her own vitality. "I can't explain it. I am constantly amazed at how good I feel 'cause I'm not supposed to feel like this. I have all kinds of problems, but I just feel so glad to be here and alive, and physically strong and healthy that it's a shock when I look in the mirror." Her father died of a heart attack a week after turning 63 ("I suddenly became aware that tomorrow is not going to be like today. I stopped looking forward to things. Back then, we thought 60 was old. It was a wake-up call about mortality.") Her mother made it to 99 and felt very well until almost the end. ("Her only real problems were emotional because it was a sad time for her knowing she couldn't be independent anymore and time was limited.") So, to what does she attribute her seemingly super powers? To Mom, it's a marvelous mystery. "I have no idea what's coursing through my veins. It just IS. This feeling is like breathing, you don't think about it. It can be frustrating to feel this good and not be able to do everything I want to try. Like skateboarding or riding a zip line."

Every Friday night, Mother and Dad go out for dinner with their circle of local chums. It's a ritual each of them looks forward to. Amazingly, my parents are the youngest of the group. "I was proud of being the only one who could read the menu when we'd all go out for dinner, but after botched cataract surgery I'm as blind as a bat. That's the only physical thing that frustrates me. I have pairs of glasses everywhere," Mom explains. Being social and maintaining those friendships are key elements for keeping my parents so active.

I should be quick to point out, however, that my folks are far from shuffling around a world full of retirees. In addition to more grandchildren and great-grandchildren than I can tally, they have an entire separate network of young friends who help them out with everything from yard work to dog walking to handyman duties (I am still pressing

Dad to turn over the car keys, even though I have to admit he's still a very cautious and capable driver.) "I relate well to young people," Mom explains. "I never feel out of place around them… or anywhere for that matter. All my friends, young and old, make me smile and give me joy."

It occurred to me while running on a city sidewalk, with its pavement made hazardously uneven by the mighty power of the lush trees planted along the street, that family trees are a lot like real ones: their roots should give you strength… not strangle or up-end you. You have well and truly reached maturity when you realize that your parents are fallible humans and, genetics aside, it's up to you to determine what traits of theirs you will carry and pass on.

You can also create your own family. Why not surround yourself with the people you enjoy and trust the most? My cousin, Keith, and I didn't meet until we were in our early 20s and, had the meeting not been orchestrated by relatives, we might never have met at all. The blood ties alone spurred our friendship, but it is our commonalities that keep us close. On the other hand, I have long considered Australian TV's Melissa Doyle my 'satellite sister', when we began a ten-year long-distance professional relationship that blossomed into a close camaraderie. Our 'in-person' times are all too brief, but in this era of Skype and texts, we are never far apart… as close as siblings… and always there to support each other. I am also "Uncle Nelson" to assorted nieces and nephews all over the world!

If you're fortunate, taking personal responsibility for your own happiness is a trait that has been instilled during your childhood… through the example set by your elders and the encouragement you received at home and school. However, as modern times have evolved, our culture has become permissive, so a lot of people have missed out on these lessons. It's never too late. Grab the reins of your own life and don't be washed along like so much flotsam and jetsam. You are a unique, one-of-a-kind creation who can achieve great happiness and success.

It is not about being anti-social or morally superior, although it can very often take a lot of strength to rise above the communal 'easy way out' that society likes to thrust upon its citizens, with its messages of 'you deserve this', or 'why should you be deprived of that?' Standing on your own two feet (or 'pulling yourself up by the bootstraps' as they said in the old days) results in a sense of mastery over a tough situation or challenge. Personal responsibility will help with all things great and small, from portion control at the dinner table to facing an otherwise frightening medical treatment.

Taking charge, seizing opportunities and controlling whatever forces are within your reach are ways to make your choices count. When I was a high school senior, Dad impressed upon me how beneficial it would be if I could manage to become class Valedictorian. It wasn't something I was pressured to accomplish… he presented it as a goal to reach. While the Salutatorian may have been in her bedroom cramming over text books and sweating it out to memorize facts and figures, I proceeded with my own usual and simple desire to perform well. Looking back, it's not surprising that I began my Valedictory speech with this poem by George Leo Robertson:

Sea of Life

Embarked on the sea of life,
Destiny and duration unknown,
Waters always changing,
Calm, peaceful, beautiful,
Fearful, dangerous, bleak,
All unpredictable, all uncontrolled.

But my ship is controlled.
For I guide it through the changing waters
With a mind and heart,
Stronger and greater than the sea.

"After forty a woman has to choose between losing her figure or her face. My advice is to keep your face, and stay sitting down."
British author, Dame Barbara Cartland (1901–2000).

I respectfully disagree with the Dame. I think sitting down is a bad idea. In fact, no one in my family is very good at sitting still! Maybe that's why we live so long: you can't hit a moving target...

I look to my grandmothers. Not a day goes by that I don't think of those fine ladies; my maternal 'Mom Mom' Anna, who lived to be nearly 100... and paternal 'Gram' Katharine who passed away at 97. These were two women who could not have been more opposite, but it's worth seeing if there might be a common link to explain their amazing longevity.

Anna was born in 1908, the eighth of fourteen children... raised poor but happy on a peach farm in New Jersey. She never ventured much further than a hundred miles from the place where she grew up, married and raised her daughters. The quintessential blue-collar homemaker of post-Depression America, she was a teetotalling, neat-nick who stuck to ironing, polishing, watching her soap operas and NFL games. You didn't put your feet on the coffee table in her home and every pillow and piece of bric-a-brac had a specific, designated location. Modest, prim and soft spoken, the most outrageous displays of excitement she exhibited were reserved for hands of gin rummy and one memorable time when she got her hand caught in the electric mixer, baking a cake.

Katharine, on other hand, was born in 1898 and orphaned shortly thereafter. All alone in the world, she was raised by a devout order of Episcopal nuns, before becoming a nurse shortly after World War I. She later married and had one son... around whom her entire universe revolved. That, however, didn't keep her from divorcing (a rarity in the 1950s) and becoming a social creature... traveling the world, smoking cigarettes and drinking Manhattans. Her little apartment was packed full of a lifetime's collection of souvenirs and mementoes, everything a little dusty and slightly yellowed by the ever-present haze of cigarette smoke.

While Anna's roast dinners and baked desserts were the scrumptious stuff of legend, Katharine routinely covered up her burned pineapple upside down cake with store-bought whipped topping. Anna chatted and crocheted afghans in a corner, while Katharine risked fracturing a hip to play a round of Twister with the kids, or would sing and dance to songs from a bygone era. Anna fretted about the weather from inside her living room, while Katharine barely took notice of it as she hopped aboard a plane, tour bus or cruise ship.

Scrutinizing their backgrounds and health histories, I can only come up with one tangible thing they had in common: their grandson... me!

What Anna and Katharine, and most people who enjoy long lives have, is what I assume to be 'the longevity gene'. While longevity is in one's DNA, I also think longevity must also have something to do with your point of view—an attitude or outlook, if you will. A happy nature and positive attitude, I believe, is not always easy to muster in the face of life's challenges (and God knows my grandmothers, like everyone else, had their share of tough times), but it's just as important as any other component of good health. Helping to support and celebrate others will also buoy your own positivity and bring good fortune.

Most people who know my Mother automatically assume that she is a sweet, happy joyful person... even her name has 'Joy' in it (Joyce Ann). Her stoicism has pulled her through many challenging periods. She'll readily admit to having a mantle filled with 'invisible Oscars' awarded for putting on a positive front when required. She taught me that sometimes it's better to paint on a smile than spiral down into a blue funk. If you try it long enough, it can actually become REAL and you may just find yourself to be happy anyway. I go one better and for many years have kept a 'book of blessings'. Just scrawling down four or five things daily, for which I am grateful, helps me keep perspective. You can't be too low when you give thanks for loved ones... health... a roof over your head... or maybe even a few hours of quality sleep. Over the decades, these journals have not only helped keep my spirits high and my glass half full, but they are treasured diaries of my life's ups and downs.

Mother taught me that a forced smile is better than no smile. If painting on a smile can make you feel happier, it may also infect others with a sense of optimism.

Train yourself to be an optimist. So what if they accuse you of being a Pollyanna? They're probably just jealous because they think you've found the secret to happiness. When I first moved into my current apartment building, I would occasionally bump into a neighbour who was obviously not a morning person. She'd slog in and out of the elevator and all but grumble to me as I cheerily chirped my sunrise salutations… either sweaty and rosy-cheeked from a pre-dawn run, or laden with laundry (no waiting for machines in the wee hours). I kept at her until she finally began to engage in little conversations. "I can't believe how much you get done before I even leave for work… For goodness sake, what time must you go to bed?" A year later, after these regular encounters, she now always breaks into a smile as big as mine when she sees me. "There's Mr Smiles!" she'll say. Or, "Here comes Happy Man." Something tells me she arrives at work a bit more upbeat… and spreads a little sunshine of her own.

Keep your eyes open for the little miracles that are all around. And when things seem as grey and dreary as can be: smile! It has the power to change the situation into a brighter one. As Dolly Parton said in *Steel Magnolias,* "Smile! It increases your face value."

LaToya Jackson said at age 57, "You can't cry when you're eating candy."

Take full advantage of the times when you're feeling good by making friends and cultivating relationships with the people around you. Then you'll have a built-in support system for when you're not in tip top condition. Research studies say that strong social relationships can increase survival odds by 50 per cent. Exercising traits such as conscientiousness and being a team player do the same. Joining a book club, neighbourhood association, PTA or doing community service work may just increase your life expectancy while boosting your brain's cognitive function and keeping your Karma sparkling! Think about it: Julia Child, even with all that artery-clogging cuisine, didn't even become *The French Chef* until she was 51 and she was still joyfully going strong until her death 40 years later! Some of Picasso's greatest master works were painted when he was well into his 50s.

For me, social interaction multiplied ten-fold when I finally moved back to NYC after 22 years in Los Angeles (you get a lesser sentence for murder!). In Hollywood, you're either isolated in the confines of your automobile bubble—and it had better be a fancy, expensive, eight-cylinder bubble, at that—or you're subjected to the loneliness of conversations revolving solely around the entertainment industry where time is delineated only by earthquakes or Academy Award ceremonies. In Manhattan, however, there are people everywhere… and showbiz is only one panel in the vast patchwork of professional, creative outlets that make up the fabric of the city. Just waiting on the curbside to cross a street, bumping along in a taxi cab or subway car, or strolling through the park provides opportunities to share some casual conversation or a smile. It can and does change your entire day if you just let it in.

My city support system is a vast network, but the core is comprised of Glenn (closer than a brother—my best friend in the world) whom I met when we were both kids working retail in Tommy Hilfiger's first-ever clothing store. My 'honorary wife' Marcia, was the first person to befriend me when I joined the soap opera *Search for Tomorrow* and we've been to hell and back together many times ever since. Darling, hilarious Marie became my 'sister from another mister' later in the run of the show and can make me laugh out loud with just a few words in an email.

I love the ability we Moderns have to create our own families; *The Golden Girls* had the right idea! I have no doubt that Glenn, Marcia, Marie and I will enjoy at least another 30 years together and perhaps one day they'll grant me permission to write a book about our loves, losses and misadventures. It would make *Sex and the City* look like a Disney Family Channel series.

Friends aren't always human. One of the best I ever had was my rescue dog, a Springer Spaniel I named Lois ('Lois Lane'... rescue, get it?). We had fifteen and a half fantastic years together and her companionship will never be forgotten... I wonder if it will ever be matched. I hope so: I'm keeping an eye out for the right pooch to come into my life one day. Meantime, I know Lois is watching over me and will be wiggling and wagging her stumpy tail when we eventually reunite at the Pearly Gates.

Don't underestimate the positive effects a pet can have on extending and enhancing a healthy life. Who can forget the images of the golden retriever therapy dogs brought to comfort the survivors of the Sandy Hook elementary school massacre? More and more hospitals and nursing homes are allowing animals to interact with patients to offer comfort, socialize and help reduce anxiety and stress. Actress Ashley Judd hardly makes a move without her licensed therapy dog, Shug. (Ashley was one of my fitness students and I've met Shug... he's a great little fellow.) She credits him with helping her cope with depression.

My parents have always had dogs and, even now with their infirmities, have two who completely delight them and dominate the household. They have a dog-walker and groomer, in addition to other dog-owning friends so it consequently opens them up to a broad social circle, as well.

I instinctively like dog owners because I think it says a lot about their nurturing capabilities (obviously that excludes the thugs who parade around aggressive curs, looking for a fight). That goes for the celebs I have met, too. Back when movie stars were first manufactured in the early part of the 20th century, little pooches were considered fashionable accessories. (There's a publicity shot of a young Joan Crawford with a tiny canine peering out from inside her overcoat with a caption reading, 'pockets are for pets!' Crawford, however, was a life-long dog lover and, by many accounts, treated her four-legged friends better than her own adopted children. Ditto legendary real estate mogul Leona Helmsley, who left the bulk of her personal fortune to her Maltese named Trouble.). Not much has changed: Look no further than Paris Hilton who seems to go through pets like most people go through socks. But, just like 'real' people, the stars who are true dog lovers are much more mellow than their footloose and fancy-free counterparts. I've had wonderful experiences with Jessica Biel and 'Tina', Charlize Theron and 'Tucker', and Jane Lynch and 'Olivia'. Drew Barrymore and I commiserated when we both lost our dogs around the same time. Bernadette Peters and Hugh Jackman keep it real, pooper-scooping after their doggies on the streets of NYC. Amanda Seyfried unwinds by teaching tricks to her beautiful Australian shepherd, Finn. If you bump into Jake Gyllenhaal, chances are his German shepherd, Atticus, is following closely behind. Jeremy Renner offered a $5000 reward for the safe return of his French bulldog, Hemi, who went missing in the canyons of Los Angeles. Hopefully the animal didn't suffer the same fate as those belonging to Jessica Simpson, Halle Berry, Ozzy Osbourne, Katherine Heigl and Demi Moore: all were victims of coyotes that roam the Hollywood Hills.

When I used to walk my springer spaniel, Lois, in LA's Runyon Canyon, she would gleefully bound up and down the rocky terrain, in tireless pursuit of her tennis ball or stick. One day, we ran into my fellow aerobics instructor pal, Bob Harper—now best known as the host of the wildly popular TV show, **The Biggest Loser.** *We met his lovely Rottweiler... also named Lois. What are the chances? Bob now has a mixed-breed small dog named Karl Lagerfeld.*

According to website WebMD, cortisol, the hormone associated with stress, lowers when you take some time out to spend with a pet (even watching fish) and the chemical associated with well-being (serotonin) is increased. Research has revealed many other health benefits for pet owners, including:

* Lower blood pressure and lower heart rates during rest.
* Lower levels of cholesterol and triglycerides, likely attributed to the lifestyles of pet owners.
* Lower risk of dying from cardiac disease, including heart failure.
* Ability to deal with/recover from depression.
* Lower risk of stroke.
* Can boost immune systems in children.

My parents have been life-long animal-lovers and, growing up, we had a menagerie of critters that ranged from cats, dogs, hamsters and rabbits to a Polish hen, pigeons, parakeets, fish, ducks, horses, a donkey and a goat named Samantha, who was more dog than our German shepherd. She'd jump a ride in the milkman's truck, hop up on the couch for a snuggle, or do tricks for guests. Unfortunately, she couldn't be broken of her incessant horn butting so back to auction she went. Mom and Dad, as they've gotten older, swear that every dog will be their last but they can never resist a canine in need of rescue and, as of this writing, dote upon a neurotic little Jack Russell/Chihuahua mix (Sonny).

Walking/playing with your pets, especially dogs, can produce myriad physical benefits in addition to the social ones. Everything from reduced obesity and arthritis pain to increased bone density. Say 'Woof!' Even if it's just pet-sitting or dog-walking, everybody wins.

> *Physical ability means next to nothing if you don't have the mental capacity to go along with it. Studies have shown that the brain benefits from being exercised, too. So tackle that crossword puzzle or organize a game of rummy and Scrabble to help maintain your noggin's agility and dexterity.*

Positivity and stress reduction affect every aspect of your lifestyle. Even your natural, inherent body clock can be put to good use. Like my Mother, I've always been an early riser. I once asked her why she supposed we were so naturally predisposed to adhering to the 'early to bed, early to rise' lifestyle. "We're excited to get up in the morning!" she immediately answered. You might laugh, but it's true—at least for us. That magical time in the early hours when I seem to have the whole world to myself is my most productive and happy part of the day. If I slept in, I might miss something. It's also my body's most natural time to go for a run… it's a bonus to be out there witnessing the first rays of sun, chirping of birds or the THWACK'ing sound of a newspaper hitting the doorstep, when the world is waking.

Of course, night owls contend that all the can't-miss moments happen while the moon is high; marathon card games, musical jam sessions or midnight screenings of *The Rocky Horror Picture Show* just wouldn't resonate in the bright light of day. Why do you think none of the casinos in Las Vegas have any windows?

"I have found that acquiring years in a way that brings joy is keenly dependent upon my ability to let go (I like to think of growing older as 'acquiring years'… an elegant collection of sorts). That would be letting go not only of anything that crowds my spirit and psyche—such as old beliefs that hold me back, resentments and such—but also letting go of trying to keep unnaturally youthful those parts of my physical being that are now insistent upon changing. I'm all for taking great care of yourself and being the best you can be, but changing as we age is inevitable, and embracing those changes with a healthy attitude is one of the best vibrancy-elixirs I know. Trying to hold on to physical youth all your life is foolish. Give me vibrancy any day! It's a much more appealing quality as the years pass. Vibrancy ignites passion within and flows out to focus on others, whereas always striving to maintain eternal physical youth focuses so much attention on self. Hopefully, by the age of 50, we have grown wise enough to see that!" My friend, actor/author/cancer survivor Louan Gideon.

I believe that keeping well-organized and forward thinking not only increases efficiency and alleviates duress, it can keep you charged up for all the years ahead. How do you organize your life? Maybe you have a wall calendar or bulletin board with sticky-notes, or perhaps all the minutiae is kept in your iPhone. Many athletes keep track of their workouts in a special watch that synchs with their computer. Are you a blogger? These days, more than ever, it is possible to record and track every piece of data that pertains to your life. Even as prone to being a Luddite as I can be at times, I think this is a great thing. At my desk, I am surrounded by diaries. The aforementioned wall calendar and bulletin board share space with my gratitude journal, my fitness log, bank books and office folders for receipts. No matter how organized I am, there are scads of business cards, scraps of notes, coupons and clippings all around me. I regularly go through them to keep as up to date as possible, but invariably things fall between the cracks.

"A goal is a dream with a deadline." Napoleon Hill

One thing all these resources have in common is that they contain my goals. Whether it's a balance I'd like to reach in my savings account, a dream job I'd love to achieve in television, or a race breakthrough to attain in running, my dreams are literally at my fingertips... reminding and encouraging me at all times. Some (or many) may never be recognized, but that's okay; isn't the journey what it's all about, anyway? My grandmothers always seemed to be looking toward something: a holiday, a milestone, a trip.

It occurred to me recently that, even with all those journals, diaries and logs, it would probably be a good idea for me to also keep a running 'list of accomplishments'. I guess my website, blog and Twitter account are akin to that, but look at all the other lists we have that seem to harangue us with their constant pressure of 'to do'. Even a so-called 'bucket list' would start to feel that way if it made you feel under pressure to hurry up and start ticking things off. Too often we exert ourselves with diligence at the office, dedication at home, devotion to our loved ones… and we may seldom get the praise or simple pat-on-the-back we so richly deserve. So why wait? Who says we can't give ourselves a high-five? Make some kind of deal with yourself to actually write out your accomplishments on a regular basis and, when you hit a designated number (25 sounds reasonable to me), reward yourself with a treat. Time to wander around the bookstore with a cappuccino, an hour of mindless television, whatever. You earned it!

Make time to dream of great things for yourself. Fantasies are not only fun, they can begin to manifest themselves into reality if you keep them in mind in a constructive way. Burying yourself in mundane tasks and constant work won't help you reach your goals, so dare to imagine everything you want out of life and write it down, or find ways to illustrate your goals tangibly. My mother, whenever she left my grandmother's house, would write a message of love with soap on the bathroom mirror. I was raised in a house where we all left notes hidden in each other's books and drawers, to be discovered later as a happy surprise. To this day, Mother and I not only inundate each other with little written 'peek-a-boo's', then we usually save them right in the spots we found them, to be enjoyed again at a later date. Every once in a while, buried in a sock drawer or between two long forgotten books, I'll find a yellowed old slip of paper that says, 'I'm thinking of you, Tootie! XXX.' What a treasure.

Just as a few simple words can wound (look at how cyber-bullying has proliferated), they can heal, encourage and inspire. Look around and see where you can add some to your environs.

Both Mom Mom and Gram were always remarking on what they were 'living' to see: a first great-grandchild…Chavah Ann getting married… Mickey finishing law school…then, a first great-great grandchild! I'm no scientist, but if I had to pinpoint the longevity gene, I'd say it can be found in your outlook: mine is the perfect combination of Nature and Nurture.

> *"Keep in your soul a friendly thought, in your heart a friendly song." Frank B Whitney*

HEALTH AND FITNESS

Everyone should have a motto. Many years ago, I found mine: 'Bodies in Motion STAY in motion'. I'm always in perpetual motion, juggling as many projects as possible, saying 'yes' as often as I can. When I have time to myself, either alone in my apartment, sipping soup at a corner table at a sidewalk café, or doing the crossword puzzle under the shade of an old elm tree in Riverside Park, I'm never lonely at all. This time is precious 'me' time.

Helping keep other people busy is good for all parties involved. Coach a kids' athletic team, plant a garden in your neighborhood, reorganize your closets, or offer to pick up groceries for a neighbor. Don't just SIT THERE. Often, when I have a day off, I'll volunteer with our local City Meals on Wheels program (in New York City, it's more like 'meals on heels' since you have to walk everywhere). I put the hot meal packs over one shoulder, the cold packs over the other, and off I go, opting for the steps over the elevator whenever possible to burn extra calories. I call it 'philanthropic fitness' and I help brighten the day for a lot of folks who might not otherwise get a nutritious meal or see a friendly smile from someone. Try to take notice of volunteer service opportunities in your vicinity or check out these websites that can match your skills with organizations that need them most:

* AllforGood.org
* ServeNet.org
* Catchafire.org
* VolunteerMatch.org

Camp Heartland for kids with HIV/AIDs, Joe Torre's 'Safe at Home Foundation', St. Jude Children's Hospital, the Children's Cancer Institute of Australia and St. Lucy's School for children with disabilities are other organizations close to my heart.

"What counts in life is not the mere fact that we have lived.
It is what difference we have made to the lives of others."
Nelson Mandela

How old are the oldest people you know? I bet they're at least 80. Maybe some are in their 90s. Do you know anyone who's 100? They may not be running marathons, but I bet they all have one thing in common: something to keep them busy. I have a very inspiring next-door neighbor, a Polish lady named Velde. She turned 100 on February 1, 2013, and her daughter (also a neighbor in another apartment on our floor) threw her a party with champagne and cake. Lots of friends were there to honor Velde's resilience and inspiring disposition. She has lost her vision and spends a lot of time in a wheelchair, but she enjoys TV, music, audio books and, weather permitting, gets outside to soak up some sunshine in the back yard and chat with other residents of the building. She and her daughter even go camping every summer in upstate New York!

I asked my Dad, born in 1925, to name one good thing about:

… being 50? "The kids are gone!"

… being 60? "Looking forward to retirement."

… being 70? "Enjoying retirement!"

… being 80? "Reading obituaries that aren't mine!"

And what does he suspect will be good about being 90? "Looking forward to 100."

Theater legend Marge Champion, born in 1919, was still dancing on Broadway into her 80s and continues ballroom dancing for her own 'health and amusement'. In a recent interview with the *New York Observer*, she related a lesson she learned from the famed theatrical caricaturist Al Hirschfeld, who lived until shortly before his centennial. "What I learned from Al was, if you're lucky enough to get these later years, you're only going to be able to do certain things, but, if it's your passion, keep it up. You can celebrate every decade for what it gives you, not for what it takes away."

What is the decade you're in right now giving you?

A survey of 2,000 people by the Pew Research Center's Religion and Public Life project found that 63 per cent of Americans believe medical advances that prolong life are a good thing, although most feel that the ideal lifespan is 90 years of age (11 years longer than the current US average). In America, as in most developed nations, ageing adults account for a rapidly growing share of the population: Approximately 41 million Americans are 65 or older, making up 13 per cent of the population, up from 4 per cent in 1900. By 2050, that number is expected to rise to 20 per cent, according to Census Bureau projections. I have always noticed how easy it is for someone in youth or middle age to throw out a number on how old they'd like to live to be. "Oh, I'd be content if I could live to be 85." Tell me that again when you turn 84! Just as expectant parents say, "I don't care if it's a boy or a girl… as long as it's healthy," so too should you consider how you want your last chapter to read. It's quality over quantity… but the earlier you begin investing in longevity, the more likely you are to achieve both.

One of the worst, if not the worst, aspects of ageing is that you are likely to begin experiencing the loss of close friends and family members. Whether it's someone whom we lose too soon, or whose passing is a blessing, it's never easy to say goodbye… even if you believe, as I do, that it really is only 'so long for now'. We all know that life can end at any moment from the time it begins, but it never seems as precious as when there is the threat or actuality of loss at hand. Author/athlete Dr George Sheehan, who died after a seven-year battle with cancer just four days shy of his 75th birthday wrote, "… health has nothing to do with disease. Health has to do with functioning and wholeness and reaching your level of excellence. … My health can be maximized even when disease is present. There is, I find, a healthy way to live your disease. Disease may change or modify my excellence, but it does not remove excellence as a possibility." Sheehan ran his last race a year before his death and was known for his credo that 'Man at any age is still the marvel of the universe' and 'Listen to your body: we are each an experiment of One'.

We all know that there are certain risk factors for shortening your life, such as smoking, drug use or even texting while driving. Michael Jackson and Whitney Houston both passed away at age 50 and, considering how they'd been treating their bodies, it's no wonder they left us so young. *Sopranos* star James Gandolfini shocked fans around with world when he passed away suddenly at 51, even though he could have been a poster-boy for cardiac risk. Well-known Dr Mehmet Oz described the late actor as "an outsize personality in a dangerously outsize body," (6 ft/ 180 cm tall and 300 lb/136 kg in weight). He speculated that stress hormones may have triggered his appetite and made him eat, even when not physically hungry. Even so, I don't believe there's any magic potion for extending your life… plenty of athletes and 'health nuts' drop dead in their 50s or 60s because of natural causes. Taking care of yourself and living healthily, however, is certain to improve the quality of your life while you're here. Unless you believe in reincarnation, you only have one life to live…so how do you want to spend it?

One major component to feeling good at any age is SLEEP. A lack of it not only leaves you 'off your game' the next day, increasing the risk of accidents, it can also weaken your immunity and leave you more susceptible to diabetes and cardiovascular disease. We hear all the time that seven hours of uninterrupted slumber is best for the average person (I've noticed that number seems to increase as people get older). That's one of my biggest challenges as I have a hard time 'turning off' my brain. I've (almost) learned to keep the iPhone out of the bedroom so I'm not tempted to roll over and take a peek at whatever email or text has come in. Gay marriage may still be an unsettled issue in many places, but someone please alert me when it's legal to marry your handheld electronic device; that may be the real love of my life. For better or worse… for richer, for poorer… in sickness and in health, my iPhone is always there.

James Bond may love his vast assortment of high-tech gadgets, but his most recent portrayer, Daniel Craig (born 1968)… not so much. He credits the boudoir embargo on electronic devices for the success of his marriage to actress Rachel Weisz, saying, "If the iPad goes to bed, I mean, unless you're watching porn on the internet, it's a killer. We have a ban on it."

The last time I moved, I went to great lengths to turn my bedroom into a haven for rest. Even if I can't manage seven hours of sleep, I want to make sure whatever time I DO get will be therapeutic. For me, that means a mattress and bedding that cradles me in complete comfort… blackout shades for total darkness when needed (I'm usually up before the sun, anyway) and, most importantly, no television. It's too easy to channel-surf the night away, and I'd rather pull a book from the stack on my bedside table and read a chapter or two until I doze off. An oscillating fan helps provide temperature control but also ambient 'white noise' to help keep me in a state of slumber. I'm especially fortunate to live on an unusually quiet block, which is virtually devoid of any city sirens or honking horns… with a marvelous cross-breeze wafting up from the mighty Hudson River.

On the nights when I wake and there is no prayer of nodding off again, I've learned to stop fighting it and either enjoy the peace and comfort of my bed… or just get up and get busy! You can get an awful lot accomplished in the wee hours before dawn. A Skype chat with friends in another time zone while doing a couple of loads of laundry is a much more efficient use of time than tossing and turning under the covers.

Taking medication to aid sleep is risky business. I don't like the 'punchy' feeling it leaves me with the next morning; sharp thinking or a rigorous workout are definitely out of the question when I've taken medication. If really in need, I will occasionally opt for a valerian herbal supplement. Meds, however, are not for me… I've known too many folks who have gotten into trouble sleep-walking or having memory gaps. Prescriptions for sleeping pills have skyrocketed (60 million reported in the USA, in 2012), but their side effects may not be worth it… especially for people older than 50, whose bodies take longer to break down the drugs. Consequently the medication lasts longer than it should, leaving some people with a groggy or unsteady morning 'hangover'. It's important to consider interaction with other drugs one may be taking, so definitely consult your physician and use extreme caution before taking a medicated sleep-aid… even one that is sold 'over the counter'.

My natural body clock makes me a morning person, but I'm also a staunch believer in 'early to bed, early to rise' for other reasons. Aside from feeling more productive by utilising the quiet, magical early time of the day, I also contend that sticking to a sensible bedtime is more conducive to so-called 'clean-living' and staying out of trouble. What good can come of being out and about after midnight, anyway? DUIs, nightclub fracas, and other assorted mayhem all seem to occur while I'm safely tucked in my bed, recharging my batteries for the next productive day.

For me, running is my 'fountain of youth'. But, thankfully, that's not for everyone or it would be way too crowded on my favourite jogging paths. As long as I can get out and exercise three or four times a week, I'm confident that I'm doing what's needed to keep my waistline intact and my cholesterol down. And there is no better tonic for a deep, long sleep than a vigorous, extra long training run.

> *It was common before the running boom of the late 1970s for non-runners to think people out for a jog were nuts. Some motorists were even aggressive... trying to force runners off the road, or frighten and taunt them from inside their vehicles. Even though running has evolved into a popular recreational activity, those who do not partake still seem mystified by those of us who do. After a recent long run, I cooled down on my front stoop with a sports drink. As I huffed and puffed to regain my breath, sweat dripping off me and forming salty little streams on the sidewalk, a woman walking two poodles edged as far away from me on the sidewalk as she could and had to comment, "... and that makes you feel good?" I laughed and answered, "It sure does. And it will all day long!"*

Any movement is better than nothing. A new study from the George Washington University of Public Health shows that a 15-minute walk after dinner can help lower blood sugar in older adults. Even people more than 70 years old should try and make time for motion. My parents were prescribed physical therapy (PT) sessions but not at some windowless, confining basement facility: they were sent to a state-of-the-art fitness center, one of the fanciest workout spots in their community... complete with spa, pool, basketball court, group exercise classes and a juice bar. Just being in that environment encouraged them to do more activities than they would have otherwise considered. Long after the PT was completed, they still made visits to the center a part of their routine. If you're not a gym rat, considering going to one just to indulge in a massage or stretch class... you might surprise yourself by getting hooked. Combining exercise with ordinary daily activities is another great way to get started... yard work, running errands, taking mail to the post-box. If possible, give up the most convenient parking spot for one that's a farther walk from the store. Every calorie expended counts!

NYC three-term mayor, Michael Bloomberg, was accused of trying to create a 'nanny state' by doing away with jumbo-sized, sugary soft drinks and enforcing a volume limit for people wearing headphones on the subway. The health-loving politician came up with a very clever (in my opinion) initiative to not only encourage people to forego the elevator whenever possible, but to make stair-climbing a functional part of architectural design. As the *New York Times* described it, he "issued an executive order requiring city agencies to promote the use of stairways and use smart design strategies for all new construction and major renovations. Mr Bloomberg has also proposed two bills that would increase visibility and access to at least one staircase in all new buildings around the city. This would include putting up signs on the walls, especially near elevators, with one central injunction: 'take the stairs'." My running partner, Amy, is a self-described 'stair taker' and, when she goes missing, it's usually because she's working out in the stairwells of her high-rise apartment building. Who needs a gym membership? (We runners are admittedly a little obsessive-compulsive: Amy also participates in the annual stair climb up to the top of the Empire State Building.)

When it comes to fitness, it's important to find the activity that's right for you. I used to think my best friend Glenn was crazy for being a runner... until I got bitten by the bug. But most of my other friends have their own diverse choices of exercise that have evolved from the pleasures it provides them. Marcia has been taking step classes for 20 years or more. Adam plays tennis for hours on end any available day he can.

Tim's a weightlifter. JoDell is a champion power-walker. Scott plays on a softball team. Marc and Carol McClure walk their rounds of 18-hole golf. My LA neighbors, the Forbes, hike as a family sport. And speaking of families, my NYC neighbors, the Doughmans, home-school their kids... so the gym class is actually a trip to the health club for designated work-outs. Neat idea!

> *I noticed a "Family Circus" panel in the cartoon section of the newspaper recently, depicting the little kids darting around the yard. The caption read, "When we get old, running won't be fun. It'll just be exercise." Obviously, cartoonist Jeff Keane is not a runner. I pledge to always find it fun, no matter how old I get.*

I've wanted to develop decent skill at tennis and golf as a pre-emptive strike against a sedentary retirement. It seems like these two sports in particular encourage not only movement, but camaraderie. I don't expect to ever be good at either of them, but just getting out there to play and enjoy the experience, fresh air and the sunshine's vitamin D, seems like common sense to me. I think, in an old-fashioned way, it's like being able to play gin rummy or speak a bit of another language... useful skills to come in handy at any given moment. What sport or recreation can you develop for fun and later use?

You have probably seen at least one performance by the Canadian circus troupe Cirque du Soleil. They have been amazing audiences around the world since the early 1980s with their dazzling effects and incredible circus arts. I've enjoyed many of their shows over the years but none as much as TOTEM when it came to play in NYC and I was treated to a backstage tour by their company manager, (another distance runner, like me) Jeff Lund. The sheer talent and beauty of the skilled performers is matched only by their intense athleticism... and I'm pleased to report that it's not just a world inhabited by youngsters.

Alexander Moiseev (born 1957), for example, not only plays a role onstage but is the coach for the jaw-dropping Russian bars act, which he originally designed three decades ago. Usually, one act is performed by three people: one 'flyer' and two 'porters'. It intricately combines the gymnastic skills of the balance beam, the rebound tempo skills of a trampoline and the swing handstands skills of the uneven and parallel bars. Needless to say, it requires an amalgam of mental focus, dexterity and strength. I asked Alexander for some insight into how he maintains his rigorous discipline.

NELSON: "First off, what do you consider to be the peak years of your athletic performance?"

ALEXANDER: "In my opinion there is no peak. Every stage in your life is, in a way, its own peak. After all, the result depends on your inner state of mind. There have been many things that I can consider peaks in my career. Starting from 1977 when I put together the first Russian bars troupe with the Moscow circus of the Soviet Union, then later moving on to a 'teeter board', doing tricks no one has done before. Winning the Golden Clown in the Monte Carlo Circus Festival in 1985, starting to travel and perform abroad, joining and working with Cirque du Soleil. All these things can be considered peaks in my career and in my life. I always set specific goals for myself, and when I reach these goals I consider myself to have reached a new peak. These are peaks in my life, but there are also everyday peaks. Every performance must be done on a maximum. Then, if a person works on a maximum the audience in turn pays with their own energy, and that gives a big boost, a change of energy, if you take that away, then you will quickly get tired from working. And in this case you will never be able to reach a peak."

NELSON: "Have you had to make any adjustments after turning 50?"

ALEXANDER: "The same adjustments one makes after reaching 20, 30, 40. Treat your body with respect, and your body will treat you the same way. Even after 60 the principle doesn't change, it is an endless process. The moment you stop respecting your body, you start encountering unpleasant situations."

NELSON: "What special challenges do you feel now on stage and off?"

ALEXANDER: "I feel a lot of responsibility, seeing that I am the leader of my group. I need to always get everyone together and in good spirits. Like it or not, I must set an example for my partners. So far it seems to be working."

NELSON: "In the circus world, what does your generation provide for the younger ones?"

ALEXANDER: "A transfer of energy and information. I teach the youngsters the various aspects and laws of presence on stage, how to give out proper energy to the audience. It's like having children, teaching them how to grow up on stage."

NELSON: "How long do you expect to keep on performing? Any secret weapon to stave off age?"

ALEXANDER: "I was 20 when I joined the circus in 1977. I can't say how long I plan to work, that depends on how much time God gives me. I have a lot of goals, ambitions and ideas. As long as I have enough energy and health I will keep at it. Age is irrelevant; the important thing is well being. Often you meet 'young elderlies' and vice versa. What you do today becomes your future. There's a quote I like from the cartoon *Kung Fu Panda*: 'Yesterday is history, tomorrow is a mystery, but today is a gift. That is why it is called the present.'"

I love to encourage and inspire people with my love of running, but I certainly don't think it's for everyone... whether it's physical limitations (bad knees, weak ankles, diminished lung capacity) or just personal preference. I'm a baseball fan, but I don't possess the skills required to play the game. Seeing Alexander and his comrades on the Russian bars is jaw-dropping, but I couldn't attempt anything like it in a million years. Thank goodness everyone has different talents and interests. What a boring world it would be if everyone excelled at the same thing. I wouldn't survive a nanosecond on a football field, but it doesn't mean I don't enjoy the Super Bowl.

As I remember from school, running laps of the playing field was a punishment. And my Mom's attitude ("You never see a runner smiling.") didn't make it seem any more appealing. Even long after I'd been working as a fitness professional, logging hours of high-impact cardio exercise every week, the idea of simply running was anathema to me. It seemed boring and pointless. I remember precisely the moment that all changed.

My then-roommate's boyfriend, Olli, accompanied me to the gym and challenged me to run five miles on the treadmill. It seemed like something impossible... that was the distance I drove to work. How could I run a distance that took me 25 minutes to drive in Los Angeles traffic? But as soon as I accomplished it (with relative ease), I was hooked. Five miles on the treadmill became my new, regular workout warm up. And as soon as I dared to try it on the street, canyon trails or Santa Monica beach promenades, my miles and speed began to dramatically increase. Some folks dislike the repetitive nature of treadmill running, but I love my time on the belt and eventually invented and trademarked my own "Brains and Brawn Workout", which incorporated exercises with book club discussions and entertainment... all executed on a moving treadmill. It was a hit and I was becoming a full-fledged runner.

On a lark, I signed up for an Independence Day 6-mile (10-km) race in the Pacific Palisades. I had no idea what to expect when the starting gun was fired, but I suddenly found myself launched forward in a pack with hundreds of runners, while crowds cheered enthusiastically, clapping and waving flags. The roar of all those feet pounding the pavement sounded like applause and I felt like I was doing the greatest thing in the world. Not exactly a 'runner's high', but definitely euphoric. Any weekend I could, I was signing up for road races… until eventually, in 2001, I dared to try what would ultimately be my biggest challenge: the marathon.

Training for and running marathons immediately suited my personality. It was time efficient, convenient, required no particular athletic talent and kept the calories off. The regimented schedule fed my obsessive-compulsive tendencies and it wasn't long before I was planning my annual calendar around racing schedules. I had just turned 38, but felt like I had discovered my second childhood. Why hadn't anyone turned me on to it sooner, I asked myself? Ironically, one of my first training partners, a young woman named Lauren (who is still a friend all these years later), memorably said to me after one of our initial long outings, "I can't believe you're that old and can run that far!" I take great delight in reminding her of those words… especially now that SHE is that old!

> *Apple's late co-founder and CEO Steve Jobs said, "The only way to do great work is to love what you do. If you haven't found it yet, keep looking. Don't settle."*

How lucky I am to have a gig on *Sunrise* that allows me to include so many stories about running in my TV reporting, from my own participation in running events to the sometimes sad and serious situations such as the Boston Marathon bombing and how Superstorm Sandy impacted the NYC Marathon. My friend, Marie, is convinced that someday I will have a TV show all about running. I'd love that. It also allows me to take on assignments other reporters wouldn't get to do, like a running tour of Universal Studios… becoming the superhero 'Flash' for a speedy story about the Justice League movie… or racing up a skyscraper with tennis legend Martina Navratilova as she prepped to climb Mount Kilimanjaro. Even in her late 50s, the breast cancer survivor had the right outlook about ageing, fitness and state of mind, "Positive attitude is a choice," she told me. "Live in the moment." That was after we bolted up 53 flights of stairs!

Twenty marathons (and scores of half marathons and countless other race distances) later, I'm delighted to be running as happily as I did that summer day in the Palisades, maybe more so, because I so greatly appreciate my body's ability to keep going. Glenn suffered a torn meniscus and is still recovering from the surgery to repair it. I live in terror of anything ever compromising my beloved running. I am not one to indulge in many personal luxuries, but I consider my running coach to be a necessity. He not only helps enhance my athletic performance, but my longevity as well. (A great coach or trainer might end up being part-therapist, too… then you really get your money's worth!) My goal is to be out there running when I'm a little old man. Heck, ageing can be great for runners… it not only helps us retain bone density and flexibility, but as we enter older race divisions, we increase our chances to improve our standings/rankings. Interestingly, I am becoming a better runner in my 50s than ever before. The other day, I was trotting along after a rigorous session with my coach and a bird in flight actually flew straight into my chest and then bounced off and continued on his way. I thought, "Man, I must be going pretty fast if birds are flying off of me!"

'Masters athletes' is a term given to 'older' sporting competitors… usually more than 40 year old, but sometimes considered as young as 35. Not only can you be a strong athlete into your 40s (and beyond), you can improve and excel more than at any time in your life. Age grading is used for most race results nowadays; like in school where certain tests might be graded on a curve of the overall students' results. Age grading compares an individual's finish time to a best time achievable for that individual's age and gender. Developed by the World Association of Veteran Athletes, it allows us each to determine a measure of our performance, even as our finish times eventually decline with advancing age. You may find that the age-graded result of your race time may, in fact, be a personal best... even if it took you longer to run that distance than in your younger years.

For example, the first race of my new 50+ age division was September 2013's 'Autism Speaks' charity 4-miler (6.4 km) in Central Park. My official finish time was a respectable 33:42 but graded for age it was 29:29. Considering my personal record for that distance was set in 2009 at 31:22, I could make the case that I am faster than I used to be.

Is it cheating? For now, I feel like it is... perhaps that will change when I start to slow down. While it's a fun statistic to analyze (how neat that some of my age-graded times can match the 'real' times of my 20-something-thing running pals), at 50 I am still running strong enough to not only compete against others but, more importantly, outperform my own past results. I used to consider logging 100 miles of running per month to be an excellent achievement. In 2013, I beat that consistently and, in August of that year, I even racked up a personal record of 131.4. And 2013 was by far my best running year yet. You can keep your age grading, thank you... but I will relish the distinction of being a 'master'. It seems that the more I run, the better I run. Consequently, my priority is to maintain an injury-free status so that I can continue to (literally) make strides.

Nelson's Mileage Tally
2013: 1323.6 miles (2130.1 km)
2012: 1175.2 miles (1891.30 km)
2011: 1200 miles (1931.21 km)
2010: 1105.6 miles (1779.29 km)
2009: 1070.1 miles (1722.16 km)
2008: 1152 miles (1853.96 km)
2007: 1300 miles (2091.7 km)
2006: 1064 miles (1712.34 km)
2005: 1143 miles (1839.08 km)
2004: 944.9 miles (1520.34 km)
2003: 834.2 miles (1342.22 km)

One of the indelible images from the Boston marathon bombings was the sight of 78-year-old Bill Iffrig faltering and collapsing to the ground, just feet from the finish line when struck by the force of one of the bomb explosions. It was his third time running the famed event and he said he'd been "feeling pretty good". After recovering from the initial shock, he was helped to his feet and able to walk the remaining distance with only scrapes and impaired hearing. He then proceeded to walk back to his hotel. He plans to return to racing at 80 when he'll be on the 'younger' side of the 80–85 age division category. Meantime, he remains in his small hometown in Washington state where he lives in the house he built himself a half-century ago with his wife of almost 60 years. Even the US President accurately cited Bill as an example of American resilience saying, "…we may be momentarily knocked off our feet, but we'll pick ourselves up".

The next year, Joy Johnson ran her 25th NYC Marathon at age 86 and, ironically, passed away the very next day. Her daughter commented that Joy had died doing what she loved. We should all be so fortunate.

After 35 years and five attempts at making the 100+ mile swim from

Cuba to Key West, Florida, without being inside a protective shark cage, famed endurance swimmer Diana Nyad finally achieved her dream in 2013. She was 64 years old. Before she set out on her journey of 200,000 strokes in the jellyfish-infested sea water, she remarked, "There's the fine line between seeing that things are bigger than you and letting your ego go. And there's another edge over that fine line where you don't ever want to give up and I am still at that place." Emerging onto the beach in the US after her 53-hour swimathon, she only had inspirational words for the excited, assembled press. "Never give up. You are never too old to chase your dreams." After some food and rest, she added, "I'm going to say to myself, never forget how this feels, always remember you can dream at any age." Her lifetime motto has been 'Find a Way', and only with the grace of time was she indeed able to. If that isn't a lesson in persistence and evidence that middle age is marvelous, I don't know what is.

In Roman mythology, Diana was the goddess of the moon. If those ancient fellows could see Ms Nyad, they might just tell Neptune to get lost and let her take over as ruler of the seas!

It wasn't just her athletic prowess that finally propelled Diana to achieve her extreme dream: it was the resolve and assurance that comes with maturity. "I think it was her belief in herself that she could do this," said Kathryn Olson, CEO of the Women's Sports Foundation. "She had such a strong belief in herself and her ability that she was able to convince all those around her as well. There was a higher calling about this," Olson says. "That desire allowed her to transcend the pain."

In the boxing world, Floyd Mayweather, Jr. (born 1977) was considered the oldster in his sold-out Las Vegas bout against Saul 'Canelo' Alvarez in September 2013. Floyd not only knocked out Father Time, he hammered in 232 of 505 punches thrown against his 13-years-younger, widely-favoured opponent. Compare that to the mere 117 Alvarez was able to land out of 526 throws.

Controversial German dancer-turned-actress-turned-filmmaker Leni Riefenstahl lived to be 101 and never stopped reinventing herself, even taking up underwater photography at age 72. Still working as a centenarian, she held the distinction for being the world's oldest scuba diver.

Days after he turned 70 in 2013, I spoke with film icon Robert DeNiro and asked him his trick to keeping in such excellent health and condition. Of all the times I've interviewed him, this was one of the few questions that actually prompted him to make direct eye contact with me. He said, for him, it was all about keeping on top of medical issues as soon as they arise and develop into anything serious. He added that having a young child (his fourth, born in December 2011 via surrogate) was also a key element in keeping him young.

No one is more physically fit or financially secure than bad boy-turned-pop star-turned-underwear model-turned film and TV mogul, Mark Wahlberg (born 1971). For all his accomplishments, 'academic' can sometimes trump 'athletic'. There was one major hurdle he was compelled to overcome: earning his high school diploma after having been a ninth-grade dropout. While continuing to make and promote movie and television series, he completed an extensive online course to finally achieve that goal. "The greatest regret in my life is quitting school. I was lucky, but a lot of my friends who did the same ended up incarcerated or dead," he said at the time. "Now I have a different perspective: that what's cool in life is being a good person, and doing the right thing. I take any opportunity I can to speak to teens and encourage them, first and foremost, to graduate high school. And today, I'm proud to say I'm leading by example by joining the Class of 2013."

Life doesn't have to, as Joan Crawford once noted, 'deal from the bottom'. One of television's pioneering and most enduring stars, Bob Newhart, was 84 when he received his first Emmy award in 2013, after seven nominations for his three eponymous comedy series. Tearfully accepting the award to a standing ovation, he said, "I just felt the kind of stuff I do doesn't win awards. I didn't want to go through the process, the disappointment." And remember *Titanic*'s Gloria Stuart? Although a moderately successful working actress in her youth, fame didn't find her until age 87. In fact, she seemed to have started an Oscar trend… now every year there seem to be nominated performers well into old age. Consequently, Jack Palance's famous one-handed push ups at age 73 back at the 1992 telecast don't seem quite as remarkable now as they did back then! It seems everywhere we look, 'age limit' is more and more of an oxymoron.

> *"To give anything less than your best, is to sacrifice the gift."*
> *Steve Prefontaine, famed runner (1951–1975)*

Runners World (RW) magazine, August 2013, cited some specific, surprising benefits of running that should reassure any naysayers who contend that we're hurting ourselves with all that mileage. It says running:
* Grows cartilage, which can safeguard joints from arthritis.
* Sharpens hearing. Exercise improves circulation to the ear, which provides more nutrients to help preserve hearing.
* Saves your skin. A caffeine/exercise combo results in fewer damaged cells developing into skin-cancer tumours. (Sunscreen always recommended).
* Fights migraines.
* Regenerates muscle.
* Eases anxiety.
* Helps prevents cancer. *RW* cites research that the more intense the exercise, the least likely men were found to die from cancer, especially in the gastrointestinal tract or lungs.
* Increases brain function.
* Strengthens bones, guarding against fractures and osteoporosis.

… And to my worrisome Mom who is convinced that it's so dangerous ("You'll get hit by a car!" "Oh, your knees are going to go to hell!" "You'll drop dead of a heart attack!"), I say that if I finally meet my maker while out on one of my runs… at least my survivors can take comfort in the fact that I died happy!

> *Not-so-fun-fact: Want to see what you'll look like in 10 years? Look in a mirror immediately after you complete a marathon. Yikes!*

Exercise will undoubtedly enhance your life in mind, body and spirit… as will having a child's sense of play. So, find a recreational sport that works to satisfy all those. Experiment with a variety—you'll know when you hit on the right one! Additionally, running has afforded me the opportunities to make new friends, travel the world, stay trim, healthy and happy. What can your hobby do for your life?

PERSONAL BESTS
2007 DC National Marathon: 4:03:46
2006 Palos Verdes Half-Marathon: 1:47:47
2011 Ted Corbitt 15k: 1:21:42
2005 Run for the Bay 10k: 45:38
2007 Santa Monica Mountains Trail 9k: 52:14 (1st Place Men 40-44, 9th Overall)
2011 Achilles Hope & Possibility 8k: 41:01
2009 Run for Central Park, 4 miler: 31:22
2006 Achievable Foundation 5k: 21:58

OTHER MAJOR RACE RESULTS
2013 Hamptons Marathon: 4:27:55
2011 NYC Marathon: 4:21:37
2011 San Francisco Marathon: 4:25:37
2010 Hamptons Marathon: 4:19:48
2009 Hamptons Marathon: 4:24:00

2008 Hamptons Marathon: 4:26:11

2008 Bermuda International Marathon: 4:17:51

2007 Catalina Eco-Marathon: 4:41:30

2007 San Francisco Marathon: 4:15:55

2006 Florence Marathon: 4:22:11

2005 St Jude's Memphis Marathon: 4:11:39

2006 LA Marathon: 4:13:37

2005 LA Marathon: 4:14:01

2003 LA Marathon: 4:23:35

2002 LA Marathon: 5:08:11

2003 Honolulu Marathon: 4:47:55

2002 Honolulu Marathon: 4:32:53

2001 Honolulu Marathon: 4:51:31

2013 NYC Half-Marathon: 2:03:41

2012 Grete's Great Gallop (NYC): 2:04:28

2012 Hamptons Half-Marathon: 2:03:05

2008 Palos Verdes Half-Marathon: 1:54:26

2005 Palos Verdes Half-Marathon: 1:48:29

2004 Palos Verdes Half-Marathon: 2:06:47

2002 Santa Barbara Half-Marathon: 2:06:50

When the great actor Russell Crowe decided once and for all to get in great shape for himself (and his kids' benefit), and not just for the acting role-of-the-moment, he discovered that he could stay inspired by sharing his workouts on social media. The Twitter-sphere follows along as he records his regimen and progress and, in the process, he evolved from tabloid's hot-tempered bad boy to amiable gentleman. I can tell you he's the real deal. He even spotted me in a New York corridor and made a point of introducing himself… and we've had a very friendly professional relationship ever since. He even follows me on Twitter and, after I'd posted the statistics of a particularly gruelling training session, he kindly responded, "You are an inspiration, Nelson." How's that for encouragement? The Oscar winner turned 50 in 2014 and is certainly in the best shape of his life. He told me a funny story about being pursued by a swarm of paparazzi while he was out cycling. Proving fitter than the photographers, he led them on a long and crazy ride and only one could manage to keep up with him. A good sport, Rusty obliged that sole-surviving snapper with a photo opportunity when he finally pedaled to his destination.

Russell is a great example of someone who improves with age. My mom used to say "Your brain is delivered when you reach 35," and maybe that's why so many showbiz 'bad boys' eventually reform and trade in their wild ways for more gentlemanly, productive pursuits. Long gone are the days when he was known as a phone-throwing hot head, now he's the guy who tweets about his workouts and brags about his kids.

> *In 2013,* **The Daily Telegraph** *cited an unnamed research study that determined 43 to be the age when men "officially grow up".*

Colin Farrell is another such transformed fellow. The hard-drinking, troublesome Irish lad he was known to be in his 20s has been replaced by a calmer, yoga-practising father, who hides his muscular physique beneath tailored designer suits and cardigan sweaters. When I first met him in 2006, he was a far cry from the dapper Dubliner I've encountered again in 2012 and 2013: a well-mannered conversationalist with a firm hand-shake and penetrating eye contact.

> *Today's celebrities are too-often given a pass when it comes to manners, which is why it always stands out when they exhibit impeccable behaviour in even the most banal press situations. Tobey Maguire, Zac Efron and Joseph Gordon-Levitt all give me hope that politeness is not lost on the*

younger generation. No one serves up more gracious star power than Tom Cruise. He may have been laughed at for jumping on Oprah's couch, but you can only be impressed when he leaps from his seat to greet you when you enter a room. He also happens to be punctual to the micro-minute and possesses the best handshake in Hollywood.

There are certain inevitable facts of age. All the sunscreen and vitamins in the world won't permanently stave off wrinkles and spots or receding hairline and gums. No one is Dorian Gray, Isn't it ironic that when we were young, we tried our best to look older and more grown up? Now, we do everything we can to try and look young. While I never say never, the idea of any kind of face-lift surgery seems far-fetched and out of the question for me. I certainly support a person's decision to do whatever cosmetic procedure they choose to make themselves feel better about their appearance, but even a 'good job' still looks phony to me… especially on men. Again, I go back to attitude: if you have a happy, smiling visage… it will be beautiful at any age. Someone once said, "You get the face you've earned." I agree.

Vivacious, talented screen legend Shirley MacLaine (born 1934) has enjoyed unprecedented popularity over the course of her long career—most recently in the smash TV series **Downton Abbey.** *Ever the trouper, she still dedicates herself to her work… but takes no prisoners when it comes to how she looks on camera, offering up strict criteria for the lighting and lens crews to carry out. Woe be to anyone who doesn't measure up. She does her job and expects the same level of excellence from anyone around her. Old-fashioned star power, baby!*

Rolling Stones' legend Mick Jagger may have an estimated net worth of

$305 million, he also has a face that money couldn't buy. His talent, energy and enthusiasm for performing made him one of the most sought-after showmen of the last century. No one would ever accuse him of being a health nut, but there's something reassuring about knowing that 'doing what you love' can sustain you well into your years as a 'seasoned citizen'. When he hit the milestone age of 70 in 2013, U2 frontman Bono paid tribute to the rocker's longevity by commenting, "… he still has a very beautiful face. The wrinkles that run through it now have made it even more beautiful. Why? Because he wears those wrinkles well. I love his wrinkles."

Enjoy the individuality of your own original face. Cosmetic procedure junkies wind up having a look of 'sameness' about them. Wouldn't Diane Keaton or Sean Connery look ridiculous with unlined, smooth countenances? Where would Julia Roberts or Jack Nicholson be without their broad, signature smiles? Cindy Crawford and Robert DeNiro have facial moles that are perceived as 'beauty marks'. Does anyone care about scars on Tina Fey or Joaquin Phoenix? Nope! There's a long list of gorgeous celebs who have shaved their head for acting roles or just because they realize that 'bald can be beautiful'. Love your looks… especially if they're offbeat.

Let's try something for a minute. Take this book and let's walk over to the mirror together. Take a good long, close look at your wonderful, unique face. Maybe you see some wonderful trait of one of your parents or grandparents. Dad's 'ski-slope' nose or Mom's rosy cheeks… there's some of your family history written right there on your face. That's a miracle. Is there a little scar under your chin or a pockmark on your forehead? I bet you have a memorable story about how it got there. Now let's look at those lines. The deep frown marks may be testament to how hard you studied in school or how serious you had to be to survive a traumatic time. And survive you did. Look at the eyes. They're not 'crows' feet', they're 'laugh lines' that represent the countless smiles that have spread across your countenance over the course of your laughter-filled lifetime.

Maybe some are from squinting into the warm, summer sunshine. In fact, those hot, halcyon days may have left you with some freckles, too. The 'fingerprint' of your face is well earned and shows the world your life well lived. Of course, maintenance is involved… polishing that table or trimming those tree branches, but you love them for their distinctive characteristics. Unless you have an identical twin lurking around, your looks are solely your own. Quirkiness rocks! Time has made you more beautiful.

Okay, you can stop looking at yourself now and keep reading.

I took a jab (pun intended) at botox twice in my 40s… the first time as part of a story I was doing on 'celebrity body parts' (I wanted 'Nicole Kidman's forehead') and the second time on a ridiculous whim at the suggestion of my friend's dermatologist. Both times I regretted it… it wasn't worth losing the expressiveness of my face: which makes me look like ME. Having a bag of frozen peas handy is great for a make-shift ice pack, or healthy snack. Having a frozen face is just ridiculous.

> *"It's not the years in your life that count, it's the life in your years." Abraham Lincoln*

As we age, there is less stomach acid secreted and less absorptive ability making vitamin replacement/supplementation more necessary for some people. I'm a fan of taking a targeted (50+ for men) multi-vitamin and baby aspirin daily. The former because, no matter how healthful your diet, you're bound to be missing some key, beneficial nutrient… and the latter because, with a family history of heart disease, the wonders of low-dose analgesics are hard to refute. I also take glucosamine/vitamin D tablets and usually throw a powdered vitamin C packet into my water bottle when I hit the gym. (I credit that, along with frequent hand washing and the use of a hand sanitizer on the NYC subway system for keeping virtually cold-and-flu-free for over three years.) My doctor assures me that the benefits of fish oil caplets far outweigh their risks and I believe their anti-inflammatory properties keep my joints and vascular system in good working order. And Saw Palmetto extract, while believed by many to aid in prostate health, demonstrated no greater benefits than a placebo. With so many choices available on store shelves these days, chances are that one tablet alone is all you may need. Check with your physician when deciding on customizing a formula for your own regimen. Whenever possible, attempt to get the lion's share of your vitamins from natural food sources. Luckily, I love eating spinach, salmon, fruit and other yummy things that are rich in nutrients.

Even though most of our body weight is water (up to 78 per cent), most people don't drink enough!. Some of the benefits of keeping hydrated throughout the day include:

* Preventing/treating depression
* Sleep disorder
* Lack of energy
* Boosts mental alertness
* Boosts weight loss

I may look and feel younger than my age, but 50 is 50 no matter what. I was having some pain in my foot that was beginning to compromise my running. My dad took a look at it (though long retired from his orthopedic surgery practice, he still gives great consultations) and declared that my collapsing arch and subsequently deforming second toe were just normal parts of middle age. Ouch! Crazy old doctor, I thought. What does he know? I was convinced it was something much more heroic… athletic… YOUNG. So I went to a fancy-schmancy Manhattan specialist who examined it and took an x-ray. His diagnosis: synovitis. A ha. That sounded very macho. Turns out, that is a joint swelling from overuse. He also uncovered heel spurs I didn't realize I had. I was strangely comforted until he explained that 'overuse' was a kinder way of saying age. Dad was right.

That doc added further insult to injury a few months later when I returned to his office to have my neck and should area examined. I was having a lot of discomfort there after several long overnight flights as well as some intense weight lifting sessions with my trainer. Another x-ray and he was able to diagnosis and dismiss this as no-big-deal and something that would go away on its own (which it soon did), but he wanted to point out something new he'd discovered: spinal compression! I started laughing aloud as he pointed out the vertebrae that were progressively closing in on each other as they went down my spine. "This is perfectly normal for a man your age," he said. Here we go again… as if I'm not already height-challenged enough, now I can say I'm SHRINKING.

As my little old Auntie Joan Raindrops always merrily says when a new age-related challenge pops up, "Right on time."

Artistically, we may have muses. Professionally, mentors. For fitness, I think everybody should have role models—not some chiseled god-like supermodels that pose, all tan and toothy, on the covers of magazines. (After Lance Armstrong looked the world squarely in the eyes and blatantly lied to us over and over, I burned out on the idea that famous folks should be put on pedestals… How many sports figures, politicians, musicians and movie stars have also fallen from the lofty heights to which we elevated them?) Look around you and find local athletes, sportsmen or trainers right in your own sphere whom you can emulate or, dare I say, even idolize. Chances are they'll be flattered and keen to offer their encouragement or tutelage. Channing Tatum openly man-crushed on Jude Law, so guys shouldn't be afraid to start up a bromance of their own. Remember in *Seinfeld* how Jerry famously crush'd on baseball player Keith Hernandez? And how jealous he was when Elaine actually started dating the Mets player? What made that such a hilarious episode was the truth behind the situation. Every guy has been there in real life.

For my money, ultramarathon man Dean Karnazes is one of the

running world's ultra-superheroes. If we had a *Justice League,* he'd be Superman. His accomplishments alone would earn him that reputation, but it is his charm and skill as a communicator and cheerleader for others that make him heroic, in my book. I was fortunate enough to become friends with him through my work (we even ran a leg of the Catalina Eco-Marathon together) and it is impossible not to be inspired by his all around mega-fitness. Christopher Reeve and Henry Cavill may have worn the big red 'S' on their chests, but Dean lives it. And he's even (a year) older than I am.

NELSON: "Is there pressure on you, being a 'role model', especially as you age?"

DEAN: "Yeah, though less about my age and more about who I am. Thankfully, I am authentically committed wholeheartedly to the pursuit of physical excellence (no junk food in my cupboards!)… "

NELSON: "Athletically and/or physically: What changes are you starting to notice in your body?"

DEAN: "I have to train harder and more intensely to achieve the same results that used to come easier when I was younger. But, I don't mind (in fact, I kinda like it)."

NELSON: "What's the best thing about life after 50?"

DEAN: "Haemorrhoids (hee hee)! Truthfully, it's the wisdom you garner (or don't) after a lifetime choked full of rich experiences. Some people say you grow more content as you age, but I'm still quite restless. Show me a man who is content, I say, and I will show you an underachiever."

NELSON: "You're a role model for me… but who is someone YOU would consider a role model?"

DEAN: "Although he has passed, Jack LaLanne is someone I long admired. Not only was he in excellent shape, he used his gift to benefit others. To me, a great champion is someone who can use their talents to help others be the best that they can be." (Note: Fitness icon LaLanne passed away in 2011 at the age of 96.)

NELSON: "You had a big epiphany on your 30th birthday, which propelled you to take up distance running. Did anything noteworthy happen on the day of the big 5-0?"

DEAN: "Other than going for a 50-mile birthday run, it was quite uneventful."

Australian paralympian champion Kurt Fearnley is another mate I've made as a result of my work and we regularly email back and forth, and dine together when we're in the same city. He was born with sacral agenesis (he is missing certain parts of his lower spine and all of his sacrum). When he was born, doctors didn't believe he would live longer than a week. But not only did his parents and four older siblings treat him like any other kid, his spirit and determination have led him to a long and unprecedented list of athletic championships and achievements. Not content to ever rest on those laurels, he is actively involved in a host of organizations bringing help and awareness for young athletes with disabilities. He is a hero in every sense of the word and one of the biggest ego-boosts I ever received was when he mused that if we could merge his upper body with my lower body, we'd create the perfect 'super marathoning machine'.

Malibu Marathon Race Director, Blue Benadum, became my running coach when I was living in Los Angeles, and our workouts are probably the one thing I miss most now that I don't live there anymore. We met at the gym and our rapport was instant: he's not only a knowledgeable champion keen to share his knowledge, but he is blessed with a physique and running style I can only dream of achieving. I had been ready to retire from marathons until he convinced me otherwise… and I sealed the deal with a new tattoo of '26.2' (the mileage of a marathon) on my lower leg. We are in touch regularly and his encouragement always gives me an extra jolt when I need it.

The next time you're in a quandary, pick one of your role models and ask yourself, what would so-and-so do?

Fit and Fabulous 40+ Females

Ladies, the next time you want to skip an exercise session, consider how dedicated these divas are to their workouts… and how it pays off for them with sleek, sexy figures! Every one of them continues to dazzle on the red carpets and runways…

Salma Hayek, born 1966

Paulina Porizkova, born 1965

Sheryl Crow, born 1962

Madonna, born 1958

Iman, born 1955

Christie Brinkley, born 1954

Cyndi Lauper, born 1953

Jane Seymour, born 1951

Cher, born 1946

Jane Fonda, born 1937

Role models work two ways. You may seek someone to help you improve you're your fitness but YOU can also be a role model to someone else, in an area in which you are an expert. The wonderful yin and yang of being human!

Over the course of my friendship with the impossibly fit,

funny and fabulous Hugh Jackman, I have often asked him why he hasn't tried to run a marathon. He always dismisses his ability to tackle the distance, although he did run a half-marathon, not too long ago. I tell him, "You're Hugh Jackman. You can do anything!" I hope one day to convince him... and wouldn't it be something if I could actually coach him?

In terms of fitness, freedom and relationships, my dear friends Roger Robinson (born 1939) and Kathrine Switzer (born 1947) are role models for everyone. Both enjoyed long careers as elite runners and are now sought-after commentators and speakers for athletic events. Kathrine made history as the first woman to complete the famed Boston Marathon as a numbered entry, even when the race director tried to forcibly remove her from the race. She opened doors for women everywhere in athletics and, alongside Roger, continues to be a committed activist for human rights. They met and married later in life and their personal and professional partnership is inspirational. I always have fun in their company... and a bonus is always getting to profit from a bit of their wit and wisdom.

NELSON: "As young athletes, what did you foresee for yourselves after the age of 50? 50+ certainly ain't what it used to be."

KATHRINE: "I remember in 1967 (I was then 20) telling a newspaper that I planned to be a little old lady of 80, still out doddering along. However, when I turned 50, I was surprised at how fit I really was, still wearing clothes I had from age 25. (They were back in fashion!) Regular running can forestall the ageing process in many ways."

ROGER: "I just wrote this sentence, Nelson, in an article about the history of 'masters' running: 'In 1964, when Bob Dylan sang "The times they are a changin," it didn't apply only to the young, as we thought at the time.' Running was a leader, even THE leader, in changing attitudes to age. When I kept running at an elite level into my 40s and 50s, I was one drop in the first wave of a surging tide. I didn't think about being 50, but I never saw any reason to stop running, something I loved. I improved late and slowly as a runner, first making an international team (England) at age 26, and I retained a simple runner's faith that if you keep working, you keep improving. Later, that becomes relative, but it's still the truth."

NELSON: "How has middle age surprised you… for better or worse?"

KATHRINE: "Menopause really surprised me; it was the first time I felt out of control of my own body… and mind. I got these mood swings—totally unreal for me. It also brought weight gain and slower running, it was frustrating. Good news: whenever I ran, I felt just fine. Bad news: I can't run 24 hours a day. So, for the better, I got a great perspective on ageing and coping with it, for worse, the sadness of knowing you are, in fact, ageing."

ROGER: "When I was 37, overseas on the New Zealand team, one young woman runner complained that several of the men's team were 'old'. 'What's so much better about being 22?' I asked her. 'I've got my whole life to enjoy ahead of me,' she gloated. 'But I'm in the middle of enjoying my life right NOW,' I replied. Yes, I'm surprised—very much for the better—how full and vital life continues to be. And thank you, Nelson, for that term 'middle age'—very tactful."

NELSON: "So, as life-long athletes, how do you advise young runners when it comes to preserving their good health and long term athleticism?"

ROGER: "I always tell young people that nothing will make them better life-long friends. Nothing will make them feel more fulfilled. Nothing will give them a deeper sense of interaction with the earth. And nothing will contribute more to their health and quality of life."

KATHRINE: "I advise them to run all kinds of events, and participate in a huge variety of sports so they develop all kinds of strengths, have team experience, and most of all have fun. When it's just running and it is the be-all and end-all, it can create performance pressure and get boring for a young person."

NELSON: "Do you have any particular regimens you follow in terms of diet or exercise?"

KATHRINE: "Over the years, this has changed from 'the more you run the better, and when you see food eat it' to: run consistently, plan recovery, and when eating and drinking, practice the 'push back' technique of pushing back a plate of food before it's finished. Always and forever I do a lot of stretching."

ROGER: "I approve of all that—for Kathrine. She looks fabulous when she's stretching. I introduced one significant new exercise discipline to my routine after age 65—a daily afternoon nap. I'm rigorous about it. In diet, the main recent change has been to switch to single-malt Scotch."

NELSON: "Who inspires you as a role model now?"

KATHRINE: "Absolutely, my husband. He is totally amazing, without in any way being an obsessive nutcase. His ability to achieve without losing balance in his life is so admirable."

ROGER: "One of the burdens of my marriage is that I have to accompany Kathrine to all these races, where thousands of attractive women run around in crop tops and shorts. Tough work, but also inspiring. But to be serious; I get inspiration from the friends and contemporaries who sadly can't run now. One close runner friend was killed in New Zealand's Christchurch earthquake. Another, a truly great runner in his day, recently had a leg amputated. I think of them every time I run, and know how fortunate I am to elude the bent pin of fate."

NELSON: "How do you maintain your youthful disposition and vitality?"

KATHRINE: "Sex."

ROGER: "None of your business. Bloody nerve."

NELSON: (After I manage to stop laughing.) "You're one of the premier power couples in the running world… but you met later in life. How old were you when you two fell in love and why was the timing so right?"

KATHRINE: "I was 36. I'm not sure the timing was so right, as I was just out of two disastrous marriages and vowed I'd never get into a serious relationship again. Besides, I was at the top of my career in New York City, and was all-consumed with it. Roger was at the top of his career in Wellington, New Zealand—8,000 miles away. That's a disaster for romance. But when I met him it was like a thunderbolt. We were sharing the speaking stage before a big marathon in Australia. Some people fall in love at first sight, I fell in love at first voice."

ROGER: "The timing was right because that was when she appeared. But only two very stubborn marathon runners could have made it work. One time, she flew from New York and I flew from New

Zealand for a weekend in San Francisco. Did we run that weekend? Can't remember." (More laughter.)

NELSON: "Did running bring you together, or was it just one point of interest?"

ROGER: "It's a great bond to have an active interest in common. But there are many others. We're both readers, we love theater, art, Mozart, and good food and wine. Friends are high priority for both of us. And family. Kathrine's parents were wonderful people, as are her brother and family. And in my family, Kathrine has become a much-loved grandmother without ever having been a mother. She's my ideal in her diverseness and genuineness. When we first met, she gave a charismatic speech, organised a high-level race, was stylishly beautiful and scintillating company at dinner, and the next day was out running with me splashing through the puddles."

KATHRINE: "All my life I'd been looking for my kind of Greek ideal of a 'philosopher-athlete'. A man who not only was an athlete, but who tested his limits, who understood excellence. But he also had to be a man who could think, and love and could use words."

NELSON: (Taking a moment to recover from the sheer romanticism of their replies.) "To what do you credit the success of your union?"

KATHRINE: "To the lack of dominance in the marriage. We try very hard to make things equal. Not only in terms of money or household tasks, but in supporting and taking each other's work seriously."

ROGER: "Totally agree. At our wedding, when friends read literary pieces, I had one friend read Chaucer's lines about dominance ('maistrie') in marriage: 'When maistrie cometh, the god of love anon, Beateth his wings, and farewell, he is gone.' But a lot of the success is also due to Kathrine's sunny benevolent disposition—she even forgave Jock Semple." (That was the race director who tackled Kathrine in an effort to eject her from his 'male-only' marathon.)

NELSON: "And how does running fit into it now?"

KATHRINE: "Running is very important as now we are both working in the industry as writers, speakers, commentators... the physical part is very important. For me it's my 'sanity and vanity' time."

ROGER: "Having running as a common work theme means we can often travel together. Since we spent so many long periods apart, that's a bonus. But we're not just a duo. We're fiercely independent as writers. Kathrine is developing her 261 brand. I still do literary scholarship, book reviews, and so on. My big moment in 2013 was being invited back to Cambridge University to give a guest lecture. Running is not the whole of life for either of us."

The number 261 was Kathrine's bib number from the 1967 Boston Marathon. Women around the world wear '261' to 'feel fearless in the face of adversity', whether it's a tough marathon, a difficult business presentation, or coping with the many challenges of life.

NELSON: "Will you ever really retire?"

KATHRINE: "Not in the sense of being away from the sport, as we love following it even in events we don't cover, for instance. Plus, in times when we can't run (such as an injury) we still are compelled to 'feel running'—to move and exercise and get outside close to nature. Mostly, I for sure cannot retire because there is still so much that needs to be done for women. Running has hugely changed women's lives socially, physically, and politically by empowering them and making them quite fearless. The biggest and most positive changes are yet to come, however. Since I was responsible for a lot of this to begin with, I feel compelled and responsible to continue to make things happen. Watch this space! It's called '261 Fearless'."

ROGER: "I've retired from committee meetings. That's bliss. I'm proud of what I did as a university teacher, scholar and manager, but the meetings drove me nuts. I thought I'd retired from running, too, when my knee gave out, but now I've had a replacement I'm running and racing again—please don't tell the surgeon. I won my age group in a 5-miler last week. Everything ends, but no one can make you retire from being interested in things."

Being an eternal student is also a key component in staying fit for life. Having a curious, inquisitive nature, setting, reaching and re-setting goals, gathering more and more knowledge about the things that spark your interest… these are ways to be sharp and vital regardless of time's passage. My current running coach and personal trainer both keep me so motivated and perpetually hungry for performance that I literally am sleepless on the nights before my workouts. Like a kid on Christmas Eve!

It's not always fun, but the fact remains that, after 50, we owe it to ourselves and loved ones to be vigilant about our health care. As easy as it is to put things off, more regular check ups are in order and monitoring statistics in regards to your 'vitals' is important for preventing problems down the line. Fortunately, I get along well with all my doctors and can go through the potentially humiliating absurdities of examinations with my dignity (and often times, humour) in tact. Even with the natural progressions/deteriorations of time, I believe your body can be 'young' at any age. Regular check-ups let you keep tabs on what's going on inside your body. It's easy in our busy lives to put those appointments aside… especially if we're feeling and looking in top form. For all the inconvenience and anxiety an annual physical may bring, it's worth it to know the results of all that poking, pricking and prodding. After my last round of lab work, the doctor called me at home and said, "I only see numbers this good maybe once a year. Keep doing whatever you're doing." What a relief. But if there had been numbers to adjust, I could get on top of the situation right away.

New York magazine selected Dr Jordan Metzl as one of the city's finest sports medicine doctors and I've gotten to know him through our mutual participation in the local running community. When he's not busy with his successful medical practice, he's participating in, or coordinating, sporting events and I regularly join his early morning 'pop-up' Iron-strength Training for Runners boot camp classes in Central Park: intense, all-weather workouts that always leave me soaked with sweat and smiling ear to ear. He, like many of my previously mentioned role models, is hovering around the age 50 mark, but is undeniably in top physical form—with a personality to match. I had some questions for him about fitness and ageing and want to share his answers with you.

NELSON: "We hear 'consult a physician before beginning any exercise program' but what is the best advice for a middle-aged person who wants to take up a new form of fitness?"

JORDAN: "You have to become an even better body-listener. Your body breaks down more easily so it's important to stop if there's a lot of pain."

NELSON: "How does the psychology of fitness change for athletes over 50?"

JORDAN: "Psychologically, I think athletes greater than 50 can some-times can feel defeated or frustrated, but I don't think they should.

They just have to keep going. Rest equals decay. Move it or lose it!"

NELSON: "You wrote *The Athlete's Book of Home Remedies.* How does a person know when it's time to see a doctor?"

JORDAN: "It's time to see a doctor when your body mechanics have changed as a result of pain."

NELSON: "What about stretching? Love it or hate it?"

JORDAN: "I like stretching, but it's not the be-all and end-all. If given a choice between stretching and a foam roller, I would pony up with a foam roller (a cylindrical piece of hard Styrofoam used by athletes and physical therapists to work the kinks out of overactive muscles). You need to continue to do anything that makes your kinetic chain (the combination of successively arranged extremity joints) happy. It needs to be strong and flexible, and all of these help to improve flexibility."

NELSON: "As a life-long athlete, what changes have you noticed in your own body and have you had to make any adjustments?"

JORDAN: "I've had to do more strength training to maintain my functional strength."

NELSON: "How much exercise is too much?"

JORDAN: "It really depends on the person, the kind of exercise, their exercise tolerance, and life balance. There are both physical and psychological factors to pay attention to. Overall, a person should think—is it healthy? Am I having a good time? Am I feeling good about myself and what I'm doing? To stay motivated, I set goals, make sure that I'm having a good time, and make it social."

NELSON: "What's an athletic accomplishment you have yet to master (or never will)?"

JORDAN: "Surfing. No matter how much I try, I still suck at it."

NELSON: "What are the most common complaints you get from patients older than 50?"

JORDAN: "General aches and pains, mostly weakness and lack of energy. But all of the athletes who come to my office in their 50s and beyond are inspiring in their own ways."

The power of peer pressure? Jordan says that you workout 20 per cent harder in a group environment than when exercising alone. So grab some friends or join a class and get moving.

Jordan recommended me to the NBC *Today Show* to take part in a stunt in honour of Kathie Lee Gifford's 60th birthday: having her carried on set by a cadre of shirtless middle-aged hunks. Not only do I not consider myself a candidate for the 'hunk' contingent, it's all I can do to get shirtless in the locker room or poolside… let alone on national television. Those days are well behind me and I do admit to thinking that showing too much skin after a certain age is a risky proposition, no matter how taut and tight you are.

Another charming experience I promised my friends and family I would endure after turning 50 is the dreaded colonoscopy. Ever since Katie Couric lost her husband to colon cancer and had her own colonoscopy procedure televised to raise awareness of the need for regular testing, it has been an important part of the mature person's routine health maintenance.

My own doctor advised me not to worry about it until I reached my fifties, since I have no family history or indicators that it would ever be an issue. But when my best friend's brother-in-law fell off a ladder while hanging Christmas lights, and an x-ray of his fractured ribs revealed a suspicious shadow on his colon (which was subsequently diagnosed as cancerous and successfully treated), I decided to move forward with it. I was referred to a gastroenterologist by my fabulous dentist (our NYC specialist physicians are truly extraordinary… a good doctor is a blessing) and, thanks also to extensive internet research, he turned out to be as great as I'd been told. You shop around for the best bottle of wine… the sheet set with the highest thread count… the right pair of sneakers. You certainly should be discerning when it comes to selecting a specialist to treat your medical needs.

Since my insurance would cover the cost of the procedure once I reached 50, I wasted no time in scheduling the appointment. Like taking off an adhesive bandage, if there's pain or discomfort involved, I want it over as quickly as possible. Everybody warned me about the prep and how unpleasant it would be. Frankly, I found it to be anticlimactic; the toughest part was abstaining from my morning coffee. Otherwise, it was an opportunity to stay home and catch up on some paperwork, phone calls, crossword puzzles and reading (brain fitness). For whatever reason, the strange tasting concoction and subsequent cleansing resulted in me being able to end the day with one of the best night's sleep in ages… nearly ten hours. Oddly, I wasn't even hungry the next morning. I felt lean and energetic. So off I went to my appointment, only half-heartedly missing my morning jolt of caffeine. (Interestingly, my doctor told me, previous attempts to replace the liquid prep with an easier-to-swallow pill form resulted in many patients experiencing renal issues… so it looks like we're stuck with the drink for the foreseeable future. Hold your nose and chug!)

There is a patient's Bill of Rights when it comes to visiting a health clinic or hospital, but there are also a few cardinal rules for us to remember when we are slipping on that backless piece of material they dare to call a gown. First, exercise patience (defined as 'the good natured acceptance of an unexpected delay'). If someone is ahead of you in line, chances are they are in more urgent need of the medical attention. Second, be nice to the nurses. In most situations, it will be the nurses that provide you with the bulk of your care… and they'll make it a whole lot more pleasant on you if you make it pleasant on them. They don't get the pay or the glory of the physicians, but they're the ones who keep the machine going.

Everyone at the endoscopy center was friendly and thorough. Aside from the sterile surroundings, it wasn't a scary place at all. The nurses were upbeat and took their time explaining every phase of what would be happening. They made sure I was comfortable on the gurney after I'd changed out of my clothes and didn't mind at all when I snapped a few selfies to post on Twitter. My friends in social media wouldn't have to go through the nitty gritty of the colonoscopy with me, but I sure appreciated their support while I was waiting for it to begin. I admit to being a little nervous especially when a nurse made sure I understood the rules about DNR (Do Not Resuscitate) in the event of an emergency. Fortunately, I had a peace of mind about all that, having long since drafted a living will, making all my personal intentions legally known, including being an organ donor. Even so, no one ever really wants to face the fact that today could be the day those wishes will be enacted.

A very friendly anesthesiologist pulled the curtains aside to introduce himself and detail how my sedation would be performed. This was followed by a nurse inserting the needle for the doctor to use once I was in the room where the examination would occur.

Finally, in came Dr Mohajer, a veritable rock star if you were to judge by the reception he received from the staff. I was his first patient for that Friday, so I was consoled by the fact that he wouldn't be in too much of a hurry to rush through so he could skip out and start his weekend. Gifted with a terrific bedside manner, he set my mind at ease and even made it feel like we were about to go out for a beer together rather than have me knocked out and a giant camera-tipped tube inserted up my backside!

I was wheeled down the short corridor to the room where it all would take place and got a chance again to greet the fleet of nurses milling about, along the way. I liked these people. I bet they have great parties.

Inside the room with Dr Mohajer and the anesthesiologist, I was introduced to a young woman who was wielding the big tube. She was young, pretty and reminded me of a snake charmer! Some upbeat music was flipped on (I don't remember the artist, but I'm guessing it was Pink? Carly Rae Jepsen?) and the lights dimmed. I was instructed to roll over on my side and the last thing I remember was the doc saying, "Have a good nap!"

Less than half an hour later, I was gently rousing back in my curtained-off area with a light blanket over me. Rested, not punchy... no pain. Piece of cake. Cake. I was getting hungry. Other than chicken broth and gelatin, I hadn't had any food in more than 24 hours. A nurse brought me a bottle of water and some Graham crackers, then Dr Mohajer showed up to deliver the results of the colonoscopy. Everything was normal and he recommended another check in three to five years for surveillance. A printed copy of his findings (along with some digital images that were significantly less palatable than, say, high school yearbook photos) detailed the results so I could digest them more comprehensively after the effects of the Propofol wore off.

> *Advice from gastroenterologist Babak Mohajer:*
> *"A colonoscopy should be done on everybody over the age of 50. There is some data that shows African-Americans could have increased incidents of colon cancer, so they should considering having one at age 45. People with a family history, rectal bleeding or a change in their bowel habits should also get a colonoscopy at an earlier age. ...The*

best way to find the right doctor for this kind of procedure
would be a referral through your primary care physician
and careful online research. …My top tips for colon health:
I recommend fiber and a probiotic. …The other most
important routines for people 50+ besides a colonoscopy
include regular PSA tests for prostate health for men. Women
should go to their gynecologists at a much earlier age for
annual physicals and a yearly pap smear."

My life-long pal Melanie came to discharge me from the center and we got a cab to my favorite local French restaurant for a big lunch. I guess this was a good preview of things to come: in the old days, she and I would go to nightclubs and parties together.

By the next morning, my colon and I were back to normal and I was even able to hit the gym and spend an hour on the treadmill. Was the whole colonoscopy experience fun? Not an adjective I'd use. But it wasn't awful and it was certainly interesting, a bit like jury duty. I'm a fortunate guy in that so much of my life's happenings are enjoyable… but the key to long-term happiness is to approach everything—especially the tough stuff with a sense of humor and curiosity. My moral of the story? Make your colonoscopy a blast! (yuk yuk)

When I moved from Los Angeles to NYC and began
'shopping' around for doctors, I realized I should be looking
for medical professionals YOUNGER than myself. Having
always associated age with wisdom and experience, my
physicians had traditionally been kindly old guys who
reminded me of Dear Old Dad. But I believe for our long-
term care, we need relationships with professionals who are
not only up on the very latest developments in health care,
but are young enough to stick around and look after us for
the long haul.

Watching my parents and grandparents go through all the medical prodding and probing that comes with age, I've learned that one cannot be modest or insecure when it comes to baring all for your doctor. There may be nothing more psychologically freaky for me than my annual dermatological body scan. My doc is a lovely guy, but it's still unnerving to be splayed out naked while he combs my entire body surface with a magnifying glass. Yikes! That's sure to bring you crashing down to earth in a hot minute!

At the beginning of my colonoscopy saga, I mentioned my dentist. Good oral hygiene is essential and something you need to keep up with as time marches on. I was lucky to find my dental surgeon through, of all things, a blind date. It wasn't a love match, but I admired my date's flawless smile and asked for a referral (See? Don't sit home… even a blind date bomb could have a silver lining). Mine led me to the awesome Dr Jeffrey Reagan. He has the cleanest, most high-tech office in Manhattan—complete with city views and fantastic music—and is the most attentive dentist you'd ever want looking around inside your oral cavity. He obliged me with some toothy tips for middle-aged mouths.

NELSON: "What are the special challenges of oral hygiene after age 50?"

JEFFREY: "Manual dexterity can become an issue for adults over 50, which can make it difficult to brush properly. Adding an electric toothbrush to your routine can greatly improve oral hygiene."

NELSON: "What are the most common age-related dental issues and what are the best ways to prevent/treat them?"

JEFFREY: "There are very few dental conditions that you can say are absolutely age related. Dental problems tend to be wear-and-tear-type issues. That being said, the longer you keep your teeth the more problems you could potentially have, including periodontal disease, caries (an infection which leads to cavities/decay), fractured teeth, or gingival recession. Seeing your dentist regularly and doing your work at home with good oral hygiene is the best way to maintain your teeth and hopefully prevent most problems."

NELSON: "Can we check ourselves for oral cancer?"

JEFFREY: "Absolutely not. Every time a dentist checks your mouth at a hygiene visit they should be doing a cancer screening and evaluating all the soft tissues as well as the teeth. There is a whole host of conditions that can happen in the mouth and it takes a professional eye to evaluate them."

NELSON: "I don't think it's ever too late to improve your smile. Do you have any stories of people older than 50 who have made dramatic improvements through cosmetic dentistry?"

JEFFREY: "I have had several people that have decided to improve their smile through comprehensive cosmetic dentistry. It can dramatically improve one's self esteem and confidence."

NELSON: "What cautions do you have about cosmetic dentistry (to avoid looking fake)?"

JEFFREY: "There is a whole host of dentists selling themselves as 'cosmetic dentists'. In my opinion every procedure should be cosmetic, meaning everything should look like a real tooth when it is done. Prosthodontists, restorative specialists, are the best in achieving this goal. The American College of Prosthodontists can be a great resource to find a prosthodontist in your area."

NELSON: "Some people outlive their dentists. How do you recommend finding a new one you can trust?"

JEFFREY: "Most dentists will do their best to find someone qualified to take over their practice when they retire. If that's not the case then word of mouth tends to be a good method. Talk to friends and colleagues."

Ha ha! He said "word of mouth"!

NELSON: "Even as a dentist, you must occasionally face your own dental challenges. Have you started to notice any changes with age?"

JEFFREY: "The usual wear and tear issues such as gingival recession and some wear from bite forces."

NELSON: "Any new, cutting-edge dental devices/tools/measures you can recommend?"

JEFFREY: "We now have the ability to do a crown in one visit with CAD/CAM technology. It's an amazing service to be able to offer someone."

After a run in with a dried pea, I was left looking like a real-life Jack O'Lantern! Unable to face the TV cameras with my toothless grin, I got an emergency first-hand experience with this amazing technology and Jeffrey had my smile back to normal in time for my afternoon live report. A lifesaver!

NELSON: "Your #1 most important tip for good dental care?"

JEFFREY: "Brush for the full 2 minute cycle and floss once a day. It's a night and day difference in homecare when people use an electric toothbrush properly. Also, you should have your teeth cleaned professionally every 6 months at a minimum. Some people do it 3 or 4 times a year just to insure their teeth are well maintained."

My friend, Colleen Zenk (born 1953), is a wildly talented and glamorous 'cougar' who was beloved by legions of fans of TV's long running **As The World Turns.** *She played the oft-married heroine Barbara Ryan (there were multiple married surnames over the course of her amazing 32-year run on the show) and her own battle with oral cancer was even written into one of her character's storylines, bringing information and awareness to the home viewers about this important and often ignored subject. Her dentist actually missed detecting the cancer initially and, when she discovered it, her first doctor misdiagnosed it. After the initial excision and treatment, the cancer returned and she had to go through a second round, including reconstructive surgery on her tongue. Today she is speaking (and singing!) up a storm, and remains a great advocate for diligence in the fight against oral cancer.*

Everyday stress reduction is also an important component in living/ enjoying a healthy, active life. Practising what I preach on this subject has been one of my greatest challenges for as long as I can remember. From being a nervous kid, I grew into a jumpy teenager and eventually wound up a worrisome adult. Determined not to become neurotic, or riddled with anxiety as my mother and grandmother both did, I have developed coping mechanisms to deal with stress when it begins to overwhelm me. While a clean diet can greatly add to your sense of wellbeing (too many carbs leave you feeling bloated and blue… too much sugar or caffeine makes your tense and jittery… overdoing the sodium solicits hypertension… alcohol, remember, is a depressant), getting plenty of exercise can quickly and efficiently change the course of your disposition and day for the better. I can't tell you how many times I've had to drag myself to the gym when all I really wanted to do was lie in bed or work on the computer. While I'm not one who experiences a 'runner's high', I definitely get a mood lift once my body is warmed up and moving with vigor. It's clear that making changes like this may retard or even reverse damage caused by everyday stress factors. Whatever stress you can't eliminate or prevent, you must manage.

A study of more than 13,000 men and women aged 40–55 years old published in the *Archives of General Psychiatry* found that those who were depressed at midlife were much more likely to develop dementia later in life. But those who reduced their stress had NO increased risk of dementia.

Any exercise is better than none at all… but why not treat yourself to some new goodies to help motivate yourself to try some new athletic activities?

I have never been one to excel at 'quiet' activities such as yoga, pilates or meditation. Heck, even a massage leaves me feeling antsy to do something more energetic. I do, however, force myself to take some quiet time to stretch or use a foam roller. It's been proven that in addition to elongating and relaxing muscles, these practises can increase one's ability to cope under pressure. With so many different types of meditation, you can try several to find the one that works for you. Tai-Chi, anyone?

I've known some people who keep a 'stress journal' to record and access things that are contributing to their anxieties, in an effort to diffuse their effects. And others who schedule 'worry breaks'—a designated time set aside to focus on their problems and concerns. It is certainly true in hindsight that almost all of the things we allow ourselves to worry about, never actually manifest themselves.

Avoid things you know will be stressful. Obviously, it is inevitable that at times there will be difficulties to deal with, but if you can pare down

that list whenever possible, it should greatly contribute to your wellbeing. Don't sign up for more than you can manage in your already busy
schedule. I had a colleague from New Zealand who fronted his network's
US news division and he cleverly referred to 'the news pig'—an insatia-
ble animal that will keep asking a journalist to deliver more and more
content, a seemingly endless supply of stories, without any regard to
the reporter's own schedule, spirit or sanity. Whenever I would become
overwhelmed trying to juggle TV assignments, press junkets, premieres
and other assorted professional duties, he would advise me, "Nelson...
stop feeding the news pig." Even the most talented and dedicated professional knows when it's time to back off and say 'enough'. Making a time
and place for regular 'you time' is vital. You deserve it, you need it and...
come on, you know you want it. In this noisy, frenetic, all-access 24/7
workaholic world, it can be difficult to 'escape' even for a few minutes.
Your sanity depends on being able to disconnect long enough to recharge
your battery or you'll end up being no good to yourself, or anyone else.
Think about it: would you want a surgeon operating on you who had
already cut into 20 people that day? Or an airline pilot that had flown for
three days without a furlough?

> *"Today, it is up to you to create the peacefulness you long
> for." Chinese fortune cookie*

Researchers at the Harvard School of Public Health concluded positive
outlook can provide measurable protection from heart disease and stroke.
Optimistic people, according to their studies, had about 50 per cent less
chance of experiencing an initial cardiovascular event compared to
others who are less upbeat. Julia Boehm, PhD, said, "The absence of
the negative is not the same thing as the presence of the positive." Remember the song, *Don't Worry, Be Happy*? A better title might be, 'Don't
Worry, Be Healthy'.

Optimism, contrary to what you might believe, can be learned. Think of it as a muscle that needs to be exercised. Even if you naturally possess it, you should practice optimism every day. Make a concerted effort to find the bright side of situations… even the most benign. 'My bus was late… but at least I got a good seat,' or 'The ball game got rained out… but tomorrow's forecast is perfect.' It gets easier and easier. Someone once said to me, "The problem with optimists is that they get disappointments too often." When you are trained to be upbeat, disappointments can almost always be shrugged off in favor of the next positive opportunity.

Try to avoid people who irritate you. Make every effort to surround yourself with positive, uplifting people. Granted, that tricky office co-worker or sister-in-law may be a fact of life, but come up with ways to limit your exposure to them. If you're prone to road rage, try and schedule your trips to miss rush hour… or at least give yourself plenty of time to commute to wherever you need to go and play soothing music on the stereo. With all the 'talk TV and radio' that blasts the airwaves these days, we are always hearing loud voices quarreling over their different opinions about politics, religion, circumcision, sex, you name it. Turn it off! You may actually find you enjoy the peace and quiet. Similarly, limit your exposure to the computer… the telephone… your iPod. You schedule time to work, do laundry, run errands, pay bills… why shouldn't 'relaxation time' be just as important to work into your daily duties?

> *"You're not really free until you're free from trying to please everybody." Joel Osteen*

As we age, we should become more comfortable with ourselves and wise to the ways of the world. Consequently, our stress should be less than ever. But if you're a tense type, old habits are tough to break. Now is a wonderful time to work on that.

So far in this chapter, I've been writing about all the marvelous things that health and fitness bring to our lives. The reality, though, is that sooner or later almost everyone experiences some kind of medical crisis or serious health event that can't be remedied with a trip to the gym or a simple out-patient procedure. Mandatory health insurance and the concept of socialized medicine are hot issues these days, but the bottom line is you want to remain healthy at all costs. (And when it comes to costs, no matter how good your insurance plan may be, it's most definitely less expensive to be healthy than it is to be sick.) Keeping your insurance premiums up to date and looking after your overall good health should always be a top priority at any age.

I'd like to tell you about Erik Fredrickson, my friend Glenn's personal trainer. He's one of the best in the business and to look at this charismatic hunk, you'd definitely want to put your money on him to win if he were on *Survivor*. Ironically, a survivor is exactly what he is. At just 35, married with his second child on the way, Erik was diagnosed with a rare, chronic disease called hairy cell leukaemia (named for the fine hair that attaches itself to the affected white blood cells). Bloody noses, night sweats, eye infections and a host of other issues went undiagnosed until a simple electric shock while plugging a cord into an outlet resulted in a dramatic reaction: petechiae, the bursting of the tiny blood vessels all over his body. On the same day that his wife went into labour, he was having blood tests that would reveal that his spleen had nearly doubled in size and his platelets were dangerously low. A bone marrow biopsy revealed that leukaemia was present in 70 per cent of his blood.

He immediately began a course of chemotherapy, which as he describes, was like pressing a reset button in his body to bring his white blood cell count to 0. New cells were created and regenerated without the little hairs attached. In true boot-camp style, he managed to work out next to his bed while still hooked up to the monitoring machines. "I looked like a puppet with strings, doing squats and other exercises to try and maintain some strength… and just to try and feel normal, too." After this treatment came pain, fatigue and fever. Another few weeks in hospital were followed by months of recovery at home. He slowly began to resume his personal training business, working with clients who were also recovering from cancer treatment. What a gift for the folks who train with him to have his newfound perspective and approach to good health. "Today I'm learning more and more to let go of what is 'normal' and just be happy with what is normal FOR ME." I'm happy to tell you that Erik now feels and looks great, although he must still be diligent about keeping track of his blood count stats with his hematologist. He led a 155-mile bike tour recently and is signed up for an 18-mile paddle board challenge in the open ocean waters off Long Island.

If you didn't know his story, you'd simply assume this strapping, smiling fellow was just another happy-go-lucky hunk who worked in a gym. Far from it. His survival experience served to make him far wiser than most of his peers and I'm proud to share some of his excellent advice and insight with you on the subject of health and fitness.

NELSON: "What was the hardest part of the treatment?"

ERIK: "Balancing self-advocacy with trying to trust my caregivers. On one particular night they didn't know what medication they could give me to control my pain and my fever went to a neutropenic (low white blood cell count) scale of around 107. I actually was worried the pressure in my head might kill me. It was an overreaction but, wow, I'd never felt pain like that."

NELSON: "Did you ever lose faith that you would recover?"

ERIK: "I never lost faith but it took faith to control the fear that I wouldn't recover. I had to trust… and with the help of friends and family I just kept believing and praying for that."

NELSON: "Did your fitness help you cope with the treatment?"

ERIK: "It provided a huge coping mechanism on a few levels. Being fit when you become sick gives confidence to the doctors who treat you. You are more likely to respond to treatment. On another level, fitness helped me to create new personal goals and have something to look forward to once I was able to move around more."

NELSON: "Did your fitness help you bounce back more quickly?"

ERIK: "There's no doubt. Being fit going into it accelerated my healing."

NELSON: "Are you back to the same level of fitness as before the treatment? Could you surpass it to be in even better shape than ever before?"

ERIK: "I think my strength is 100 per cent again. Now, it's about what I am going to do with it. I need to continue to set goals and challenge myself. You don't need something like cancer to begin to lose your fitness, but it sure reminds you to make the most of the time you have. I don't exercise to prevent disease. You can't control that. All you can do is make the most of the time you are given. You can live those days with more energy and vibrancy, and exercise will do that for you. I am setting new goals and doing things I never tried before I had the HC leukaemia. That makes me feel I can be in better shape than I was before."

NELSON: "What do you tell 30-somethings who think they are invincible? What's your advice for check ups and maintenance?"

ERIK: "It is hard to go to the doctor sometimes, but doctors don't make us sick as some people I know may think. They can identify something that is wrong and provide correction. Early detection is very important for almost all conditions. Most importantly: believe the diagnosis but not the prognosis. No one can predict the future, so just stick with the facts and do whatever it takes to heal."

NELSON: "What are the biggest challenges you see for clients as they get into their 50s?"

ERIK: "Careers and families can take up a lot of time. It is so important to carve out time for yourself to exercise and make conscious decisions about health. Every decision we make impacts on our body in some way. I also think finding the energy to exercise gets more challenging as we get older, but the other option is a lot more painful!"

NELSON: "Does your experience with leukaemia give you new insight into dealing with clients older than yourself?"

ERIK: "It showed me how fast the body can deteriorate when you stop moving. Muscle atrophy begins about four days after inactivity begins. The process is slow but it catches up with you fast. Although I'm not 50 yet, I feel like I may have extra empathy about feeling lethargic or immobile and how painful it can be to move through that."

NELSON: "Off hand, what would be your top fitness tips for folks 50+?"

ERIK: "Make time for conscious movement and enjoy what you do for exercise. Keep your routine consistent but freshen it up with variety. Be kind to your joints by avoiding high-impact activities and be sure to include stretching in your workouts. Stay hydrated with coconut water; it has more electrolytes naturally than any energy drink you can find. I can't tell you how many clients I've seen walking around dehydrated not realizing that was the primary source of their pain and discomfort."

NELSON: "What do you say to someone who wants to start an entirely new regimen?"

ERIK: "If you don't find the right exercise, chances are you won't stick to your routine. Find someone or something that keeps you motivated, safe, and your enjoyment high."

NELSON: "How diligent are you about diet/nutrition (for yourself and for your clients)?"

ERIK: "Although there was no known cause or prevention for my type of leukaemia, I am certainly more diligent now than I used to be. We need to keep our alcohol, sugar, red meat, and quantities of all food in check and eat a colorful array of foods when possible as well as staying hydrated."

NELSON: "What do you consider to be the biggest no-no's?"

ERIK: "Skipping workouts (it can kill the habit and then you have to start a new routine again). Thinking 'moderation' is just a cliché. Alcohol and soda are two quick ways to gain unwanted weight, slow your metabolism, and make your body work harder to filter out the bad stuff."

NELSON: "Do we ever have to succumb to age?"

ERIK: "'Succumbing to age' sounds too much like giving up. We need to have fun with what seems like a fight sometimes. There are so many ways to exercise and feel young. Enjoy the journey without needing a destination. Just get in your body and go somewhere!"

There is a certain satisfying degree of self-acceptance that comes with reaching middle age. If you haven't achieved that rock hard six pack by now, you probably never wanted it badly enough in the first place. Frankly, very few of us can attain the bodacious bods of a Bundchen or Beckham… and even if we somehow managed to, it would likely be an agonizing exercise in 'maintenance'. So if there's a little extra wiggle around your middle, you don't have to beat yourself up. In fact, I saw a very large woman on a recent airplane flight (sitting beside her beanpole scrawny husband, by the way. Isn't it funny how that so often happens?) who needed a strap extension to get her seat belt to buckle. She wasn't fazed in the least at having to ask. In fact, I got the impression that this was something she was not only accustomed to, but had no qualms about whatsoever. We ended up chatting later in the journey and she was an incredibly lovely, self-assured lady who just happened to be overweight. And she wore it well.

Even as a 'work in progress', remember to embrace whatever size or shape you may already be. Don't waste a second of life's enjoyment. Transition times are as precious as the moments when you reach your goals. Plus, keeping on top of your body's evolution may not necessarily prolong your life, but it can certainly improve the quality of it. In the end, it's not whether you win or lose but how you play the game.

FISCAL FITNESS

As we age, it's not only prudent to have more money in the bank…
it's vital. Those rainy days pop up more and more often and being prepared is everything. The fewer dollars you have, the more
urgently you need to devise a financial plan. By now many of us will
have settled into a routine of income/expenditure so buckling down to a
budget is do-able, even if it's not exactly what you'd call fun.

That said, I learned to manage money from my Dad… who made it
a game with the net result that I did think of 'saving' as fun. I wish more
parents would take the responsibility to teach their children about money
in the same way that they teach them to tie their shoes, ride a bike, or
drive a car. It's as much a philosophy as a skill. Alas, schools don't teach
financial skills and really they should; it's certainly one of the most
important aspects of surviving in the real world.

Many modern economic crises can be attributed to people living
beyond their means. From the indulgent 1980s onward, consumers were
told they 'deserved' luxuries including state-of-the-art appliances and a

new car every three years. Where I grew up, you only 'deserved' what you could afford to buy.

But back to Dad and how he taught me about money. Dad is an avid numismatist (coin collector), paper money aficionado, and co-founder of the Currency Club of Chester County, which just celebrated its 42nd anniversary. His passionate hobby became a second career for him, serving not only on President Ford's Assay Commission but as a consultant to the Bermuda Monetary Authority. He was a history buff, and he had me recite every face on every denomination of coin and currency by the time I was three. While most kids have piggy banks to save their loose change, Dad gave me an official bank book. I didn't receive a weekly allowance… I had to earn spending money by answering general knowledge and trivia questions (I got to be very adept at multiple choice quizzes!) each night after dinner, then once a week, father and son took a trip to the bank together to deposit the loot. It was fun to see the balance gradually rise… and oh boy, it was extra special when that monthly interest was added on. I was hooked on watching those numbers… and I evolved into a frugal kid. If a relative sent me some cash in a birthday or Christmas card, I didn't spend it on comic books or records (I got plenty of hand-me-downs from my four older siblings)… it went right into the bank.

The same principle should apply to adults. Putting any extra money you acquire into the bank leaves you less likely to make impulsive, frivolous expenditure.

Recently, I queued at the ATM to deposit my paycheck and I overheard the following conversation between a young mother and her daughter, who looked to be about five years old:

KID: "Do you have enough dollars?"

MOM: "No. If we come to the bank, it's because we need MORE dollars."

I realized that child was now on her way to forever thinking that the bank is a vending machine that dispenses currency as needed. I was taught that the bank was a place to put money into. I predict a rude awakening for her one day.

Don't misunderstand me: I don't deprive myself of anything I really want. But I always make sure I can pay for it first. Knowing the golden rule of finance, 'no debt, no regret', resulted in my cultivating inexpensive tastes and enjoying simple pleasures. That makes extravagances extra special. Ask yourself: does the gourmet coffee really taste better than the less costly brand? (Don't get me started on what a rip-off Starbucks is for coffee-lovers!) Do you really need a personal trainer when you already know some buff buddy who'd find it flattering and fun to be your workout partner? Does that insanely expensive scented soap from Tuscany really get you any cleaner than a good old bar of Ivory?

TV's highest paid actor and tabloid-darling Ashton Kutcher may be perceived as a 'hunky doofus', but don't let the exterior fool you. He's a canny businessman and philanthropist who knows the value of a strong work ethic. He beautifully expressed the importance of this to the young audience at the 2013 Teen Choice Awards when he recalled, "When I was 13, I had my first job with Dad carrying shingles to the roof, and then I got a job washing dishes at a restaurant, and then I got a job in a grocery-store deli, and then I got a job in a factory sweeping Cheerio dust off the ground. And I never had a job in my life that I was better than. I was always just lucky to have a job," said Kutcher. "And every job I had was a stepping stone to my next job, and I never quit my job until I had my next job. And so opportunities look a lot like work." Let's hope some of that sank in with the crowd.

Fiscal fact: According to the Bureau of Labor Statistics, by 2016 one-third of the total US workforce will be age 50 or older, up from 28 percent in 2007.

Not all of life's sacrifices are monetary… but even choices we make that aren't money-related impact on financial situations. I always assumed I would one day fall in love and become a parent, but it never worked out that way and being a single dad wasn't something I ever wanted to take on. Having lots of nieces and nephews, and being a surrogate uncle to the children of friends and fans around the world really suits my personality. But by not raising any of my own I have consequently been able to save a lot more of my income than my child-rearing counterparts. More and more people aren't just letting fate determine whether or not they're child-free, they're opting out altogether. In fact, the US birth rate is the lowest in recorded American history.

"Everybody with a womb doesn't have to have a child, any more than everybody with vocal chords has to be an opera singer." Gloria Steinem.

"My songs are like my children… I expect them to support me when I'm old!" Dolly Parton

Gloria Steinem, Margaret Cho, Oprah Winfrey, Dolly Parton, Katharine Hepburn, Condoleezza Rice and Janet Jackson are some notable females who have all claimed that they never felt raising offspring was an essential component to a fulfilled life.

One thing is certain: kids cost money! As a parent, you feed, clothe and care for the children you bring into the world… and the money to do so must always take precedence over everything else, at least until they leave home. For those who want children but physically can't have them, it is becoming increasingly easier to become a parent, regardless of sexuality or age. Surrogates, IVF, adoption are great alternatives for those folks but the often exorbitant costs associated with them should always be taken into consideration.

For all of us, health care is a financial concern. No matter how good your insurance, it is unquestionably more expensive to be sick than be healthy. So, if your instinct is to complain the next time you have to pay for your gym's monthly membership dues, a doctor's visit, or if you're curiously 'disappointed' when a check up reveals no major issues ("I paid all that money for lab work and nothing's wrong with me?"), remind yourself that staying healthy is an important investment in your overall physical, mental and financial wellbeing. *The Journal of the American Medical Association* found that, compared to 34 other countries, US citizens may be living longer… but not necessarily better; long-term chronic disabilities such as depression, diabetes, lung disease and musculoskeletal disease are the most prevalent problems, although we are better than other nations in treating stroke, breast cancer and colon cancer.

Money and friendships don't mix. Whenever possible, take Shakespeare's advice and "Be not a borrower, nor a lender be." This doesn't mean you shouldn't support your pals by attending their concerts or book signings, sponsoring their charity endeavors or picking up some Girl Scout cookies when little Sally is selling, but set a limit for spending on each that is within your budget and that you will be prepared to match when the next person in that social circle comes along with a solicitation.

My buddy Roy cleverly calls this 'go away' money. "Here's twenty bucks for you… and twenty bucks for you… and another twenty bucks for you… Now, GO AWAY!" Approach is everything, so if you're looking for a donation or a loan: be nice and be BRIEF. If someone declines, don't take it personally… don't be offended and move on.

The relentless guilt-trips a former friend was laying on me to contribute to help fund her latest money-making venture nearly cost us our friendship. For 20 years, she and I had been very close… doing favours for one another without thought or hesitation. However, when she began equating dollars with devotion, I had to walk away. It wasn't about the money. It was her belligerent disrespect for repeated, polite refusals that took its toll. True friends don't put conditions on each other.

Reciprocal generous gifts are one thing… but loans are another thing altogether. Unless you treat it as a professional transaction (and get the terms in writing), don't expect to get your loan back, no matter how well you think you know and trust each other.

Did you know that being prudent might be good for your love life, too? Studies suggest that single folks are more attracted to good savers than lavish spendthrifts. It's believed that the discipline exercised in financial self-control extends itself to other areas of responsibility and maturity prized by partner-seeking individuals. Hey, why splurge on a dozen roses when one single stem says as much?

In this era of online piracy and identity theft, it's never been more important to keep a close eye on your dollars. Knowing your financial institution's up-to-date guarantees and liabilities regarding your holdings, routinely checking your credit score and balancing your account are must-do's. I proudly restrict myself to one credit card, but three times in less than a year it had to be cancelled because of ID theft… a major inconvenience, especially with all the auto-billing and online purchases we enjoy these days. A debit card or a cash-stash is a good back-up plan for these kinds of unforeseen occurrences.

I'm also an unapologetic coupon clipper. If there's a discount code or 'members price' I make sure to use it. Comparison shopping and the time-tested practice of haggling are also tools I use for just about every-thing from groceries to appliances to wardrobe. Those few dollars I save at every purchase really add up by the time I do my year-end accounting. Look through your wallet and you might be surprised at all the bargain opportunities you may already be offered through your insurance company, union membership or employment status.

As you can tell, no one appreciates a bargain more than I do… but being 'cheap' is crass. There are times to economize and times to spend the dough. So what if your friend had an extra drink at dinner? Split the bill evenly. If So and So is really taking advantage of the situation, you'll know next time to avoid him as a dining companion. Be a generous tipper: consider it 'cash karma'… what goes around comes around.

In 2012, the National Endowment for Financial Education conducted a survey of parents who had adult children living at home. It revealed that 26 per cent had taken on debt to support their kids and 7 per cent had delayed retirement. Parents' intentions may be good, but they're doing their offspring no real favors by keeping them cushioned in the nest well into adulthood. A child's poor financial habits may never reprove and then comes the cycle of guilt/resentment and further dependence… not to mention a probable loss in ambition from the children. One of the greatest gifts my Mother and Dad gave me wasn't monetary: it was the education and confidence to leave home and pursue a career.

Increasingly, it's not just the next generation that is putting a stress on our savings, it is reported that 13 million US adults are financially supporting their parents and their children at the same time. Subsequently, homebuilders are now offering floor plans for multi-generational houses specifically designed for these families. A 2012 survey by Pulte-Group found that 31 per cent of adults with grown children expect their kids to move home at some point and 32 per cent expect to eventually share a home with an elderly parent. In addition to the costs associated with the care and feeding of those 'extra' families under one roof, there will subsequently be a raise in basic utility costs such as power and water. If you're likely to be one of those 'sandwiched' in between caring for both an older and younger generation of family members, resist the temptation to splurge on luxury items.

The renowned capitalist John D. Rockefeller was known to fanatically record his expenditure down to the last penny… from his boyhood onwards. The oil baron passed this habit on to his son, John Jr., who ultimately became one of modern history's greatest philanthropists, giving away unprecedented millions in donations and endowments. When you visit majestic Rockefeller Center in NYC, you will no doubt be impressed by the grandeur… but take a moment to consider the prudence and planning that went into creating it!

I have a close friend who happens to be an heiress. She was bequeathed a lot of dough, which she inherited as a very young adult after her parents' tragic, untimely demise. She's now closing in on 60. It may be easy to blithely say, "well, she'll never have to fret about money a day in her life." Probably not but that's because she's fretted about it in her youth and lived a thrifty life… right down to checking the prices on the back of greeting cards. But acquiring a fortune when young—and under such terrible circumstances—also instilled a sense of anxiety. That inheritance seems to represent a 'living' link to her folks and consequently a responsibility to be meticulously managed and preserved. Fortunately, her pecuniary instincts have served her well and she is enjoying an enviable retirement.

> *"Always borrow money from a pessimist. He won't expect it back." Oscar Wilde*

It's not always easy to save, especially when you have little or no control over what money you have coming in. There have been two occasions in my life when I had to borrow significant amounts of money (ie, mortgages) to facilitate some dramatic life changes, I was relentless about paying the debt down until it was finally behind me. Sometimes that meant taking on second or third jobs… I even sold off my prized celebrity autograph collection on ebay and regularly held garage sales. I survived a series of housemates that would make any sitcom scenario pale in comparison. Some of my most wacky 'survival jobs' and situations turned out to be helpful though: making lasting friendships or taking unexpected professional paths.

> *Maybe there's a part-time job or lucrative sideline you haven't yet imagined. What are your hobbies, talents or*

interests? I turned my joy of running into extra income by giving running tours of Central Park and dog 'jogging' for harried pet owners. Get creative. Good with math? Do some book-keeping. Like kids? Babysit, coach or tutor. Movie fan? Be an usher at the cinema. Think of all the films you'll get to see for free. If you're a 'people person', there might be positions as a receptionist, greeter or personal assistant. Browse online at sites such as craigslist.org ('services available') for some ideas.

In my mid-forties I took a long, objective look at all the things I had managed to amass over the course of my adult life. There I was, a single guy in a three-bedroom house with a yard and a garage stuffed to the ceiling with... stuff! For the next phase of my life, less would be more. As soon as I started the process of downsizing, it was as if I had been liberated. The shackles of having all that STUFF came off and so did the burden of its upkeep: both physical and financial. Honestly, what did I need with grandfather's Wedgwood and silver? My sister was thrilled to have it and I was thrilled to be free of it. My gorgeous player piano from the 1920s and the scores of original music rolls were a collector's dream. I enjoyed them for decades... now it would be someone else's turn. Now, whenever I go over to my pal Louise's house, we have singalongs for old times' sake. Maybe I don't get to tickle the ivories as often, but I don't have to polish them, either. Any books that didn't have a special and significant place in my heart were donated to the local library (and I gladly took the charitable tax deduction) for others to enjoy. As the song says, "The sweet things in life, to you were just loaned... so how can you lose what you never owned?" Life is just a bowl of cherries, right? So don't overpay for the pits!

Throwing off the shackles may provide you with unimaginable freedom. Say 'yes' to opportunities... even the strangest ones. You never know where it might lead. It may be an adventure... or it may be part of some divine plan. Joan Crawford used to say that she welcomed problems and advised, "Turn a problem into a challenge and enjoy it!" That certainly may be easier said than done when it comes to monetary matters, but rising to the occasion undoubtedly builds character and beats the alternative of giving in to a purely emotional response. Money matters affect everyone differently… anger, anxiety, depression… all stressful. Try to counsel yourself to handle these with the same rationale and detachment of any other important adult circumstance. If your basement flooded or car had four slashed tyres, I bet you wouldn't have a temper tantrum: you'd knuckle down and solve the problem as calmly and efficiently as possible.

> *"Magic is believing in yourself, if you can do that, you can make anything happen." Goethe*

Everybody's different (thank goodness) so if you don't have a financial planner, or a father like mine, with whom to consult… talk to a well-off friend you can trust for advice. So far, my primary success outside of some dividends from family stock and traditional bank savings accounts has been through real estate. Even that was serendipity… I was in the right place at the right time, when the housing market turned to my advantage. For all the methods there may be to make money, sometimes nothing beats timing.

While I like the security and stability of having my money in a bank, I am well aware that simply having it sit there will not get me much return. Paltry interest rates come nowhere near to the cost of inflation, so it's important to put your money to work for you through investments. One of my goals is to become more educated and aggressive about the stock market… even though my prudent side will only allow me to make ultra-conservative, 'blue-chip' safe choices. I am starting slowly with mutual funds and have also arranged for a small monthly amount to be automatically debited from my savings to be placed in an individual retirement account. I'll keep you posted on how that goes.

Definitely talk to a financial advisor or someone whose personal money management impresses you. Take a 'slow and steady' approach and don't be swayed by the daily pendulum swings of the stock market… and best not to listen to nerve-wracking Cable News hysteria every time it moves one way or the other. If you want to increase your wealth, it will take time and patience. When the numbers go down (which they inevitably will), remind yourself that you are in it for the long haul. If you want short-term gains, have a yard sale or try your luck at the Powerball lottery.

Fortunately, I love to work and have a job I enjoy. I have no dreams or plans for retirement any time soon. That's good news not only for my bank account (in the US, the longer you can delay retirement, the more dollars you stand to collect) but for health. A Harvard study showed that retirees are 40 per cent more likely to suffer a heart attack or stroke than people who are still working. Even if you have a career/job you love that feels safe and secure, it is smart to keep your resumé up to date and, if you have professional marketing tools such as a website or social media pages, keep them current.

Want to save some money to pass down to the kids or stash in the bank? Skip the traveling and plan a 'stay-cation'. You can bloom where you're planted and maybe catch up on some enjoyable projects you've been putting off, and you won't need to worry about having someone retrieve your mail or water the lawn.

Making wise everyday choices can add up to significant savings. I'm a big coffee drinker, but not a fussy one. Just as I am perfectly content with my inexpensive coffee maker at home as opposed to an expensive contraption that does everything but hula dance. I pretty much eschew the big over-priced coffee houses who charge five bucks a pop for a

mediocre cup and instead swing into a Bodega or by a street
vendor and plop down a dollar for a good old steaming hot
cuppa. On a daily or even bi-weekly basis, those savings
really add up.

Lucky for us, so many great stars continue working into their 70s and beyond, providing not only first-rate entertainment to audiences as well as
inspiration that you need never be too old to do what you love. It will be a
sad day if treasures such as Carl Reiner, Christopher Lee, Sydney Poitier,
Cloris Leachman, Christopher Plummer, Gene Hackman, James Earl
Jones, William Shatner, Rita Moreno, Debbie Reynolds, Ellen Burstyn, or
Angela Lansbury ever decide to take to their rocking chairs. When asked
at the most recent Venice Film Festival if she planned to one day wind
down her stunning film career and retire, Judi Dench quickly retorted,
"No, no! That's a really dirty word. 'Old' and 'retiring' are really dirty
words!" What do you suppose has kept the indomitable Carol Channing
belting out show tunes into her naughty 90s? As the song says, *Applause,*
Applause! As long as there's an appreciative audience, these troupers
keep trouping. Maybe that's why these folks seem to have no 'sell by'
dates. There really is 'no people, like show people'.

He may be best known for playing eccentric villains and
other assorted oddballs, but when asked what real-life
person he would like to play in a film, talented Johnny
Depp explained with all seriousness that he planned to do a
biopic that indicated he was serious about his plan to play
nonagenarian Channing. He also revealed, that as a child,
one of his favorite dress-up characters was, in fact, the great
lady of the Broadway stage. Hmm... like filmmaker Ed
Wood, whom he famously portrayed, Johnny's certainly in
touch with his feminine side.

The old adage, 'If you love what you do, you'll never work a day in your life,' rings true for many in the creative arts. In addition to actors continuing to work for a lifetime, dancers and singers often turn to teaching up-and-comers when their own skills eventually get rusty. That's the bright side of 'those who can't DO, teach'.

And there must be something about cartoonists. Charles Schulz changed the world infinitely for the better with his creation of *Peanuts* and kept good old Charlie Brown and the gang shiny and new until his death in 2000. Bil Keane met and married his wife Thel while stationed in Australia during World War II. He chronicled their domestic misadventures in *The Family Circus* until his death at age 89, but the cartoon clan continues delighting newspaper readers to this day under the similar style of his son, Jeff. The late Bob Kane co-created *Batman* and forever sealed his place in popular culture history. When I met him in his 80s, he was still with pen in hand... delighting fans with his wonderful renditions of the caped crusader. *Beetle Bailey*'s, Mort Walker, is now in his 90s and still cranking out the daily strip, which celebrated its 60th anniversary in 2010... with no plans of stopping.

While we're on the subject of advanced planning, in addition to making sure your living will/DNR (do not resuscitate), organ donation wishes and last will and testament are in order and legally binding, make sure you have chosen and notified a responsible executor to carry out your wishes. You may also be wise to consider pre-planning and paying for your final expenses. If you don't have the funds currently available, consider a life insurance plan that will help defray the costs for your survivors. There are many affordable policies available to choose from.

Whatever you do, don't get all melancholy or fearful about it. Dying is as much a part of life as birth... and the great common denominator. Wouldn't you rather get the details arranged to your own specifications, and while you're fit and vibrant enough not to get emotional about it? My parents, in their infinite macabre wit and wisdom, decided to make a game out of it. They invited the mortician over to their home, dressed head-to-toe in black outfits and served Bloody Marys while they went through catalogs of caskets, urns and headstones. How very Herman and Lily Munster. The undertaker wasn't much amused, but it was a lot of fun for Mother and Dad and will ultimately save me and my siblings extra stress and sadness. (More on marking after-life milestones later.)

I guess the summation of this chapter is that you don't have to be Ebenezer Scrooge, but you'd better develop a savings plan pronto, if you haven't already. We have all seen those unimaginable 'rainy days' wash away even the most seemingly prepared individuals. Preparation is a key quality in most of life's issues… especially when it comes to fiscal matters.

FOOD AND DIET

We've all heard the adage 'you are what you eat' so many times that the philosophy may seem to have lost its meaning… but it really is the essence of living. What you put into your body directly manifests itself by what you get OUT of it. I don't mean the physicality of human waste but in terms of the wonderful things you can exude: from an energetic personality, to happiness and vigor… and the more esoteric benefits such as sparkling eyes, a bright smile and a luminous complexion. As we age, these qualities become more and more evident… and important. Compare the skin tone, vitality and effervescence of a 60-year-old who pigs out on sloppy Joes and beer, with a seafood-, fruit- and vegetable-loving counterpart and you'll see what I mean.

When it comes to my favorite recipes, I've published three books in which I purged my file of healthy and indulgent kitchen concoctions. They should all be available on ebay by now, so for a buck or two, you'll be all set.

* *Let's Dish Up a Dinner Party!* (2008)
* *Hollywood Insider: Exposed!* (2009)
* *Dinner at Nelson's* (2011)

What about your approach to food? As a habitual over-eater and gourmand, just eating until satisfied has never been a reasonable option for me. While being a runner helps keep excess weight off, it also increases my already voracious appetite to the point where, if I'm not conscientious, I can actually gain weight while training for long-distance races. I have a small frame, so a few pounds makes a big difference on me even if it doesn't show on camera. One advantage of having an elongated face and high-cheekbones (thank you, great Grandfather Cherokee Indian.) is it always looks thin on TV. Don't believe what they say about the camera adding ten pounds.

The notion that our metabolism slows as we age hasn't proven true with me… yet. I haven't encountered a 'middle age spread', but I have battled the same waistline bulge my whole life. Unless I want to go have it cut off or sucked out (I don't), it looks like it's here to stay. I don't get too uptight about it since there aren't many times a 50-year-old man is expected or encouraged to be shirtless. That said, my manager did enquire about my interest in joining a short-lived competition show, *Celebrity Splash*. I only had to consider a minute before declining; a) I didn't want to risk any injury and b) the idea of parading around in a swimsuit for three months on high-definition television was a deal-breaker. It's a sign of maturity to recognize your limitations.

Popular New Jersey Governor, Chris Christie (widely believed to be prepping for a 2016 presidential bid), revealed that he had gastric-band surgery to lose weight but denied it had anything to do with prettying up for a potential presidential run. "This is about turning 50 and looking at my children and wanting to be there for them," he said.

The National Institute on Aging recommends these tips for
healthy eating after age 50:
* Eat many different colors and types of different fruits and
vegetables.
* Make sure at least half of your grains are whole grains.
* Eat only small amounts of solid fats and foods with added
sugars. Limit saturated fat (found mostly in foods that come
from animals) and trans fats (found in foods such as store-
bought baked goods and some margarines).
* Eat seafood twice a week.

I've tried all sorts of diet regimens over the years from fasting to vegetarian, South Beach to vegan. What works best for me is to eat as much
fresh food as possible with lots of vegetables for fiber and lean meats and
fish for protein. I manage to avoid most 'bad' choices such fast-food, fried
dishes, saturated fats and processed sugar. I don't like soda, so that helps.
Coffee in the morning, water in the afternoon, wine at night… that's pretty much always worked for me (and sports drink when exercising).

But proper hydration isn't just important for athletes. Getting the
necessary replenishment of electrolytes, sodium and calories is a
balancing act you should strive to master. I have experimented with many
over the years that I've been a distance runner and find that good old
Gatorade and Gu carbohydrate supplements work best for me. I'm even
wedded to particular flavors. Hey, whatever works…

Of course, there are times when you just have to let your body tell
you what it needs. Note, I didn't say 'craves'! Just as there are moments
when I feel a genuine, physical urge to put a good piece of steak down
the hatch, there are times when my gut calls out for some crispy, crunchy
fresh veggies. It's interesting that two of our past presidents, Bill Clinton
and George W. Bush (both born 1946), were both runners but suffered
with heart ailments after they left office. The former was a notorious

fast-food junkie while the latter a fastidious teetotaller. Mr Clinton is now a contented vegan, keeping chefs around the world on their toes when he shows up for state dinners. Their predecessors, George H. W. Bush and Jimmy Carter (both born 1924), never seemed to fuss much over cuisine. Bush was known for his hatred of broccoli, while Carter, a former peanut farmer, loved fatty Southern fare. They're still hanging in there and President Bush was still skydiving as of his 85th birthday.

Whenever we hear from the current 'world's oldest person' it always seems their dietary regimens are unremarkable. Admit it: you know when you're putting healthy choices into your body and when you're not.

Deprivation and starvation tactics are never a good idea no matter how desperate you are to lose weight. That irritable feeling you get when you haven't eaten won't get you very far in public if you give it a voice. Get over yourself and have a granola bar.

At one of the clubs where I work out, there is an emaciated Upper East Side housewife with a very obvious eating disorder. She works out like a maniacal Olympian, only pausing to sip from her cup of ice coffee, and tears around the facility like a cross between a whirling dervish and a Tasmanian devil. Her behaviour sparked a conversation with my then-coach, Scott Fishman, about the rage associated with folks who don't eat and/or work out to extremes. He told me that one of the biggest meltdowns he ever witnessed was in a juice bar.

Scott told me, "Post-workout rage occurs in individuals who work out, often solely with the intention of losing weight, and it leads to nasty screaming and shouting at health club employees, gym managers and even strangers on the street. People should always bring along a post-workout snack/meal with them. Even picking up a bottle of low-fat chocolate milk can help stave off that feeling. The post-workout rage does not always hit right after a workout. It sometimes creeps up on the individual later in the day unexpectedly and for no apparent reason. Eating less, doesn't meant you should eat nothing. It's all about finding the balance to maximize your energy and minimize your hunger. And don't neglect carbohydrates. People hate carbs too much. They are important to have before and after your workout. Healthy carbs consist of nuts, blueberries, strawberries and raspberries. They are not a bag of chips or candy. Stay away from processed foods. A deceptively bad choice is having a banana all by itself in the middle of the day without working out after. It spikes insulin levels a lot." To bounce back from a bad binge, he recommends drinking lots of water and eating dark green veggies. Better than a traditional scale, Scott thinks the best way to monitor the effectiveness of your diet is through regular Body Mass Index (BMI) tests and performance assessments.

The juicing craze that is so globally popular has resulted in a new word coined by its devotees: 'hanger', meaning the combination of 'hunger' and 'anger' that results from food deprivation. Some juicers are actually becoming addicted to the feeling of being 'hangry'! Walk away from the blender, folks, and go make a sandwich.

Certain foods are thought to help fight stress and, as a bonus, they're delicious. Are these staples in your diet?
* *Blueberries*
* *Dark chocolate*
* *Fatty/Oily fish (Salmon, trout)*
* *Flaxseed*
* *Walnuts*
* *Soybeans*
* *Sunflower seeds*

Keep in mind that having a distorted body image is a psychological issue, not a physical one. So what's the best way to help a person with obvious symptoms? Scott wisely advises, "Don't talk about their body. They won't believe you, anyway. I like to focus on the development of athletic ability. I try and shift the attention to performance."

Don't you hate it when you spend good money on beautiful produce only to have it spoil after only a day or two? I found out that this actually has nothing to do with the quality of the food... it's actually because of a gas certain fruits and vegetables emit as they ripen. If you place one piece that releases this gas (ethylene) next to another that is ethylene-sensitive, it will go soft or spotted. Here is a list of delicious, nutritious ethylene-producing items you should not place near other produce: apricots, avocados, bananas, cantaloupes, honeydew melons, kiwis, mangoes, nectarines, papayas, peaches, pears, plums and tomatoes.

Living in a city such as New York (where every kind of food is available around the clock and can be delivered in an instant to your door), it should be easy to eat like the ultimate health nut. I have found it to be just the opposite. Even in the world-famous gourmet Zabar's Market, which I pass every time I come and go from my apartment and where there is a vast selection of delectable, nutritious cuisine, my mouth invariably waters for all the naughtiest things. On a daily basis, I'm faced with black-and-white cookies, bagels and bialys, knishes, and the greatest pizza parlours on the planet. Even while dining in restaurants you're at the mercy of the chef controlling your portion size. It's usually too much. I don't know about you, but I've always been a 'clean your plate' kind of guy and wish I could be more like my Dad, who's never left a restaurant without a 'doggy bag' of leftovers. I'm trying more and more to limit my courses, but it's one of my biggest challenges. (If there's salmon on the menu in a restaurant, I invariably order it – that's an easy way to make sure I get those omega-3 fatty acids renowned for their immunity-boosting powers.)

I've never been to a nutritionist and, without any food allergies or other dietary related issues, I haven't felt the need to visit one. I enjoy all the different things I eat. When I overdo it in one food group or another, my body tells me pretty quickly. Myriad industries are built on trying to tell people how a certain diet or lifestyle will work wonders for them. Maybe some of them do. I can't help being turned off by the assault of all those books, info-mmercials, DVDs and gimmicks. Here's a surefire way to lose weight: put down the fork and go burn some calories. By all means, knowledge is power... so listen to what the experts are saying, but also take into account your individual needs, lifestyle and desires. Customize your own plan and remember that fad diets are so named because they (and likely their results) are only temporary.

> *A study published in the* Journal of Alzheimer's Disease *found that a diet high in carbohydrates (in which two-thirds of daily calories are derived from carbs) not only increases the risk of mental decline among seniors by as much as 89 per cent, but also those seniors who eat the highest percentage of protein and fat are least likely to get dementia. 'Bad' carbs are considered those made from refined starches and sugars as opposed to the 'good' carbs found in fresh vegetables and fruit.*

Stock up the kitchen with plenty of fruits and vegetables and you're more likely to eat healthily. I simply refuse to keep fattening things in my home.

I'm not Gordon Ramsay and neither are you, but I do think it's possible to 'eat like a star' if you combine quality ingredients with simple recipes and pay a little extra attention to presentation... really savor and enjoy what you're putting into your body. It's never too late to start bringing healthy eating habits to the table. Consider a Mediterranean-inspired meal plan with lots of fruits and vegetables, whole grains and legumes, and healthy omega-3 (wild salmon, walnuts, flax) and monounsaturated (olive oil) fats. Trout, wild salmon, olives and avocados are not only versatile and delicious, they are considered to be cancer-fighting foods. Low-fat dairy products and leafy greens will help keep your bones strong. You'll find many of the savory and nutritious recipes I am including here to be influenced by these guidelines.

MIXED GREENS WITH TOMATOES AND WHITE BEAN

Is there anything more convenient than the 'salad in a bag'? I love grabbing a bag of mixed greens, giving them a quick rinse and making a meal by adding in whatever healthy ingredients I happen to have in the pantry or refrigerator. Spinach, Swiss chard, arugula (rocket) and kale are among my favorite greens for their flavorful, leafy loveliness. This recipe has become a quick and easy lunch or side dish that is low in calories and fat, but supplies a tasty dose of good carbohydrates, fiber and protein. Canned beans and tomatoes (more nutritious than fresh) should always be in your cupboard.

Serves 2 as a meal, 4 as a side dish.

* 11 oz (300 g) bag of mixed greens, rinsed
* 2 tbsp (30 ml) olive oil
* 1 tbsp (15 ml) chopped garlic
* 1 tsp chopped or dried thyme
* 1 tsp ground cumin
* red pepper flakes, to taste
* 15 oz (400 g) can diced tomatoes (no salt added)
* 15 oz can (400 g) white beans (drained and rinsed)
* salt and pepper, optional

Bring a large pan of water to the boil, add the greens, return to the boil and boil for approximately 3 minutes. Drain and blot with kitchen paper and set aside.

Heat the oil in a saucepan over medium heat. Add the garlic, thyme, cumin and pepper flakes while stirring continuously. Add the tomatoes and beans and cook until the mixture is hot. Stir in the greens, add salt and pepper to taste, if desired.

CRAB SALAD WITH CANNELLINI BEANS

As Dad used to sing, "Beans. Beans. The magical fruit. Don't worry about the 'toot'." Their healthy qualities far outweigh that occasional side effect! Another quick, easy lunchtime meal or side dish for a summer's soirée.

Serves 2 as a meal, 4 as a side dish.

* ⅓ cup (2 oz/55 g) red bell pepper, chopped
* ⅓ cup (3 oz/85 g) red onion, chopped
* ⅓ cup (1½ oz/45 g) chopped celery
* 2 tbsp white wine vinegar
* 1 tbsp fresh lemon juice
* 1 tbsp olive oil
* red pepper flakes, sea/kosher salt to taste
* 6 oz (175 g) lump crab meat (drained)
* 15 oz (400 g) can cannellini beans (rinsed and drained)
* 11 oz (300 g) bag mixed greens

Combine all ingredients except the greens and toss gently. Cover and chill for 20 minutes, then serve over the greens. Cool and colorful!

COLESLAW WITH YOGURT AND APPLE DRESSING

I adapted this recipe from the venerable *Bon Appétit* magazine and love it as a refreshing side dish or even on its own. Low cal, low fat, low cholesterol, Big taste. Keep a supply in the refrigerator and you can always scoop some into a taco shell with some flakey white fish, sprinkle with Tabasco sauce and have an instant fish taco.

Serves 2 as a meal, 4 as a side dish.

* 1 cup (8 oz/225 g) non-fat Greek yogurt (strained plain)
* ½ cup (4 oz/115 g) low-fat mayonnaise
* 2 tbsp white wine vinegar
* 1 tbsp fresh lemon juice
* 1 tsp chopped garlic
* salt and pepper to taste
* 8 cups (1 lb 1¾ oz/540 g) shredded cabbage (mix red and green for a colorful dish)
* 12 oz (350 g) broccoli, shredded
* ½ cup (75 g/2½ oz) carrots, shredded
* ½ cup scallions (spring onions), finely chopped
* 1 green apple

Whisk the yogurt, mayonnaise, vinegar, lemon juice and garlic in a medium bowl until smooth. Add salt and pepper to taste. Cover and chill.

Twenty minutes before you are ready to serve, combine the cabbage, broccoli, carrots and scallions in large bowl. Toss to mix well.

Core the apple and slices into julienne strips. Add the apple to the vegetable mixture and toss until evenly mixed. Add the chilled dressing and stir until evenly blended.

CITRUS CHICKPEA SALAD WITH CHEESE AND HERBS

Serves 2 as a meal, 4 as a side dish.

You can have some fun with this easy, nutritious salad, also adapted from *Bon Appétit*, because you can substitute or add whatever choice of herbs or cheese you happen to have on hand, or are craving. Good healthy carbs also make this dish a real cardio boost to energize you, or to help you recover from a rigorous workout.

* 15 oz (400 g) can chickpeas (garbanzo beans), rinsed and drained.
* 2 tbsp fresh basil, chopped
* 2 tbsp fresh Italian parsley or cilantro (coriander), chopped
* 2 tbsp fresh lime juice
* 2 tsp olive oil
* 1 tsp chopped garlic
* ⅓ cup (2½ oz/75 g) feta cheese, crumbled
* salt and pepper, to taste

Combine the chickpeas, herbs, lime juice, olive oil and garlic in a medium bowl. Add the cheese on top, then salt and pepper, to taste. Cover and chill. Serve chilled, or at room temperature.

ORZO PASTA SALAD

Here's a hearty and heart-healthy salad that is delicious served warm or chilled. It's easy to make too.

Serves 2 as a meal, 4 as a side dish.

* 1½ cups (300 g/11 oz) dry orzo pasta
* 2 tbsp olive oil
* 2 tbsp lemon juice
* 1 large cucumber (peeled, seeded and chopped)
* 1 tbsp mint, chopped
* 1 tbsp Italian parsley, chopped
* ½ cup (4 oz/115 g) fresh mozzarella, crumbled
* ½ cup grape (small plum) tomatoes, halved
* salt and pepper, to taste

Cook the orzo pasta until *al dente*, according to the packet instructions. Drain in a colander and transfer to medium bowl. Mix in the other ingredients.

RAW CORN SALAD WITH BUTTERMILK DRESSING

Buy corn in season from a farmer's market or organic grocer, and it won't even need to be cooked. It can be sliced right off the cob and tossed into a bowl. It is a fresh and sweet source of antioxidants, carbs and fiber.

Serves 2 as a meal, 4 as a side dish.

SALAD

* 1 shallot, thinly sliced
* 3 cups (1 lb 3 oz/525 g) sweet corn kernels
* 4 cucumbers peeled, seeded and thinly sliced
* 1 red bell pepper, seeded and diced
* ¼ cup fresh parsley, chopped
* ¼ cup fresh dill, chopped
* ½ cup (4 oz/115 g) feta cheese, crumbled, to serve

DRESSING

* ¼ cup (2 fl oz/50 ml) buttermilk
* ⅓ cup (¼ pint/150 ml) plain (natural) low-fat yogurt
* 1 tbsp white-wine vinegar
* 3 tbsp sweet onion, minced (finely chopped)
* 1 tsp garlic, chopped
* ¼ cup (2 fl oz/50 ml) olive oil
* salt and pepper, to taste

In a large bowl, lightly toss the corn until the kernels separate. Add the remaining salad ingredients, but not the feta, and toss again to combine.

In a smaller bowl, combine the buttermilk, yogurt, vinegar, onion and garlic by whisking. Slowly pour in the oil and whisk until combined. Season to taste with salt and pepper. Serve chilled, garnished with the feta.

PESTO PASTA AND PEAS

Serves 2 as a meal, 4 as a side dish.

There are plenty of good quality pesto sauces to buy, but with a food processor, it's easy (and tastier) to make it fresh at home. I prefer using gemelli, mostaccioli or penne pasta because the sauce really clings to it.

* 3 cups (12 oz/350 g) pasta
* 2 oz (55 g) pine nuts
* 4 cups basil leaves
* 2 cloves garlic
* 2 tbsp Parmesan (plus extra, for serving)
* ½ tsp salt
* ½ cup (4 fl oz/120 ml) olive oil
* juice of 1 lemon
* 1 cup (4 oz/115 g) peas
* salt and pepper, to taste

Cook the pasta according to the packet instructions, until *al dente*. Reserve the cooking water.

Lightly toast the pine nuts in a pan over medium-high heat. Allow to cool. Place the nuts, basil, garlic, Parmesan and salt into a blender or food processor. Drizzle in a little olive oil and slowly pulse until a thick, liquid consistency forms. Continue adding in the rest of the olive oil this way and then add the lemon juice. Season with salt and pepper to taste.

Put the cooked pasta in a large pan with a ½ cup (4 fl oz/120 ml) of reserved pasta water. Over medium heat, stir in the peas and cook until warm. Toss in the pesto sauce and heat until hot. Scatter additional Parmesan on top of each serving.

QUINOA WITH GREEN VEGGIES AND LEMON DRESSING

Serves 2 as a meal, 4 as a side dish.

DRESSING

* 3 tbsp olive oil
* 3 tbsp lemon juice
* 1 tsp honey
* 1 tsp garlic, chopped
* 1 tbsp fresh basil, chopped
* salt and pepper, to taste

SALAD

* 2 cups (16 fl oz/475 ml) water
* 1 cup (6 oz/175 g) quinoa
* pinch of salt
* 2 tsp olive oil
* 1 cup (4½ oz/135 g) fresh asparagus, chopped
* 1 cup (4 oz/115 g) frozen peas
* 1 avocado, diced
* 1 tbsp fresh basil, chopped

In a small bowl, whisk the dressing ingredients to combine.

Pour the water into a large pan, add the pinch of salt and bring to a boil over medium heat. Add the quinoa, return to a boil and boil for 5 minutes. Lower the heat and simmer for 15 minutes until the water is absorbed. Fluff the quinoa with a fork.

Meanwhile, heat the olive oil in a frying pan over medium heat and sauté the asparagus with the lemon juice until tender. Stir in the peas and cook until they are thawed.

In a large bowl, combine the quinoa and vegetables. Mix in the dressing with salt and pepper, topping with the remaining basil and diced avocado.

LEAN-GREEN VEGETABLE SOUP

Serves 4.

* 3 tbsp olive oil
* 2 cloves garlic, chopped
* 2 medium onions, chopped
* 2 medium white potatoes, cubed
* 2 medium zucchini (courgettes), chopped
* 4 cups (1¾ pints/1 litre) vegetable stock
* 4 cups (10½ oz/ 290 g) fresh spinach leaves
* 1 cup coriander (cilantro), chopped
* 2 tbsp single (light) cream
* juice of 1 lemon
* salt, to taste

Heat the olive oil in a large pan over a medium-high setting. When hot, add the garlic, onions and a pinch of salt. Sauté for a few minutes until softened. Stir in the potatoes and zucchini. Gradually pour in the stock. Bring to a simmer and cook until the potatoes are soft throughout, about 15 minutes.

Stir in the spinach, which will quickly wilt, then the cilantro. Using a hand blender, blend until smooth. Add the lemon juice and the cream. Mix again until combined. Serve drizzled with extra olive oil and salt, to taste.

AMY'S LENTIL SOUP WITH PENNETTE

One of my longest friendships is with chef Amy Casale, whom I met as a teenager, about five minutes after I moved to NYC and we wound up in the same acting class. She's one of the funniest people I know and nothing brings me more joy than laughing with her as she prepares one of her incredible meals. Being her kitchen helper always leads to hysterics and she puts all that love and good humor into every dish she creates. Many of her recipes are from or adapted from those of her late, great mother, famed Italian chef Ann Casale. This recipe, she says, Ann always served on New Year's Day… as lentils are considered good luck and are thought to bring wealth for the year ahead. Luck and wealth are great… but don't discount the healthy bonus of all that fiber.

Serves 8.

* 8 oz (225 g) dried brown lentils
* 5 tbsp olive oil
* 4 oz (115 g) pancetta, finely diced
* 1 large leek trimmed, split in half thoroughly washed and thinly sliced
* 4 large celery ribs, strings removed, cut into ½ in (1 cm) cubes
* 3 large carrots, peeled and cut into ¼ in (6 mm) cubes
* 2 small parsnips, peeled and cut into ¼ in (6 mm) cubes
* 1 cup (14 oz/400 g) canned Italian plum tomatoes, coarsely chopped, juice included
* 4½ cups (1⅞ pint/1.1 litres) beef broth, heated
* 2 tsp coarse salt
* 2 tsp freshly milled black pepper
* 1 cup (4 oz/115 g) pennette or any short tubular pasta
* 1 tsp salt
* fresh Italian parsley, chopped

* freshly grated Romano cheese, to serve

Spread the lentils in a single layer on a large plate and discard any bits of foreign matter. Rinse in a strainer (sieve) with cold water.

In a large pan, heat the oil over medium heat. Add the pancetta and cook, stirring constantly, until soft but not browned, about 3 minutes. Add the leek, celery, carrots and parsnips. Sauté, stirring frequently until slightly softened, about 5 minutes. Add the tomatoes and stir frequently for 5 minutes. Stir in the lentils and add the heated broth. Season with salt and pepper. Cover the pan, turn the heat to low, and cook, stirring frequently, until the lentils are tender, about 1 hour. Remove from the heat and let the soup rest for at least 1 hour.

Cook the pasta in salted boiling water until *al dente*, according to the instructions on the packet. Drain well and add to the soup. Reheat the soup over low heat. Ladle into individual bowls and serve with fresh chopped parsley and Romano cheese.

CHILLED AVOCADO SOUP

Zabar's Market is my neighborhood secret weapon. Aside from groceries and kitchen supplies, they have every imaginable gourmet treat. Their chef, Andrew Regnier, came up with this fantastic recipe, which is delicious on a warm summer night and perfect to take along on a picnic.

Serves 4 – 6.

* 2 medium red bell peppers
* 1 lb (450 g) sweet corn kernels
* 10 cloves garlic
* 4 ripe avocados
* 1 red onion
* ¼ cup cilantro (coriander)
* 5¾ cups (46 fl oz/1.3 litres) chicken broth
* 3 fl oz (90 ml) lime juice
* 32 fl oz (950 ml) plain (natural) yogurt
* salt, to taste
* chili powder, to taste
* ¼ tsp chili powder

Preheat the oven to 400°F/200°C/Gas 6. Core and halve the red bell peppers and place on a baking sheet. Put the corn and garlic on separate baking sheets. Roast each in the oven until they give a little to the touch, 3–5 minutes. Allow to cool, then chill in the refrigerator.

Purée the avocados, onion, roasted garlic, lime juice, cilantro and a small quantity of chicken broth. Combine in a large bowl with the rest of the chicken broth, yogurt, chili powder and salt. Cut the roasted pepper into small dice and add to the mixture along with the corn.

DATING, SEX AND RELATIONSHIPS

In June of 2013, I wished Johnny Depp a happy 50th birthday on Twitter and it was almost as if the internet heaved a heavy collective sigh of disappointment. People found it hard to fathom that Captain Jack Sparrow, Gilbert Grape and the heart-throb of *Chocolat* could possibly be a half-century old. (I wondered if his manager, agent and accountant were lamenting it, too.) It was as if this milestone somehow signified the beginning of the end. Fans (remember, 'fan' is shorthand for 'fanatic') can be fickle and shift their focus to the next guy in line, who's eagerly awaiting his turn in the spotlight. That's showbiz.

Fans, both male and female, seem to be openly crushed when a sexy celebrity announces their engagement, elopement or pregnancy. Once the celeb seem to be 'off the market', the audience's fantasy bubble that they might somehow have had a chance to be close to that star is suddenly burst. Oh come on, people! How does Ryan Reynolds getting married, or Jessica Alba popping out babies make them less desirable?

If the fantasy world of romance is daunting, the actual real world of dating is just as tough... at least for me. I have had a lifetime of abundant blessings and a bounty of friends and family with whom I live, laugh and love... but a lasting romantic relationship has always eluded me. Fortunately, I have always thought of myself as 'alone, but not lonely'. I consider myself an old-fashioned, monogamy-minded romantic... so I remain undaunted in my quest to find a soulmate. Are you out there?

I remember an old episode of *The Flintstones* in which Wilma met up with an old friend, Greta Gravel, who had never married. Wilma asked her why and she replied, something along the lines of, "I guess I played too hard to get. And didn't get got." That stuck with me... even as a kid... and I knew that, to use another childhood analogy, one had to kiss a lot of frogs to come upon a Prince Charming. And if you don't meet Mr Right, you may at least come across Mr-Right-for-now.

I've always been open to dating people who don't strictly conform to my ideals of perfection. And you know what? I've met some really fascinating, fantastic people that way... and had memorable, positive experiences I'd have otherwise missed. When it comes to dating, I believe you should take a few chances. The great German poet Johann Wolfgang von Goethe said, "Plunge boldly into the thick of life, and seize it where you will. It is always interesting."

One dating aspect that definitely appreciates with age is the ability to be honest. If you have enough self-esteem to put yourself out there, then don't lie about your date of birth, height, number of children, income or anything else... the truth will always find you out, especially with a Google search at everyone's disposal.

Remember that book *The Rules* and all its so-called guidelines for courtship? It made finding a partner like hunting prey! At this time in our lives, there's nothing to be lost by being openly candid and caring. You're wise enough to recognize a red flag when you see it, so you can be confident in avoiding trouble. If you keep falling into the same destructive patterns, you don't need a romance… you need psychoanalysis! By the time we reach middle age, we've been around the block enough to know that we can't fight chemistry. If it's not there, wish each other well and move on. Why prolong the agony by delaying the inevitable? NEXT!

Being honest with a potential partner doesn't mean you need to play all your cards too soon. Resist the urge to talk about your romantic resumé… especially if it's extensive. A potential new love doesn't want to hear your track record or war stories. Nor would he/she want to hear you wax nostalgic for 'the one that got away'. Let your personality be discovered gradually. You'll be so much more attractive if you don't expose everything all at once. No matter how tempted you might be to rattle off your criteria for the ideal mate, focus on the good stuff. If your knees start to creak when you get out of a chair or you have to whip out your reading glasses to read the menu, don't make a big deal out of it. Keep it to yourself. Nothing says 'old' like people sitting around complaining about their degenerative conditions. Look at it this way: your knees are creaking because you're still moving and those chic little magnifying specs only cost about ten bucks at the drug store!

The biggest change to modern dating since I came of age is the invention of the internet. Classified ads in *The Village Voice* or meeting potential partners in singles bars were the order of the day when I was a young adult. While I think online dating is a great way to meet interesting people you might otherwise never encounter, it also comes with a slew of warnings… especially for middle-aged folks. As great as online dating can be (and I've met some wonderful people that way), like every other aspect of the internet it has its downside. Be vigilant about protecting yourself from the crazies and keep your personal information close to your vest until you can manage to schedule an actual date IN PERSON. With the ease and convenience of e-dating, it can be all too easy to forget that real chemistry relies on good old face-to-face interaction. All the sweet messages and emoti-cons in the world can't make up for the way someone's eyes twinkle or how they smile, shake hands or smell!

Love online has its pros and cons. While I love texting way more than I ever loved gabbing on the telephone, I have to remind myself to know when to put down the darned device. Certainly, 'sexting' is a big no-no. Naked selfies and videos, similarly, are taboo. Who do you think you are, Paris Hilton? They're tacky for grown-ups and you'll find that if you break up with your new partner you'll have added anxiety wondering in what online corner they are floating around.

> *"I've never done online dating. It's another way to meet people, but I think if you're a person on TV it's a little different. I could get murdered or something." Aziz Ansari, born 1983*

Be careful about over-sharing. I know how tempting it is, especially in the blush of a new intimate relationship, to want to expose yourself and the treasure trove of secrets you've amassed over a lifetime. I'm not suggest-ing you need to whip out a confidentiality agreement to be signed and notarized, but remember that there's nothing more alluring than allowing someone to gradually peel back the layers of what makes you special. No one needs to know every detail, every thought, every friend in the vault of your life. Dole them out prudently and with forethought. Then if things don't work out, you won't have to worry about them writing a tell-all. At this marvelous stage of your life, you deserve to be extremely discerning about whom you allow to get close to you. Knowledge is power, after all.

> *It's a good rule of thumb to avoid talking about your exes altogether when interacting with a potential new love interest. If you say nice things about the ex, the new person will think you're still carrying a torch. If you say too many nasty things, you'll sound bitter or insecure. No matter*

how tempting it is to launch into a conversation about the person you knew so intimately, it's a lose/lose proposition for moving on with someone new. Save the uber-personal venting for when you're with your friends and, if the subject DOES come up while you're on a date, be diplomatic and vague. "We had a good run while it lasted... it just wasn't meant to be," is an agreeable way to handle it. Likewise if your date prattles on about his/her ex, then that's a likely indicator that they haven't healed or moved on sufficiently to begin something new and healthy with you. Split the tab, head home and curl up with a good book.

If you split with a paramour, I suggest you immediately delete them from your phone and unfriend them on Facebook. In a weak moment, the temptation may arise to reconnect... even if, deep down, you know you shouldn't. (Someone would make a fortune if they invented an iPhone with a breathalyzer.) Besides... when you move on to greener pastures, you don't want them to be privy to any of the juicy details. That's how stalkers are born.

Our virtual fingerprints exist forever, so erase, wipe, delete and reboot whenever possible. I went into the studio one afternoon and jumped on a public computer for everyone's use, after a certain well-known TV newsman had been using it. He hadn't cleared the cache or deleted the browser's history and the first time I hit the letter combination "s u" the website SugarDaddy.com popped up and he was logged in. It was especially shocking given his squeaky-clean reputation as a married family man.

There's a saying 'beauty is only skin deep', but being beautiful sure comes in handy. Always look your best, especially for a date, but also if you're just hanging out with friends or running around doing errands. You never know who you're going to meet. Your wardrobe should be

Above: Ring bearer at my big sister's wedding, 1968.

Above: A happy reunion with TV star John Schneider.

Above: A theatrical night on the town with my gals Anita Gillette and Colleen Zenk.

Above: Reporting on location in New York City.

Left: Eleven years and counting… I've become a fixture on the Oscars red carpet!

Left: …and on the Hollywood red carpet for the SAG Awards.

Left: Working "from the waist up" for my Aussie TV show.

Above: With luminous Julianne Moore, who also got her start in "soaps".

Left: My running partner and fab friend, meteorologist Amy Freeze.

Above: Tickled to meet Elmo!

Right: I couldn't help
photo-bombing Il Divo.

Top: I'm proud to be an honorary member of The Wiggles.

Above: With Dr Jordan Metzl for his "Ironstrength for Runners" workout in Central Park.

Above: Nothing beats running in Central Park....even in the dead of winter.

Left: Twenty marathons, so far...and still smiling!

Below: My 50th birthday bootcamp on the beach.

Top: With my "brother from another mother," my best friend Glenn.

Above: Birthday bash getting underway. Nelson-tini, anyone?

age-appropriate. That doesn't mean 'old', it just means that trying to pass yourself off in the styles worn by the likes of One Direction or Selena Gomez will just make you look silly. When I first moved to LA I had an actress friend who got up every day and did her hair, put on her make up, and dressed as if she had a screen test... even if she had nothing whatsoever on her schedule. One day, out of the blue, a call came to ask if she were available for a last-minute interview and she was ready! She was at the studio before anyone else and wound up getting a starring role on the comedy series **Perfect Strangers** *that lasted seven years.*

If a person is only attracted to 'youngsters' chances are he or she is either a shallow individual or has some kind of age fetish. Either way, why would you want to get tangled up with that? Naturally, the media is constantly cramming crazy, almost criminal, images of unattainable/inappropriate youth down our throats with everything from food to fashion. Since it is true that 'beauty is in the eye of the beholder', it should begin with YOU finding that the traces of Time that come with age are what is most attractive in a person (including yourself)... both inside and out. This may take practise in a world where we are bombarded by 20-somethings frolicking on every movie screen and billboard.

"I am now 59 years old, which is an awkward age to define. At 59, I am no longer middle-aged. I have, after all, no 118-year old elders among my acquaintances. Yet I could hardly be called elderly. An awkward age, then, to define but a delightful one to live. I am ageing from the neck up. Which means I am elderly enough to have attained a look of wisdom; middle-aged enough to have a body that allows me to do what I want; and a face that lets me get away with it."
Dr George Sheehan

By the time you reach 50, chances are you've established a place in life that isn't going to change for someone else. In our youth, we either want to change our partners to be the kind of person WE want them to be… or try and mould ourselves to fit the needs and desires of our partners. Always a mistake! Be the best possible person you can be and I believe the 'right' mate will be attracted. That doesn't mean you shouldn't compromise with a partner when it's appropriate, but being someone you're not… or settling for anything less than you truly feel you deserve… never works for long-term happiness.

> *Music goddess Stevie Nicks (born 1948) says: "I don't feel alone. I feel very un-alone. I feel very sparkly and excited about everything."*

Maybe it's been a while since someone told you how great you look. If you haven't been active on the dating scene for a while, your day-to-day encounters with friends, family and co-workers may mean that your physical charms are taken for granted. But when you're meeting new people, expect to receive some flattering words. While it's good to be humble, it's also important to know how to graciously accept a compliment. If someone says 'you have lovely eyes', or 'you're in terrific shape', try not to blush or, even worse, find some fault with yourself to negate their praise (ie. 'Oh, how can you even see my eyes with all these crow's feet?' or 'I've gained ten pounds since my divorce… I used to be much leaner.') For goodness sake, don't act defensive either. I actually overheard a woman say to a man, 'You certainly look nice today,' to which he replied, 'Don't you think I usually look nice?' I had to speak up and point out how lucky he was that someone was paying him a compliment at all. He was embarrassed and apologized to the woman (For the record, he did look nice… very well groomed and nattily dressed; I suspect he's too used to being flattered by women. I hope I taught him a little lesson!).

Practise giving compliments, too. Don't be afraid to start out with the people around you. Neighbors, colleagues and even/especially your kids will like hearing that you think their new haircut, singing voice, writing skills or iPhone case is terrific. Consider that there is an art to flattery, too: It's much better to say, 'You look great in that jacket' than 'that's a great looking jacket'. Why should an inanimate piece of clothing get all the glory?

"One of the greatest joys of being 50+ is a much more secure sense of who I am. I'm calmer, and don't have as much of a need to prove myself... and I enjoy my own company. That's key." Artist/actor Christopher Durham (born 1959)

What about dating and age difference? It may feel hot to have attracted the attention of a younger mate, but ask yourself what you two may really have in common beyond physical chemistry. How's the conversation? Do you like their circle of friends? Would your families get along? Are they self-sufficient? There's nothing wrong with a casual fling, but you want to make sure you're communicating with each other about your mutual intentions. I try to keep my romantic liaisons within a decade of my own age. Relationships are tough enough without bringing age-related issues into play. That said, I have had some great experiences with people younger (but wise beyond their years) and older (young at heart) than I. Sometimes you just have to let fate do its thing.

Just when Michael Douglas and Catherine Zeta-Jones seemed to have made their marriage work in spite of a quarter-century age difference and seemingly more downs than ups (her ongoing struggle with bipolar disorder, his son's incarceration, his oral cancer and subsequent embarrassing remarks about oral sex), their separation was announced after 13 years. 'Taking a break!' How about 'Give me a break!' Call me cynical, but if it hadn't been for the mutual limelight benefit given to them by the union, I think it would have ended years sooner. Several months later, I seem to have been proven wrong when they publicly stated that they were trying to work things out. During this time, I interviewed Michael and he actually cited his famous father, Kirk, and stepmother Anne who married in 1954 and have weathered all the subsequent years' ups and downs by sticking together. Will it work for Michael and CZJ? Time will tell.

Calvin Klein got burned badly by his 'boy toy' paramour, who's rumoured to be brokering a salacious tell-all book. Demi and Ashton? Never had a chance, if you ask me. Clint Eastwood, more than 30 years older than wife Dina, split after 17 years of marriage, but the talented octogenarian seems far from remaining a bachelor too long. How many younger wives have Hugh Hefner, Bruce Willis and Kelsey Grammer had now? Imagine what Rupert Murdoch's 38-year-age difference with Wendi Deng cost him, in more ways than one!

Nearly 30 years separate Alec Baldwin and his most recent wife, yoga instructor Hilaria, whom he married in 2012. Do you think they're a forever couple? So far, her spiritual discipline of finding peace hasn't seemed to have had much of a calming affect on him.

Of course, there are exceptions and every situation is different, so keep your eyes wide open if you're starting a relationship where there's a big age difference… especially if you're easily dazzled.

A middle-aged friend of mine who recently worked on set with Clint Eastwood told me that the famed director gave him some terrific advice on how to avoid slowing down over time, "Don't let the 'old man' in!"

Age differences in relationships seem to work a little differently for women. Like Tina Turner and her mate, whom we'll discuss later in this chapter; Joan Collins (born 1933) seems to have found lasting happiness with a significantly younger groom, even if it took five tries. Rather than credit her seemingly endless reign of glamor on her animal print and sequin-laden wardrobe, assortment of flowing wigs or dazzling array of jeweled baubles, she says the secret to her long-lasting beauty is, "lots of laughter, hard work, to never get too thin or too fat, and a husband 32 years younger!" As for keeping busy, she adds, "If I hear the word retire it makes me want to throw up. And then do what? Sit around all day watching television? I still love life, so I live it."

Perky TV chatterbox Katie Couric, widowed in 1998 when she lost her husband to colon cancer, managed to juggle prime time and daytime broadcast duties while raising two children and conducting a years-long and well publicized relationship with a good looking 'entrepreneur' 17 years her junior (she must have one heck of a personal assistant). In late 2011, she began seeing John Molner and said of him, "He's really funny and very successful in his own right. A little more age appropriate." (For the record, Molner is 6 years younger than 'Cougar Katie'.) In September 2013, the pair became engaged so the financier is now her fiancé.

Jane Fonda (born 1937), while never a stranger to controversy, is undeniably talented and gorgeous. Famed for her breakout aerobics workouts in the 1980s, she continues to defy traditional ageing, even if means admitting to a few nips and tucks. At 75, she became a 'cover girl' for L'Oreal cosmetics in addition to her many other awards and accolades. Three high-profile marriages to French director Roger Vadim, politician Tom Hayden and CNN founder Ted Turner all ended in divorce, but in her mid-70s, she appears to have found some lasting romantic satisfaction with music producer Richard Perry, who is only four years younger than her. With him, she admits, she feels as if she has found the true intimate connection for which she's spent her lifetime searching. "I feel totally secure with him. Often, when we make love, I see him as he was 30 years ago. At 74, I have never had such a fulfilling sex life," she said. "When I was young I had so many inhibitions—I didn't know what I desired." The moral of the story here, it seems, is to have faith and put yourself out there!

There is probably no greater example of the success potential for a woman having a younger husband than Deborra-Lee Furness (born 1955) who has been wed to Hugh Jackman since 1996. Aside from having to share her handsome hubby with rabid fans around the world, she endures the slings and arrows of the frenzied tabloid media who are always mongering for scandal and discord where none exists in their otherwise busy and happy family life. After suffering miscarriages, the couple adopted two children (Oscar and Ava) and Deb works tirelessly to assist with streamlining international adoptions, particularly in her native Australia where it still remains especially challenging. Benefitting not only from Hugh's obvious adoration and devotion, Deb keeps it real by pursuing her own personal, professional philanthropic goals… all while running the gamut from flying to Africa with former President Bill Clinton to picking up the kids from school or soccer practice. Most dynamic duos enjoy partnership compatibility precisely because they are so individually fulfilled. The Furness-Jackmans thrive in New York City because they remain so unaffected by the publicity hype thrust upon them.

The fact is that some cities lend themselves more to dating than others. Part of the reason I missed sailing aboard the 'love boat' in my younger years may have been that I was trapped in Los Angeles… land of the hard-bodies, youth-obsessed and showbiz ladder-climbers. I moved from small town USA to New York shortly after my 17th birthday in 1980 and stayed there, blissfully, for ten years. What an exciting time and place to experience one's own salad days. TV work had all but dried up by the end of the decade, so in 1990 this young man headed west to La-La land (My mentor, daytime TV great Mary Stuart, was so sorry to lose me to Tinseltown, I can still hear her voice trying to muster up an ounce of enthusiasm: 'Hollywood… wow').

Of course there are plenty of wonderful things about LA, and I made some amazing friendships there while forging a successful career in entertainment journalism. I even had a few serious relationships (though none could compare to the 15+ years I spent with Lois, the world's most amazing springer spaniel). But as the season-less years passed, I came to recognize that, while Tony Bennett may have famously 'left his heart in San Francisco,' mine was still back in the Big Apple. The isolation of always being in the car, sitting in traffic, enduring the road rage and distracted drivers all around, combined with the fact that 99.9 per cent of the population is only interested in one topic (showbiz) can gradually convert you into the stereotypical bubble-headed, one-dimensional character straight out of *Valley Girl* or *Bill & Ted's Excellent Adventure*!

I think it's much more desirable to date someone who isn't in the same line or work as you. The entertainment industry is all-consuming, incestuous and competitive. Who wants to bring that home with them? I like dating people who have an appreciation and curiosity about what I do, but aren't wrapped up in it professionally.

> *Some celebrity marriages do succeed. Notorious diva and showbiz legend Barbra Streisand (born 1942) seemed like an impossible tiger to tame in the romance department, but she found the yin to her yang in her mid-50s when she met actor James Brolin (born 1940) through a friend. The pair wed in 1998 and still surprise many with the success and harmony of their long (by Hollywood standards!) union. The key to their compatibility may be found in their differences. "She thinks everything has to get done right now," Brolin said of his beloved, a notorious perfectionist. "My theme is, 'What's your hurry?'"*

I was in a great position with my job as entertainment correspondent for Australia's top-rating morning show, *Sunrise*, to become 'bi-coastal', jetting back and forth between the America's East and West coasts. However, three years and hundreds of thousands of frequent flyer miles later, I was able to make Manhattan my home base once again.

Of course, I still go back to Los Angeles frequently for red carpet events, press junkets and other celeb-related assignments. It is, after all, a 'factory town'. But New York City, in addition to TV and film, has art, culture, fashion, theater, design, dance… you name it. How great is that for dating? Most big stars agree with me that New York is 'home sweet home'. Hugh Jackman, Matt Damon, Naomi Watts (won over to the Big Apple by her partner, Liev Schreiber, who said "I am really crazy about you, but I don't know that I can live in LA, and is that okay?"), Sarah Jessica Parker, Sting, Madonna, Hank Azaria, Robert De Niro, the list goes on and on. Sally Field, in fact, finally fulfilled her life-long dream of becoming a Gothamite at the age of 65. She refers to it as her 'third act' and it certainly appears to agree with her. She is as beautiful and professionally busy as ever.

> *In a* **Good Housekeeping** *interview, Sally Field said, "I see myself on TV and I say 'Oh, I wish that weren't happening with my neck'. But I care more about having the opportunity to play roles that I haven't played before than I care if my neck looks like someone's bedroom curtains. [Happiness] is about having a good solid feeling about your health and yourself as a healthy person."*

At the risk of sounding like a male version of *Sex and the City*'s Samantha, I have to admit that New York works for me as a single guy. There are fascinating, funny, attractive, self-sufficient and eligible people of every age, size and shape. Sure I would like to find the right person to settle down with… but I'm making the most of life in the meanwhile!

Curiosity may have killed the cat, but it's not going to do YOU any harm. To find success in dating, just as with athletic pursuits or monetary investments, I think it helps to take smart, calculated risks. An online-dating profile may ask you to set guidelines when it comes to your ideal match's age range, height, income, and so on, but in real life, it can be more rewarding to be less rigid. Doing what is simple and safe probably won't reap the rewards you could get from going out of your comfort zone. Maybe you'll get a happy surprise and meet an unexpected dreamboat!

I made friends with bombshell Rachel DeAlto when we met at a TV studio a few years ago. She was there to promote her book, *Flirt Fearlessly*, and dazzled me with her charm and confidence. As a communications expert (and self-confessed 'flirt expert'), I had some questions for her about the prospect of making successful matches in middle age.

NELSON: "How does someone over 50 flirt without coming across as sleazy or lecherous?"

RACHEL: "Flirting over 50 is all about embracing your 'inner flirt', and flirting appropriately. Ten years up and 10 years down is your safe zone for anyone age over 35—if the person you approach is in that zone, go for it! Also, flirting isn't always about seducing someone. Use flirtation to make a connection without a focus on the ulterior motives."

NELSON: "Is a person ever too old to flirt?"

RACHEL: "No! You are never too old to flirt."

NELSON: "If you misinterpret something as a flirtation, what's the best way to recover and not embarrass yourself?"

RACHEL: "Laugh it off! There is nothing that shows confidence more than not taking yourself too seriously. Follow up with a comment or question that is completely platonic."

NELSON: "How do the rules of flirting change in middle age?"

RACHEL: "They don't! The desire for companionship never disappears, and flirting will always be the first step to connecting with someone romantically. The best part of flirting at 50 is that you are more likely to know and love who you are compared to your 25-year-old counterparts. Confidence grows with age, and confidence makes flirting immensely more fun."

NELSON: "Where do you suggest middle-aged singles go to meet others?"

RACHEL: "Online is a fantastic place to meet people. You can search at your leisure, and nowhere else will you have thousands of singles in one location. A great website is meetup.com (join a group with a shared interest—there are groups for everything from running to wine tasting to museum lovers), and your friends. Enlist your friends as your matchmakers. Let them know you are interested in meeting people!"

NELSON: "Any suggestions on first dates for the over 50s?"

RACHEL: "My advice for a first date is universal—keep your expectations in check and have fun! Every date is a chance to meet someone that could change your life for the better, so remain positive. Take chances, and date outside of what you think your 'type' is. You may be surprised."

NELSON: "Who should pay on a first date?"

RACHEL: "The guy should always pay for the first three to six dates. Yep, it sounds archaic and some women are making just as much money as men, but chivalry is not dead. For same sex couples, the person who asks should pay for the first date."

NELSON: "It's easy to be flattered by the attention of a much younger person. How do you know if/when they're for real?"

RACHEL: "Listen to their words, but also pay attention to their actions. Do they do what they say? Are they showering you with compliments and then disappearing? Do they only call occasionally as if you are an afterthought? Regardless of your age or theirs, you deserve someone who appreciates you and respects your feelings. They should be willing to put in the effort to date you, no matter the age difference."

Did you know? The first personal columns appeared in England in the 1690s, only a half century after the birth of the newspaper.

Rachel even had good advice for me. I explained to her that, for me, mixing my career with romance is taboo… but because so much of my life revolves around work, it's nearly impossible for me to accommodate that personal side. She immediately and bluntly called it as she saw it, "You just don't want it enough." Yeah… I acquiesced, "I guess I'd rather work." On the bright side, she said, "If you did, you would make concessions for that… and you will when you decide you want it badly enough." I'll be sure to get back to you on that, Rachel.

Nothing can complicate or complement the dating process like sex! You have to decide when the time is right for you and your partner, but quite honestly I have never been one to deprive myself of carnal pleasures. Nor do I think that physical relations between two people will jeopardize their ability to develop a meaningful interpersonal relationship. Besides, I like knowing that the person I am dating is not only as highly-sexed as I am, but that we are mutually attracted to each other in that way. You can convince yourself of many things… but sexual chemistry is either there or it isn't. It's not something you can manufacture.

When it comes to sex, by this time of life you've probably seen or tried pretty much everything on your sexual bucket list at least twice. (If not, get busy.) Being comfortable with your sexuality will only serve to enhance the moments of intimacy you do have. You know how your body works and responds… and what you do and don't like. That's a wonderful place to be, so you can relax and enjoy yourself. So what if some body part happens to jiggle a little more than it used to, as long as you're movin', you're grooving'.

> *I've been friends with my favorite movie star, Carol Lynley, since we first met when I was 15. It has been a wonderful adventure being her pal and I always delight in the fantastic, bawdy sense of humor that belies her delicate, doe-eyed beauty. Her body language and bon mots often make me laugh because they're seemingly so out of character. The woman is a riot! After a lifetime of ballet, yoga and ice-skating, she suffered from arthritic hips and eventually underwent double hip replacements. She didn't let the temporary infirmity keep her out of action, though. We kept our usual lunch date at Wolfgang Puck's famed Beverly Hills eatery, Spago, and she made her entrance into the dining room sans cane, but clutching onto the backs of chairs as she moved slowly, step by step, from the entrance. The ever-attentive maitre d', Gianni, rushed to her side and asked if she was all right. "Too much sex!" she quipped back, with a deadpan expression. I still laugh out loud when I remember that!*

It is said that regular sexual activity releases hormones such as testosterone and estrogen, helping you maintain strength, mental clarity and cardiovascular health. It also helps you sleep better, another important component to health. Chances are, by now there are no kids in the house and any concerns about pregnancy and contraception are a thing of the past.

Of course, at any age it's important to engage in sexual conduct responsibly. Practise safe sex if you are not in a trusted, monogamous relationship with a partner whose health status you know. Be open with your mate about your health issues and theirs just as you would be about your likes and dislikes. It's also important to talk to your health care provider about any concerns you may have when it comes to matters in the bedroom. If you can't be 100 per cent up front with your doctor, it's time to find a replacement. Like a lover, that's one of your most intimate relationships.

Academy Award winning actress Shirley Jones' memoir was leaked to the press (accidentally?) with the following tidbit, "I still want to make it clear that I believe that a woman can remain sexual right through her 70s and 80s and beyond. I am living proof of that. Despite my advanced years, that hasn't changed a bit, although it can take longer than before for me to achieve sexual fulfillment these days." Shirley, who turned 80 in 2014, sounds a lot more feisty than the 'Mrs Partridge' we remember from television.

Speaking of medicine: it's awesome that pharmaceuticals have advanced to help older folks out with some of the biological challenges associated with age. Like any prescription, medication should be used with extreme prudence and caution. The only one I have been compelled to investigate is Propecia, which has proven very successful at re-growing hair. I eventually opted against it after knowing a 50-something actor who, in spite of an impressive lion's mane of hair, suffered from the drug's most common side effect: loss of sexual desire/performance. He said, "I'd rather have hair than have sex." Everybody has to pick their poison! Personally, I think sex has never been better than it is today… Sorry, but unlike the Kardashian clan, I don't kiss and tell.

Some interesting facts about dating and relationships from the website RandomHistory.com:
* *In a survey of 5,000 singles conducted by Match.com, 43 per cent said fresh breath mattered the most before a date, 17 per cent said stylish clothes, 15 per cent said sexy fragrance, 14 per cent said good skin, and 10 per cent said great hair.*
* *When a man first approaches a woman, she will base 55*

*per cent of her initial impression of him on his appearance
and body language, 38 per cent on his style of speaking, and
7 per cent on what he actually says.*

*• A recent AOL survey says that 40 per cent of women view
an appropriate time frame to wait for sex as being one to
three months, while 35 per cent of men think the third date
is fine. On average, couples have sex within about four to six
dates.*

*• Four common date blunders include showing up late,
talking about yourself too much, revealing too much about
your ex, and an obvious over-eagerness.*

Someone who is a professional when it comes to these complex interpersonal relationships is clinical psychologist John Aiken, whom I had the
pleasure of meeting while working on a panel discussion for Australia's
Morning Show programme. You can read more about his methods, practice and 'marriage boot camp' (sounds like it could give new meaning
to 'fatigues'!) at www.johnaiken.com.au. In the meantime, he obliged me
with this fascinating question and answer interview.

NELSON: "If you're 50+ and still single, should you hold out hope for a
relationship?"

JOHN: "Absolutely! Being 50 is a great time of your life to find love.
You've got money, experience, great friendship networks and you've
let go of the insecurities you had in your 20s and 30s. Not to mention
the fact that with lots of people getting divorced, there's plenty of
50-somethings out there in the market looking to get hitched again. It
can happen anywhere anytime. The key is staying patient and being
open to letting someone new into your life.

NELSON: "If you're 50+ and newly single, what's the best approach for jumping back into the dating pool?"

JOHN: "Embrace a disciplined approach. Take some time out and learn from your previous relationship mistakes: get an appearance make-over, commit to a healthy lifestyle (exercise, diet, limit alcohol), and tear down any toxic obstacles (such as too many work hours, negative friends etc.) Then take on a positive dating mindset whereby you're going to be open to all opportunities, and be picky and selective, wait-ing for the right one to come along rather than just anyone. Remem-ber—the key to finding the right one is getting good at saying no to the wrong ones."

NELSON: "Online dating seems to be about matching up specific crite-ria. What happened to the old theory that opposites attract?"

JOHN: "The idea of opposites attracting can occur when the differenc-es are at a surface level. In this case, some couples can have different likes and dislikes… that can be entertaining and novel. However, when it comes to core values and beliefs, you need to be on the same page. For instance, religious and political views, cheating, having kids, parenting styles, marriage and money habits are big issues that you need to be a team."

NELSON: "Marriages were once considered 'til death do us part'. Now that we're all living so much longer, is it acceptable for a relationship to come to a happy ending or conclusion? Are we failures if our relation-ships don't last 'til death?'"

JOHN: "Any relationship can come to end and sometimes it can even finish on good terms. The end shouldn't be seen as a failure, but instead as a learning experience. All sorts of factors can influence what happens in a relationship (some you control, some you don't).

You need to understand all these factors and then learn from them moving forward. It's a growth experience not a failure. It will also make you better at your next relationship."

NELSON: "Do you support gay marriage and if so, how do you see the marriage between two men or two women as being different from a heterosexual union?"

JOHN: "I do support gay marriage and have a number of gay friends that have tied the knot. I see the marriage of a same-sex couple as being different from heterosexuals, in terms of the discrimination and social disapproval and criticism that they receive from some sectors of society. However in time I'm very hopeful that this will change."

NELSON: "Is marriage passé?"

JOHN: "Not for me. I'm married and I love it. I met the girl of my dreams and I love wearing my wedding ring each day. And I think that there are still many people out there who see marriage as a public commitment that has continued meaning and value in today's world."

NELSON: "Once the kids are out of the house, often couples flail. What's your best advice to these couples?"

JOHN: "The process begins before the kids leave. Couples need to start planning in advance, so when it does happen they're already up to speed. That means spending time developing your own individual interests and passions, connecting with friends and creating new routines for yourselves. The couple should spend more time together sharing activities, taking time to connect, showing an interest in each other and creating shared goals for the next few years ahead."

NELSON: "Kids are living at home longer these days. What kind of stress does that put on a relationship and how should couples try to handle it?"

JOHN: "There are plenty of stressors that kids put on parents when they continue to live at home. They can create mess, spend your money, give you attitude, and engage in high-risk behaviour (including binge drinking, drugs, unprotected sex, and so on). They can be unpredictable and moody, rude and obnoxious and hold you back on your plans for the future (such as travel, moving house, living in a different city...). The end result, is that the couple can struggle to spend time with each other, become financially strained, experience a tense household and get stuck waiting for the kids to leave. To combat this, create rules that you enforce consistently with the kids; prioritise one-on-one time as a couple, get out of the house together whenever you can and have some fun, and run to a budget. If possible, also establish a timeline for the kids, so that you're all on the same page about future family plans and expectations."

NELSON: "Many of my peers feel like they're stuck in a generational limbo. No sooner are the kids raised, than they have elderly parents to care for. What stresses does this put on a couple and how is it best to cope?"

JOHN: "Caring for elderly parents can be financially draining and time consuming. It may restrict your ability to plan and travel, and can be psychologically upsetting to witness their deterioration in terms of health. To manage this, it's important to share the caring around where possible, have time out together away from the situation, have good open lines of communication with their medical support team, and regularly offload your difficulties and worries on each other."

NELSON: "What's the best thing about being 50+ and single? And about being 50+ and in a long-term relationship?"

JOHN: "Being 50+ and single: you have freedom, money and the opportunity to try out new and novel experiences. The world is out there waiting for you and the key is to have a positive mindset and be excited about how you decide to take it on. Being 50+ and in a long-term relationship: you have found your life partner, you have raised your family, and now you have the chance to spend some real quality time together making the most of your friendship and love. You've got lots of opportunity, and you can now embrace this with the most important person in your life."

In my opinion, the increasing legality, popularity and public acceptance of gay marriage hasn't done much for the overall institution. High-profile gay spouses seem to be splitting up as quickly as their heterosexual counterparts. Likening love to a Broadway show, actor/singer Cheyenne Jackson described his kaput marriage to Monte Lapka as "a good long run, almost 13 years". *Glee* funny lady Jane Lynch divorced Dr Lara Embry after only three years and, in spite of having a young daughter together, remarked that "It's not a horrible thing". Most couples omit 'til death do us part' from the nuptials along with that bit about 'obeying'. Why does it seem, in this day and age with all the freedom of personal choice, that some couples are so nonchalant about marriage NOT being a lifetime commitment? Watch for 'gay divorce' to be a lucrative business for lawyers in the years ahead. Fortunately for celebrities, break-ups are always spun as 'amicable' with the couple 'remaining good friends'. Seriously... how many divorced couples do you know, gay or straight, who are good friends?

Proving it's never too late to walk down the aisle, in the summer of 2013, music legend Tina Turner wed her partner of nearly 30 years, German-born record executive Erwin Bach. The bride was 73, the groom,

57. Go girl! It is noteworthy that, after divorcing her notoriously abusive ex-husband Ike Turner in 1978, Ms Turner was not only able to move on with her own professional success, but found a long-term romantic relationship with a guy she could obviously trust. What is especially remarkable is that they decided to seal their commitment to each other with the formality of a marriage license, after already being successfully, happily committed without one. Maybe they'll inspire Goldie Hawn and Kurt Russell? "What's Love Got to Do With It?" Obviously, everything!

> *"Young people listen to the love songs that declare a love higher than the sky and deeper than the ocean. But they often confuse love with the sexual urges that now overwhelm them. As life goes on they will be saddened as those urges dwindle. Sex may fade, but love... love lasts. They don't realize that the most important element of love will be waiting for them. Romance. Beautiful romance." Kirk Douglas (born 1916), written at age 96.*

THE FAMOUS FACES OF MIDDLE AGE (AND BEYOND)

Have you noticed how certain celebrities such as Justin Bieber and Miley Cyrus use their youth as an excuse for questionable behavior? While there is no doubt that knowledge and grace come with age, I know plenty of young adults who are upstanding citizens, responsible parents, hard-working employees and all-around delightful human beings. Similarly, there are plenty of oldsters around who seem to have never grown up. You only have to check out their mug shots to know what I mean.

The celebrity culture is so ingrained in my life because of my career that 'stars' are liberally mentioned throughout this book, but this chapter is a chance for me to focus on the ones whom I hold in the utmost esteem and respect. Even if you only know them by their on-screen work and what you read in the magazines, I bet you like 'em, too. It's not a coincidence that they are all middle aged (and beyond).

I've been interviewing celebrities for two decades. Ironically, my first assignment back in the early 1990s was with everyone's favorite Golden Girl Betty White who, now in her 90s, is still amazing us with her sweet-nature, comic timing and constant grace. I will never forget what a good sport she was as I swept into her Brentwood home with my camera crew to shoot a story on 'fitness for pets'. She not only played along as I staged an aerobics class for her and all her pooches, but she opened up her house for us to stay and film as much extra footage as we needed. I've seen her on a few red carpets since and continue to enjoy her work on the big and small screens. If she doesn't make the case for 'life begins at 50', then I don't know who does!

> *"Forty is the old age of youth; fifty the youth of old age."*
> *Victor Hugo 1802–85. At the time of his death, the average*
> *human life expectancy was 45.*

It's fair to say after all this time, I've met and/or interviewed just about all of the stars. I bring up the subject of celebrities here to point out the ones who, like a fine wine, are improving with age. I don't mean just physically… although, it's fair to say that many celebs certainly do get more attractive as time goes on. Dame Helen Mirren, Daniel Craig, Robert Downey Jr, Gwyneth Paltrow, Elizabeth Hurley and even Hugh Jackman seem to just get hotter by the year! Supermodels such as Christie Brinkley, Heidi Klum and Cindy Crawford have all managed to beat the clock without drastic procedures or radical surgeries. Others are so brimming with presence and charisma that time only enhances their appeal… hello, Lynda Carter, Alec Baldwin, Mariska Hargitay, Kylie Minogue and Patrick Dempsey. It's nice to notice, too, that the most popular shows on television seem to feature mature characters; *NCIs*, *The Good Wife*, *CSI*, *Downton Abbey*, and *Hot in Cleveland* spring to mind.

Look at the 2013 prime time Emmy Awards: 'Grown up' stars not only sparkled on the red carpet, but stole the show as winners and performers.

Julia Louis-Dreyfus, Michael Douglas, Alfre Woodard, Stephen Colbert, Michael J. Fox, Jessica Lange, Jane Lynch, Bob Newhart, Melissa Leo, Blair Underwood, Allison Janney, Bryan Cranston, Jeff Daniels and Elton John all showed the youngsters how it's done!

> *"You have to keep trying and improving. Coasting is dangerous. I can't just play* **Bennie and the Jets** *over and over again." Sir Elton John, born 1947*

It used to be that Hollywood leading ladies were relegated to supporting or character roles after age 40, but that has certainly changed. Remember Archie and Edith Bunker on *All in the Family*? Their characters were only 50 years old, but watching the reruns today, they seem like senior citizens!

> *"Actors get older, actresses get old." Ava Gardner (1922–90)*

Thankfully, these days, audiences not only want to see grown-up ladies on screen, but those actresses' power and salaries have skyrocketed. Dame Helen Mirren, Dame Maggie Smith, Dame Judi Dench and Meryl Streep spring immediately to mind. Gone are the days when only a handful of women were wielding industry authority and consequently branded 'bitches' (think Barbra Streisand, Sherry Lansing, Roseanne Barr) for displaying the same tough, aggressive qualities as their male counter-parts. Many of today's leading ladies control some of the most import-ant, lucrative deals in Tinseltown. Sandra Bullock, Julia Roberts, Halle Berry, Glenn Close, Susan Sarandon, Holly Hunter, Kyra Sedgwick, Sarah Jessica Parker are hot properties in TV and film… and only a few years younger with no signs of stopping are Jennifer Aniston, Nicole Kidman, Jennifer Lopez, Cate Blanchett and Helena Bonham-Carter. It's certainly a far cry from the era when 40-year-old females were put out to pasture only to occasionally be given a supporting, character role. Have you seen Bo Derek (born 1956) lately? Va-va-va-VOOM!

*RuPaul Andre Charles, better known simply as the drag
artist RuPaul, was born in 1960 and looks more stunning
than ever when dressed as a woman. His male alter-ego,
however, looks true to his real age which may be a novelty
he enjoys along with the smoke and mirrors of his craft. I
requested an interview with RuPaul for this book, but he
declined. I guess some people prefer to keep their beauty
secrets secret!*

One star who has made maturity always seem sexy is Kim Cattrall, a
surprisingly versatile and accomplished stage actress. On Broadway, she
dazzled in Noel Coward's *Private Lives* and followed that up at age 56
playing Alexandra Del Lago in Kevin Spacey's West End Theater production of Tennessee Williams' classic, *Sweet Bird of Youth*. The character, a
faded film star, made Cattrall reflect in an interview with the BBC about
the issues that "a lot of women my age are dealing with… Feeling that
you're still valid and you're still attractive and you still have something to
say— that time has not passed you by. These are messages and things
that I'm dealing with in real life, not just on the stage. So they resonate for
me in a very specific way." Isn't her candor refreshing?

"I don't think it's just Hollywood that's youth-obsessed," she continued
in the interview. "I think we're all youth-obsessed— and why not? It's
great to be young. But I don't really feel old. I feel a little wiser, a lot more
patient, and also more courageous. I was so worried when I was younger
what people thought of me. Now I don't care as much. I care more about
what I think of myself."

Kim also credits physi-yoga (created by a New York based yogi/phys-
ical therapist) as the workout that 'saved her life'. "As I get older, I find
that cardio is less important to me," she told *The Times* of London. "What
I want to do is more intense stretching. I'm not worried about injuring
myself because a regular yoga instructor isn't versed in the way of the

body like a trained physio is." More proof that every person has to find what works for them, individually.

I marvel at my own mother, well into her 80s, who still has men eating out of the palm of her arthritic hand. Her dazzling smile, twinkling eyes and natural effervescence have always served her well in every situation, at all ages in life. In other words, she's a natural born flirt! I try to emulate that and it can take years off your appearance (I was actually ID'd buying wine as late as 2013, for goodness sake. I can't vouch for the sales clerk's vision, but I was more than delighted to whip out my driver's license and give her a surprise.)

> *"People often say beauty is in the eye of the beholder, and I say that the most liberating thing about beauty is realizing you are the beholder." Salma Hayek, born 1966.*

There still remains a double standard when it comes to the sexual prowess of movies' leading men. Certainly no one blinks at the guys hovering around or well beyond the 50 age mark such as George Clooney, Brad Pitt and Tom Cruise, but even much older guys such as Michael Douglas, Richard Gere, Antonio Banderas, Kevin Costner, Daniel Day Lewis, Mel Gibson and Bruce Willis not only get big roles… they get on-screen romances with younger, sexy females. Look at the success of *The Expendables*. Obviously old action heroes never die… they just start up a new franchise and keep the fires burning! And in many ways, art imitates life. Many fellows don't have an expiration date when it comes to taking advantage of the singles' market, while it undoubtedly gets tougher for women as time goes by. Fortunately, that is changing.

It's always mesmerizing when you're standing in the supermarket checkout line to thumb through the tabloids' plastic surgery nightmares editions. Maybe we've become desensitized to what famous females have started doing to their faces. Many, such as Sharon Osbourne and Joan Rivers make their routines tabloid fodder. Hey, laugh and the world laughs with you, right? When men go under the knife, which seems to be happening at an alarmingly more frequent rate, it still seems shocking. Why, oh, why? By going under the knife I don't mean fixing crooked teeth (Tom Cruise) or routine rhinoplasty (as rumored to have been performed for Ryan Gosling, Bradley Cooper, Brad Pitt, Robert Pattinson and Zac Efron), but the full-on Stallone route. Michael Jackson's facial alterations were legendary, but look at all the macho men who have succumbed over time. Kenny Rogers followed in the face-steps of his famous friend, Dolly Parton, and I'm not sure how he can croak out a note with his face held so tight. Mickey Rourke admitted in 2009 he "went to the wrong guy", so he wisely wears giant sunglasses and distracts you with outrageous behavior and colorful language. Just as we were getting used to Burt Reynolds' hair piece, his rugged good looks began twisting into Kabuki proportions. To me, the greatest offender... and I can't help but feel sorry for him... is Bruce Jenner. His Olympian good looks of yesteryear have been so pulled, pinched and feminized that he is unrecognizable from that guy on the cereal box. Something else to blame on the Kardashians, perhaps?

TV presenter Julie Chen shocked audiences when she revealed she'd undergone extensive plastic surgery in the early days of her career to "look less Asian". The dramatic 'before' pictures show a very different looking person from the woman she is now. Too bad she didn't have a talk with savvy news woman and ground breaker Connie Chung. Chen admits that her new look definitely got 'the ball rolling' for her career. I don't suppose it hurts, either, that she is married to the president and CEO of the top US television network. I think this just goes to illustrate how messed up most people still are about the perception of what is 'beautiful'.

Allow me to explain my approach to interviewing famous folks and how it informs my opinions (mostly positive) of the stars I meet. The reality is, it's often fun but it's rarely easy. If it looks that way to the audience, then I take satisfaction in knowing I've done my job well by a) doing my research, b) putting my interview subject at ease, and c) asking inter-esting, unusual questions they actually enjoy answering. I've never had aspirations to be a David Frost or Mike Wallace… grilling an interview subject for some heretofore unknown revelation, leaving them sweating and squirming in their seat. I like to build people up… not tear them down. Celebrities, showbiz insiders and newsmakers happen to be among my friends, neighbors and colleagues… so for me, it is about drawing them out and sharing a conversation.

Preparation is, of course, vital. Sadly, a command of the English language may not be as important as it was a generation ago, but jour-nalists who possess good spelling and grammar and know how to write a structured article stand out.

> *We've all seen so-called journalists who deliberately set up their interviews to go awry, put their subjects on the spot, or draw inappropriate attention to themselves in an effort to make a name for themselves. 'Viral videos' are all the rage, but these reporters should remember that there's a reason Johnny Knoxville's moniker is 'Jackass'. Besides, that kind of crass notoriety all but assures your '15 minutes of fame' will be just that: short-lived… not an actual long-term career. To paraphrase Ron Burgundy, "You stay classy!"*

Nothing is more awkward than being trapped in a bad interview. If you've ever been stuck at a dinner party sitting between two people with whom you have absolutely nothing in common, you know what I mean. In the glory days of the silver screen, celebrities were trained in public relations as much as they were in elocution, dancing or stage fighting. While it's nice to live in a more spontaneous age, it's disheartening to encounter a star who can win Oscars and rule the box office, but can't carry on a few minutes of stimulating chat.

One of my many sidelines is media training for actors, athletes, authors and other professionals. Sooner or later, many of these people are interviewed on TV talk shows, news programmes or in some other arena of public speaking. It definitely pays to be prepared. Of course, not everyone has access to a media coach, but we can all hone our verbal communication simply by sitting down to a meal with friends and family. Turn off the TV, games and gadgets… eliminate those distractions and engage in face-to-face discourse. Lean in, make eye contact. Remember, it's important to listen as well as talk (you want repartee, not a mono-logue!)…and ask questions. Even if it's your grandma or the old man next door: make their day and ask them to share some stories or observations. You'll not only be showing them some attention, you might learn some-thing fascinating. Next thing you know, you'll probably be bantering back and forth, finding a level of kinship you never expected.

The feedback I most often get from my interviews is that my subjects always seems extraordinarily relaxed and at ease. I would certainly hope they'd feel that way… after all, isn't that exactly what a 'host' is supposed to do for his 'guest'?

Never talk down to anyone… it's the height of rudeness. Toddlers and puppies may be exceptions, but note that I do not include cats—they may, in fact, be our intellectual superiors. If you truly feel like you have a significant degree of greater intelligence than the person to whom you are speaking, then you should be smart enough to figure out some common ground for your conversation. That said, no matter what TV, radio or live event audience I may address, I never dream of 'dumbing down' anything I have to say. People are smarter than you may think… and if there's something that they miss or goes over their heads, leave it to them to figure out. Personally, I am enthralled when someone introduces me to a new thought, concept or even a word for me to go look up and re-invigorate my vocabulary.

To illustrate how perceptions of age have shifted, take for example this list of some famous folks who were born in the same year as me: 1963. Do you think of them as old? Johnny Depp, Quentin Tarantino, Brad Pitt, Jet Li, Helen Hunt, Mike Myers, Elle Macpherson, Michael Jordan, Dermot Mulroney, John Stamos, Lisa Kudrow, Benjamin Bratt, Vanessa Williams, Edie Falco, William Baldwin, Lisa Rinna, Eric McCormack, Nicolette Sheridan, Conan O'Brien, Dylan Walsh, Alexandra Paul, Tom Cavanagh, Rob Estes, James Denton, Kathy Ireland, George Michael, Seal, Bret Michaels, Julian Lennon, Natalie Merchant, Brian Boitano.

In his fight for tolerance and civil rights, Martin Luther King Jr. famously gave his 'I Have A Dream Speech' that year and remarked "1963 is not an end, but a beginning". It certainly was!

> *"Just to be here still is pretty amazing... Every day should be some sort of celebration. So yeah, I guess when you hit 50 finally... I'm just happy to still be around." Johnny Depp*

I had a chat with my agent, John Derr, about the catch-22 of being middle aged in the TV news business. Experience counts, but too often Youth Rules on the 'boob tube'. If you are older than 50 but not considered beyond your 'sell by' date, it's probably because you have settled into a particular area of expertise and therefore have the authority/gravitas to make you not only credible in that field, but indispensable to your workplace. It's not hard to find a good-looking young bimbo or him-bo to smile and read off a teleprompter, but if a presenter can offer a smart and original take on a given subject matter, he or she probably has a job for life. Here is a bit of John's perspective as a representative of on-air news talent...

NELSON: "What percentage of your on-camera clients are older than 50?"

JOHN: "I would say around 10 per cent of my clients are over the age of 50."

NELSON: "Does age give them more credibility and respect?"

JOHN: "I think age can give a journalist/anchor more credibility. It's about more than age, but it is easier for a 50ish anchor to have credibility than an anchor in his or her 20s."

NELSON: "Do women on TV have a shorter shelf life than men?"

JOHN: "It certainly seems that way. If you look at newsrooms across the country there are fewer veteran women anchors and reporters than men."

NELSON: "Short of silly dye-jobs and radical face lifts, how can TV journalists keep themselves 'hot properties'?"

JOHN: "Stay up to date on technology. The responsibilities of journalists have changed greatly in the last few years. You should be using social media as part of your daily routine at work. Veteran sportscasters are being let go because they can't or won't shoot and edit. Don't get set in your ways. Adapt with the business."

NELSON: "What's the best way for a 'retired' TV personality to reinvent him/herself after the gig ends?"

JOHN: "It's difficult to get back in the business when you've been out for a while. It's even more difficult if you are over the age of 50. So it's important to get back on the air in any market and show you can still get the job done and you can still relate to viewers."

I think news personalities such as Diane Sawyer, Bob Schieffer, Barbara Walters and the *60 Minutes* staff have greatly extended the 'life span' of TV newsers. Even in local markets, if an older on-air journalist finds him/herself out of work, there seems to be many alternative opportunities in parallel positions such as producer, coach or writer. One thing many of us did when starting out in the business was pick up freelance work opportunities through agencies. That is a great option for any mature folks to consider for employment. A solid work ethic, experience and organizational skills all make for a desirable temp in the eyes of prospective employer. And there is the bonus of not having to worry about a bad hair day on camera!

One mistake many people (not just public figures) make is to dress and/or behave in a manner 'too young' for their age. It is especially glaring on people in the spotlight. Who hasn't cringed at the sight of an older lady with her breasts flopping out of a dress cut too low at the front, or a hemline that's too high? Or snickered at the older fellow with the hair dyed shoe-polish black that barely manages to distract from the bristles poking out of his ear lobes? When Geraldo Rivera famously posted a selfie snapshot of himself clad in nothing but a low-slung bath towel and a pair of rose-colored glasses (how appropriate!) with the caption '70 is the new 50' the media world collectively gasped. Congrats on the flat tummy, Geraldo, but do you really think we want to see that from a senior citizen?

Ladies and Gentlemen…I give you my favorite 'grown up' celebrities. These are stars that I have met who shine more brightly with every year. I hope you'll agree.

GEORGE CLOONEY (BORN 1961)

As Cary Grant was to his generation, so is Mr Clooney to ours: the quintessential star on each side of the camera (which could explain why he is the only person nominated for Academy Awards in SIX different categories). Equally adored by men and women of all ages, I'd say he ranks second only to Tom Cruise in his ability to work a crowd. He's a talented, intelligent, multifaceted guy who can be the perfect gentleman while testifying about advocacy for a serious humanitarian crises or an impish prankster while horsing around with close pals such as Brad Pitt or Julia Roberts. He is the A-list-er of all modern A-list-ers, with an armed security detail discreetly nearby at all times, without ever losing the common touch that makes him the darling of fans and peers, alike. When he flashes that mega-watt smile, makes eye contact or pats you on the shoulder, he owns you! Fortunately for him, he's also one of those rare individuals whose real life charisma translates to the big screen... with the talent to back it up, resulting in so many memorable performances.

Like Jackman and Beckham, he rocks a tuxedo with the same casual elegance as a polo shirt and khakis. Like DiCaprio and MacGuire, he can play hard without ending the night having his mug shot snapped. Like Damon and Craig, his words and deeds do not offend. In fact, the only time I can recall him having any real ruckus with the press was when he slammed aggression of their tactics in the wake of Princess Diana's death in the Paris car crash. A lot more gallant than, say, an Alec Baldwin encounter.

Whatever his personal reasons for remaining a bachelor (and, as always, there are plenty of theories about that... most of them inaccurate), his brisk personal life only endears him to us more. He may not marry the women he dates, but he always treats them with the utmost respect, generosity and appreciation. His self-effacing humor and natural confidence have allowed him to weather with time from hunky heartthrob to Leading Man. I'd say it's a sure bet he will keep going in the tradition of Sean Connery, Sidney Poitier and the aforementioned Mr Grant to become a celebrity emeritus. Who will follow in his footsteps? Many try, but few succeed... which is what makes him so extraordinary. To know him is to like him and his affable nature is a testament to the loving parents, Nick and Nina, he still so obviously adores.

DICK VAN DYKE (BORN 1925)

Thanks to his body of work as a song-and-dance man, it's easy to forget that this great star is also a talented actor and beloved friend to the Hollywood community. His ability to find the humorous side of any situation has served him well offstage including being able to survive a brush with alcoholism, assorted medical issues and even a fiery car crash at age 87. He's extremely generous with his time and talents, too. When I spoke with him on the set of his series *Diagnosis: Murder*, he spoke extensively and eloquently about the topic of ageism in show-business. It was the first celebrity interview I'd ever conducted that felt like an actual conversation… not only because he is a great speaker, but a great listener as well. That was a very exciting experience for me, because it made me feel assured as a young reporter that I was moving precisely down the right path in my life. Thank you, Dick.

JULIANNE MOORE (BORN 1960)

The delightful redhead has a mantle full of awards for her acting work, but the role that she admits satisfies her most is that of Mom. Well known for her prolific, diverse work in a variety of roles in both Hollywood blockbusters as well as independent art house films, she keeps it real by keeping out of the limelight as much as possible and spending whatever spare time she has doing such things as charity work and writing her successful series of children's books. An 'army brat' who moved around frequently until she eventually moved to NYC after college, she is earnest and hard working… but it might explain why she's also a homebody. More luminously beautiful in her 50s than ever, she (so far) claims she wants nothing to do with cosmetic surgery, saying "I feel like it doesn't make people look any younger. It [just] makes them look like they've had surgery." What I love best about her, from my own interviews with her and from others I have seen her give, is the pride she still takes in her early career as a soap opera actress. In the mid-1980s, she was starring in the dual roles of twin cousins (long story!) Frannie and Sabrina Hughes on the venerable sudster, *As The World Turns (ATWT)*. She credits it with teaching her about focus and discipline… tools that would serve her well in the acting trade. In a display of grace that epitomizes just how down-to-earth she is, Julianne asked to come back to the show in 2010 for one final appearance before the series ended its stellar 54-year broadcast run. Without Tinseltown fanfare or bravado, she walked into an 'anniversary party' scene and her fictional family and legions of loyal viewers felt treated to a visit from a loved and missed heroine. Good work and good deeds are the hallmarks of this marvelous, talented lady.

> *"I think the thing about Julie is that she has stayed true to herself. When she came to* ATWT *right out of college, she was green and game for anything. She was thrown into a major storyline with the vets and played two roles: Fully fleshed-out characters from opposite sides of the world. One was my sister, the other my cousin. And she was a pro from the start. One of the things I remember is that a couple of years into her run on the show, we went out one night and she wanted to pick my brain about how I balanced career with motherhood and a private life. I also guided her to a financial manager who she stayed with for decades. She has always remembered her daytime roots and was never embarrassed by them. Of course, when she came back for our anniversary, it was old home week for all of us. She hasn't changed a lick… She's still just Julianne!" Colleen Zenk, 'Barbara Ryan Stenbeck' on* As The World Turns.

> *"She was gracious and delightful and I'm sure her [participation] was due in no small part to her love for the show and especially Don and Kathy (Don Hastings and Kathryn Hays, the long-time cast members who portrayed her parents)." Christopher Goutman, Executive Producer,* As

The World Turns.

"Julianne Moore's return to As The World Turns *in its final months meant the world to fans. There are so many examples of actors who started their careers working on daytime soap operas but act as if it never happened once they land a primetime series or their first big movie role. Julianne has always been incredibly appreciative of her time on the show and how everyone involved treated her like an adult and professional. Soaps and their fans often get diminished in the eyes of the media. Julianne coming back was not only a tribute to her roots but a thank you to long-time fans as well. I remember thinking she had a really bright future ahead of her and am so glad I was right. She's deserved all the accolades she received over the years."*
Roger Newcomb, Editorial Director, We Love Soaps.

The last time Julianne and I met up was in late 2013 and we got so carried away reminiscing about 'the old days' in soapland and catching up on the gossip, that a production coordinator in charge of keeping her appointments to schedule, finally had to break up our party. To my happy surprise, she insisted on waiting until we took a couple of pictures together. A fine lady who deserves not only her 'star' on the Hollywood Walk of Fame, but a gold star just for being such a great, unaffected person.

HARRY CONNICK JR. (BORN 1967)

I had long admired this versatile singer/writer/actor so was particularly excited to score an exclusive half-hour sit down with him, ostensibly to promote his new album *What Every Man Should Know*. That in itself would have been enough to fill the time… finding out about the close relationship he had with his parents and all the personal things he was willing to share for the first time. In my research I uncovered so many other fascinating facts about the debonair Louisianian that I couldn't wait to ask my questions. A lot of that went out the window, though, when he warmly greeted me in the scenic interview suite: I couldn't believe what a handsome, impressive specimen he was. Even wearing his specs and a simple crew neck shirt, I was really surprised. Most 'stars' are more diminutive in person... but Harry is larger than life! Of course, we discussed his music (I was most fascinated by his skills as an arranger and the fact that he holds a US patent on an computer invention that essentially eliminates the need for orchestras to use sheet music), but also his faith in God, his hands-on philanthropic deeds and his obvious genetic gifts. Already a fan, he won me over for life. A true Southern gentleman who exemplifies the saying that 'it is better to give than to receive'.

ANITA GILLETTE (BORN 1936)

This legend of Broadway, film and television could fill an encyclopedia with her credits... which is why it is ironic that we first met during the dying days of *Search For Tomorrow* in 1986. I'd grown up watching her on TV and the first Broadway musical I'd ever seen, *They're Playing Our Song*, in which she had starred. It wasn't until a quarter century later that we reunited on a red-carpet (how showbiz!) for the series finale of the sitcom *30 Rock*, which also co-starred another SFT graduate, Jane Krakowski. She played Tina Fey's mother Margaret Lemon, and was enjoying her umpteenth career rebirth... now playing Mother to a wide variety of A-list TV and movie stars... most recently on *Modern Family*. It turned out we're neighbors (along with Jerry Stiller and Anne Meara, Richard Kind, Annette O'Toole and Michael McKean, Matt Damon, Jerry Seinfeld, Téa Leoni... they're everywhere!) and she graciously came over for a batch of my homemade Anita Margaritas and obliged me with an interview for my web series, '... @ *Nelson's!*' Her latest gig is a one-woman show, "After All", which proves her talent and timing are as sharp as ever. The key to Anita's vitality at every age is her work ethic. She can't/won't stop. And that's lucky for the millions of people in the audience she continues to delight.

HUGH JACKMAN (BORN 1968)

His name comes up frequently in my reporting, not only because he's arguably the most popular celebrity in the world, but one of the most down to earth. Everyone knows this gentle giant is a 'triple threat' actor/singer/dancer. He's also a philanthropist, upright citizen, doting dad, loving husband, loyal friend and arguably the best Oscar's host since Bob Hope. Through mutual family friends, I've gotten to know him outside of the limelight and can vouch for the veracity of his status of pretty much being a superhero without a secret identity. Even with the craziest fans or the most obnoxious press members, Hugh always remains a gentleman in every sense of the word… with the unique gift of making everyone he's speaking to feel like they're the only person in the room. He is the perfect example of 'you reap what you sow'. Never forgetting to acknowledge/credit his wife since 1996, Deborra-Lee, in any conversation, he says, "I would be a quarter of the man I am without her." Whatever 'midlife crisis' he may be experiencing off-camera, he has his characteristic charm and humor to handle it with aplomb. After being teased for tweeting a gym piccie of himself dead-lifting an estimated 210 kilograms worth of weight, Hugh was as red-faced with discomposure as he'd been with muscle strain. Ever self-effacing, he admitted in an interview, "I'm a little embarrassed about that. That was a moment (of) just showing off, completely showing off… I'm about to turn 45, I will never do this again and I want to document it." You have nothing to be ashamed of, mate. Everybody loves ya!

VIGGO MORTENSEN (BORN 1958)

While you might think of him primarily as a fine actor—or forever as Aragon in *The Lord of the Rings* trilogy, Viggo would probably first consider himself an artist. This painter, poet and musician also publishes the works of little known authors and artists and is politically active and remarkably fair and bipartisan in his views and responses. If you saw 2007's *Eastern Promises*, you know he's no slouch when it comes to hitting the gym. He's lived all over the world and is multilingual (I've witnessed him impress international reporters with offers of conducting interviews in their native tongues…) even though he was born and raised in good old New York City. This revered, respected and awarded actor is humble enough to not mind having a chuckle about his early acting days. I suspect it is sense of curiosity, love and pursuit of artistry and a traveler's sense of wanderlust that keep him a leading man at any age.

MERYL STREEP (BORN 1949)

Who doesn't love Meryl Streep? She's indisputably the most gifted actress of her generation and there is something about her self-effacing humility that makes us love her just as much off camera as on. In the many times I have interviewed her, I've come to recognize that she has a routine that works for her: arriving only after the room has been lighted to her stylist's specifications and seated to favor the right side of her famous, fabulous face. Because she is so respected and revered, most people are understandably nervous in her presence… so she always goes the extra distance to put others at ease. With major stars, not-so-common courtesies such as asking "How are you today?" or "How did you like the movie?" or "That's a nice color you're wearing… may I ask where you found it?" make all the difference. Sure, she's a cinematic chameleon, but it is her ability to interact with anyone that makes her the truly great star that she is.

JOHN TRAVOLTA (BORN 1954)

Why is everyone so hard on John? Is it because of his toupée? (Lots of stars wear fake locks on film or the red carpet, including the guys! Many are convinced *The Vampire Diaries'* Ian Somerhalder sports a variety of hairpieces, and you never know what's going to appear atop Nicolas Cage's noggin…) Is it that he's a Scientologist? Since when is a person's religion anybody else's business... even if they're a celebrity? He's a real gent with a ton of talent and a pretty impressive body of film work. He has survived the tragedy of losing both his first partner, Diana Hyland, and his son, Jett. Gay rumors and scandals have swirled around him for most of his career and he has always conducted himself in a dignified manner even under the most intense scrutiny. Whatever it is that gives him and his wife, Kelly Preston, strength and the ability to always choose a smile over a frown should be commended.

LIAM NEESON (BORN 1952)

The Irish actor is a commanding presence onscreen and off... and there aren't many actors who could still be perceived as heart throbs well into their 60s. Having boxed from the age of 9, he's also known around his Upper West Side neighborhood as a man who enjoys a drink and a laugh with his mates. It's not unusual to see him striding or strolling the sidewalks with an arm slung affectionately around one of his sons, or chatting with his in-laws, the equally radiant Vanessa Redgrave and Joely Richardson. I've interviewed him a few times and he's perfectly polite and professional... but when a female reporter enters the room, something really switches on! The eyes twinkle, the body language changes and even the timbre of his voice shifts to another level. And the ladies always respond. Being comfortable in his own skin, something we should all strive to learn over time, is obviously the secret to his critical, box office and personal success.

JODIE FOSTER (BORN 1962)

Shortly after turning 50 and finding herself single, Jodie gave a bizarre speech when receiving a career achievement award at the Golden Globes in 2013. It seemed as if she were 'coming out' but it ended up being more of a plea for the seemingly contradictory conditions of both privacy and love. "If you'd had to fight for a life that felt real and honest and normal against all odds, then maybe you too might value privacy above all else...

I want to be seen, to be understood deeply and to be not so very lonely." In addition to her career challenges and the turmoil of her relationship break-up, she was caring for her beloved mother, a dementia patient, while continuing to raise her two fine sons, Charles and Kit. The gal had a lot on her plate at the time, to say the least… and it would probably have been a better idea to script an acceptance speech rather than extemporaneous gush. Be that as it may, she continues to be one of the most gifted, creative actors and directors in the industry. Having met her a few times, both in interview and social situations, she is utterly charming. In spite of spending almost her entire life in the public eye, she is the person you'd most want to sit next to at a dinner party or a baseball game. She has somehow managed to pass that quality on to her children who strike me as the most well-adjusted, bright and good natured young men in Hollywoodland. Let's hope they stay that way. With Jodie's common sense approach to working in a crazy business, it seems entirely possible.

JULIE ANDREWS (BORN 1935)

I've written at length in previous books about this darling dame, but I will just add here that one of the traits that serves her even better than her natural poise and grace is her loyalty to friends, family, fans, colleagues and journalists, like myself. Her performance prowess is legendary, but she is also, more quietly, a role model for adoption/parenting and children's literacy. She has a dignity that comes with being secure of her legacy, and a sometimes ribald sense of humor than can be surprising coming from that elegant exterior.

ADAM SANDLER (BORN 1966)

The Brooklyn-born native has become one of filmdom's most successful movie makers in spite of the critics. Audiences can't seem to get enough of his often lowbrow comedy, probably because always evident is the big heart of the family man behind it all. When I lived in LA, he was shooting *Bedtime Stories* in my neighborhood; usually when a film crew invades, it's a chaotic mess of noise, litter and disruption. Adam's Happy Madison production company made sure to leave our streets even better than it found them, donating dough to our local park's refurbishment and a thoughtful goody basket left on every resident's doorstep. His good sportsmanship and consideration obviously has a trickle-down effect on everyone who works for him and it's always a pleasure to interact with anyone connected to his projects. Consequently, I've interviewed him many times and those are always pleasant experiences. I've mentioned it to his colleagues such as Jennifer Aniston and Kevin James and they all concur. Our most recent chat was during the promotion of *Grown Ups 2*, a film that pokes fun at the foibles of middle age… and we had a very good time comparing notes; fondly remembering our mullet hair-do's (or were they hair-don'ts?) and padded shoulders.

JACKI WEAVER (BORN 1947)

For decades, this talented lady was one of Australia's most recognized working actors, delighting audiences with her diverse abilities on stage as well as screens large and small. Her personal life seemed to rival Elizabeth Taylor (although she cites Esther Williams as the idol of her youth), with a colorful cast of boyfriends and husbands… including two marriages to controversial media commentator Derryn Hinch. Marrying actor Sean Taylor in 2003 proved lasting and lucky: after a long, enviable career, she became an 'overnight success' for her intense role as the matriarch of a crime family in 2010's *Animal Kingdom*. It landed her an Oscar nomination and the attention of film fans worldwide. She's had non-stop Tinseltown A-list projects ever since, including more Award nods when she starred in *Silver Linings Playbook* alongside Bradley Cooper, Jennifer Lawrence and Robert De Niro. However, meeting the diminutive dynamo, you can't help but be smitten with her giggly, girlish demeanor and seemingly shy, sly sense of humor. A charmer. I had a memorable afternoon with her when she was appearing on Broadway with Cate Blanchett, Richard Roxburgh and Hugo Weaving in a smash-hit revival of Chekhov's

Uncle Vanya. I got to sit down with the fabulous foursome for a lengthy and intimate conversation and Jacki couldn't help but be a scene-stealer even off-stage! "I'm just a tiny cog in a big wheel," she demurred, "So lucky to be working with the big kids." Her humility may be the secret to her longevity and later-in-life notoriety. "I don't count myself as 'successful'. Sometimes I think I'm a hopeless flop," she told me, laughing. Lucky for us, she has been a frequent fixture in New York City for more than 40 years and admits, "Nowhere in the world does a martini taste like it does in New York."

DENZEL WASHINGTON (BORN 1954)

In addition to his Golden Globe and Tony Awards, Denzel is a two-time Academy Award winner and widely regarded as one of the finest actors in cinematic history. It is hard to dispute that when you see the commanding, ultra-realistic performances in his long filmography. He has also been awarded several honorary degrees for his work and philanthropy. He credits his mother's decision to send him to a strict military academy for saving him from the streets and a life of crime. To date, I've interviewed him three times. The first two encounters, he was polite and cerebral... even admiring of a tie clip accessory I was wearing (I arranged for one to be sent to him; celebrities, like everyone else, love a freebie). He has long endured the tabloid whispers of marital discord with his wife of more than 30 years, Pauletta, to deliver consistently great performances on stage and film. When I met him last in 2013, he not only looked as handsome, solidly built and unlined as ever (a shaved head at the time removed all his gray hair), but he possessed a lightness of spirit I'd never seen in him before... either onscreen or off. He even spontaneously burst into song when I jokingly suggested the only thing left for him to try was a movie musical. And then I couldn't get him to stop singing. Besides his religious faith, work ethic and good deeds, I believe it may just be his sense of humor, and ability to stop being too serious, that is allowing him to age so very well.

MEREDITH VIEIRA (BORN 1953)

This lovely woman is not only one of the most respected and beloved TV journalists in her field, she also happens to be my lucky charm. She and I shared a light-hearted social encounter back in the 1990s at a launch party for *The View*. I never forgot her humor, wit and beauty and applauded as I witnessed her meteoric rise to television stardom… always managing to strike the right chord, balancing her personal and private lives with grace and seeming ease (it is ANYTHING but easy).

Years later, in 2007, when Paris Hilton gave her first post-prison interview to Larry King, I commented on Australian television that I thought Ms Hilton had made an odd choice in deciding to whom she's spill her guts and that, if I were in her shoes, I would have opted for Meredith. In the lead-up to the 2013 Oscars, Meredith and I were on the same early morning flight from NYC to Los Angeles to cover the Awards. I re-introduced myself and told her the story. She was so warm and welcoming, physically and verbally effusive and immediately welcomed me into the circle of colleagues with whom she was traveling: an unnecessary but enchanting and appreciated gesture I will always remember. Ironically, Meredith informed me that the Network had wanted her to go for the Hilton interview and she passed. "I found the subject matter so ridiculous…" but as time and circumstance would prove, she good naturedly added, "Of course, since then I've gone on to cover many stories equally, if not more, ridiculous. Oh, well, show-business!" We have been regular email buddies ever since; her personal and professional enthusiastic encouragement more a touchstone for me than she might ever imagine. She balances her career with a rich family life (her husband of nearly three decades, Richard M Cohen, has multiple sclerosis and they have three children) and is a striking example of how a smart and charismatic person can reach extraordinary heights. In late 2014, she is set to debut a new daily talk show that is already a hot commodity at syndicated stations across America. I'm betting on it being a huge hit because she's not only a trustworthy journalist, she's the kind of company everyone would like to keep. I can't say enough good things about this great lady.

MARY LOUISE PARKER (BORN 1964)

This busy beauty has Golden Globe, Emmy and Tony Awards on her mantle, but you'd never suspect it when, chances are, she's chasing after her kids. Her priorities are as a mother. In fact, the last time I interviewed her, she was an hour late because she insisted on accompanying her son to a doctor's appointment. I appreciated the fact that she took the responsibility of our meeting seriously enough not to cancel, but that she also had her personal priorities in order. She's been quoted as saying that the mean-spiritedness of online bloggers and trolls has her considering 'taking a break' from showbiz, but I hope that's not the case and that she continues to strike the right combination to keep fans and family alike, happy and satisfied. She won my admiration forever when, even running late, she paused before the cameras rolled on our interview to alert me to a tiny speck of spinach caught between my teeth. Most stars wouldn't have cared how I looked! It speaks volumes about her generosity. Naturally, I kicked off my interview by thanking her for looking after me so kindly... and why aren't more celebrities as thoughtful with us 'mere mortals'. She spoke beautifully about how the sycophantic cycle of fame and fandom affects many so-called stars and I greatly admire her powers of observation and self-confidence.

"The movie business and show-business infantilizes you in such a way that people tend to buy into it," she explained to me. "You get there in the morning and everybody's trying to be ingratiating. 'Good morning... can I get you a coffee... come sit in your playpen for a moment and then we're going to get you dressed!' People are always trying to keep you 'okay' and when you end up managing people, what actually happens is you agitate them. Like with children: if you manage them too much they actually become more unrelieved. Does that make sense? I'm not a psychologist!"

It makes perfect sense. It also sums up why so many celebs act like spoiled brats. I wonder if MLP has always been so enlightened or if she acquired that with age. Either way, she's terrific.

"Can you imagine what you would do if you could do all that you can?" Sun Tzu

JENNIFER ANISTON (BORN 1969)

What can I say about Jennifer Joanna Aniston that hasn't already been relentlessly repeatedly by every magazine, tabloid, blog and TV news segment since she burst into the public consciousness in 1994 as a breakout star of the sitcom *Friends*? She's arguably the most photographed, talked about, scrutinized celebrity on the planet and the fact that she remains almost (I said 'almost') normal throughout it all says a lot for whatever support system she has in the tiny little bit of private life she is able to maintain. The fortune she amassed through that show's long run allows her to choose roles in 'smaller' films. The result has been her portrayal of a diverse collection of characters from the dramatic to the outrageous. Whichever direction she takes, she continues to woo and win fans. She's one of those rare women who seems to appeal equally to all demographics. I worked with her dad, soap veteran John Aniston (still on TV, these days as unscrupulous Victor Kiriakas on *Days of Our Lives*) back when Jen was a teenager, so every time I talk to her—we briefly reminisce about those grand and glorious days of yore. She had auditioned for a part on *Search For Tomorrow*, which ultimately went to blonde phenomenon Jane Krakowski, who parlayed that into a stunning Broadway and television career. Jen would have to wait a bit longer to grab her brass ring... which certainly seems to have turned out to be GOLD! She is understandably shy, seeming to seek approval not only from the journalists she meets and the audiences for whom she performs, but from those within her own entourage, trusted allies who tend to her hair, security, wardrobe and dietary needs. That said, once we start chatting, she's every inch a 'Rachel Green' type… girlish and fun, playing with stray wisps of hair and giggling easily. We chatted in late 2013 after her hilarious and stunning turn as a stripper in *We're The Millers*, showing off a body that would have supermodels cheering from the sidelines. She admitted to me that she had to take her workouts 'up a notch', but seeing her in person is always a reminder to me that, 'Yeah… she really does look THAT good'. With the support of her yoga instructor and personal chef, it's easier for her than most other 40-something gals, but it still requires resolve and discipline; qualities she obviously possesses in abundance. She's paid to endorse moisturizers and bottled water, which she obviously puts to use: her skin is lustrous. (I will admit that a bonus of getting to interview Jen is that the lighting in her suites is beyond fabulous… we all benefit!) As for her always-noteworthy private life, she admits that when she's happy, she actually enjoys working less… and happens to be one of the few famous faces who doesn't find NYC more celebrity-friendly than its West Coast counterpart. I guess even blasé Gothamites can't help but be dazzled by her star power.

The last time I interviewed Jen, the world was still waiting with bated breath for her to announce her wedding date to fiancé Justin Theroux (whom I have also interviewed; intense guy, strikingly sexual and probably has 1 per cent Body Fat… one of those celebs who's surprisingly tiny in real life). I was under strict instruction from my Australian executive producer to make sure and get at least one sound bite from her about the big day. That would be a coup for Oprah or Barbara Walters, let alone for me who was there ostensibly to discuss her latest film for Warner Brothers Home Entertainment, a Chinese news outlet and my Aussie show. I was slated to have a 20-minute sit-down with the leggy lovely and we had a fun, laugh-filled chit-chat until minute 19, when I got the signal from someone behind the camera that it was time to 'wrap up'.

I had to address the elephant in the room, so in the nicest possible way started, "The world is watching and waiting for your happiness…" Cleverly, she just said, "Waiting? It's here!" "You know what I'm talking about," I chided with a wink. "That big day. Everybody loves you. Are you ready for it?" I think she was probably more ready for a wedding than for the question and she gave me a solid response, "I love that. And I'm always ready. I mean, it's an exciting day to sort of anticipate. And it'll be a beautiful day." Whew… mission accomplished. Certainly not a Pulitzer Prize-winning bit of journalism, but I was glad I'd asked and everybody was happy.

Let that be a lesson before you react to a news story or interview you read or see in the media. I reported a story on Russell Brand's admission that he would imagine being with other women while in bed with his then-wife, Katy Perry. My disdain for his tacky jab at his ex was obvious, but on Twitter a woman immediately shot at me, "It's called fantasy, everyone does it." Oh really, ma'am? She had told me a lot more about herself than I'm sure she intended. Life is too short to engage in those kinds of social media debates, so I ignored her… but if I had replied, I would have said, "If I don't like who I'm having sex with, I stop having sex with that person!" Obviously she doesn't feel she has the same option.

TOM HANKS (BORN 1956)

Romping around in drag on the short-lived early 1980s sitcom *Bosom Buddies*, it was not apparent to many that Tom would go on to be a multiple Award-winning film actor, producer, writer and director. In the cut-throat world of show-business, the talented and likeable California native is also good for the bottom line. According to Wikipedia, "as of 2012, Hanks' films have grossed more than $4.2 billion at the United States box office alone, and more than $8.5 billion worldwide, making him the highest all-time box office star". In an industry where 'who you know' is as important as 'what you can do', it was the combination of both that earned him his big break: the male lead in Ron Howard's romantic comedy classic, *Splash* (Tom had guest-starred on an episode of *Happy Days*). The rest is Hollywood history still being written, but it's safe to say that his filmography is as diverse as Meryl Streep's… with comparable track records for critical acclaim, financial success and personal reputation. His marriage to Rita Wilson (they wed in 1998) is regarded as one of filmdom's rarities in terms of its longevity and happiness. When he came to Broadway in 2013's *Lucky Guy*, he proved he could draw crowds for his stage presence, too… and fans clamored outside the theater after every performance with the kind of fervor usually reserved for rock stars and teen idols. A space geek (did you know he has an asteroid named after him?), political activist and philanthropist, he maintains a busy schedule but still manages to make time to be a doting patriarch to the Hanks' clan, which includes four children and two grandchildren. Perhaps, in spite of his fame and fortune, it is commitment to being a responsible citizen, a diligent worker and 'regular guy' that make him so believable as the everyman he so seemlessly portrays in his screen roles.

MICHELLE PFEIFFER (BORN 1958)

Long regarded as one of the most beautiful women in the world, she also happens to be one of the most talented. After her nine-year marriage to actor Peter Horton (who blamed their divorce on their mutual devotion to their work, rather than their relationship), she entered into a three-year affair with another actor, Fisher Stevens, which raised a few eyebrows. She married prolific TV and film producer David E. Kelley in 1993… one of Hollywood's most romantic success stories! She's known for being vigilant about diet and exercise (that cat-woman costume didn't hide much!) and continues to radiate the same healthful beauty in her late 50s as she did when she burst onto the scene in *Grease 2* and *Scarface*. As for cosmetic surgery, she's said, "If that nose or those jowls bother you, do it! But this epidemic of people losing sight of what looks good, the distortion that has been going on is creepy." I have been fortunate enough to interview her on several occasions and have to confess she looks just as good in person as she does on screen. If she HAS had any work done, it's been subtle and beautifully executed. Once I asked her about maintaining those good looks and she really thought about her answer before responding. When she did, it was perfect. She told me that she not only avoids toxic foods, but people and situations she also considers toxic. Good advice! She's very obviously comfortable in her own skin, which enables her to act in such a wide range of genres, always effectively. I might also add that she is content to expose her bare feet when parked in a chair for a long interview session. As you can imagine: she sports a perfect pedicure. Excellent news for fans, she plans to keep on making movies. "I can't see myself ever retiring. Ever. I started working part-time when I was 14 and still at school. And I've never stopped. From the moment I started, I loved it, and I feel like I always need to be productive in some way. But who knows? I may not always be acting; I hope I am."

JEFF BRIDGES (BORN 1949)

Alongside his big brother, Beau, he began his acting career as a tiny tyke on the TV show *Sea Hunt* (even though technically his screen debut was at four months of age in the film *The Company She Keeps*). The series starred his talented and versatile dad, Lloyd Bridges, with whom he went on to co-star in stage productions. Eventually a distinguished motion picture career followed... and somehow, no matter how grey and grizzled he became, Jeff always was able to maintain his status as a heart-throb leading man. Iconic roles in now-classic films include *The Last Picture Show*, *Tron*, *Starman*, *The Fabulous Baker Boys*, *Against All Odds*, *Seabiscuit*, *The Big Lebowski*, *Crazy Heart*, *Iron Man* and the remake of *True Grit* helped earn him six Academy Award nominations and one win for Best Performance by an Actor in a Leading Role. It certainly hasn't gone to his head, though... probably because he has been in the show-business industry from such a tender age that little about it impresses him. That could also explain the success of his marriage to wife Susan (since 1977) and his keen interest in other pursuits such as music and photography. Always more casual and laid back than his 'intense' peers such as DeNiro, Pacino and Hoffman, Bridges always seems happiest when he's kicking back, smiling and just shooting the breeze. That was certainly how he was when I met and interviewed him. With age and success he has found the pleasure of picking and choosing his film projects (some flops, some not) so he can devote time to his hobbies, philanthropic work and grandfather duties. "Everything in your life teaches you something," he says.

BRAD PITT (BORN 1963)

He's one of the biggest movie stars of all time. In addition to the extensive critical acclaim and box office success he has achieved through this work, he is equally renowned for his philanthropy as well as involvement in social and political issues. His personal life, too, receives the kind of attention usually reserved for presidents and royalty. Partnered (in every sense of the word) with the equally famous Angelina Jolie since 2005, they are raising six children and continuing to prove themselves extraordinary on both sides of the camera. When I interviewed him in 2007, he told me that nothing, "keeps it real" for him like changing a dirty diaper. While he may no longer be the body-beautiful young hunk of *Thelma and Louise* or *Troy*, he is still considered one of the sexiest men alive and generates throngs of excitement and attention wherever he goes. Finding fame was a hard fight for Brad, who moved to Los Angeles from the rural Midwest, determined to be a movie star. Through a classified advertisement at the Screen Actors Guild, he found a 'survival job' as a personal assistant to my friend, soap opera writer Thom Racina (best known for creating the famous Luke and Laura love story on *General Hospital*, winning over millions of devoted fans including Dame Elizabeth Taylor). Thom recounts how struck he was by the boy's earnest career intent and dedication to its pursuit… even while he was running errands and skimming the swimming pool. Thom created a role for him on the show *Another World*, but producers were unimpressed by Brad's talents and looks, deeming his complexion impossible for television. Still, Thom kept encouraging the young man who, in return, encouraged his boss to continue writing novels. Both succeeded. Thom went on to write several best-selling books and Brad graduated to a recurring part on TV's

Dallas and the rest is history. Brad mused that one day, in addition to a big film career, he'd have a house full of kids and sit on the front porch watching them play in the yard. He has achieved all that and more on a much grander scale than he ever dared imagine. For not only sticking to his dreams of fulfillment and success, but using his powers for positive change once he achieved them, Brad is certainly one of the most remarkable and admirable men of his generation.

SHARON STONE (BORN 1958)

We still see the stunning lovely leggy on the red carpet as well as crossing a Beverly Hills street, or bikini clad on Malibu Beach. In her own words: "I think I am ageing but I'm enjoying the process. I think that's really it. I'm enjoying my years, I'm enjoying my life, I'm enjoying my family. I'm just happy. My secret is no secret. I just do all the things you're supposed to do. I eat right, I sleep, I work out, I'm happy. I have a beautiful family and nice friends. I choose the good things. I choose the happy, healthy things. I don't choose the bad, unhealthy, unhappy things. What if you just don't do the dumb, stupid, unhappy things? Took me a long time to figure that out, but I think that's what it really is." Good for Sharon for making smart choices. She also exudes the confidence to show off what she knows are her best assets. If you have it, make sure you flaunt it.

ANTHONY FIELD (BORN 1963)

Best known as 'The Blue Wiggle', this founding member of the wildly successful musical group The Wiggles remains the only original band member and was made a Member of the Order of Australia 'for service to the arts, particularly children's entertainment, and to the community as a benefactor and supporter of a range of charities'. To me, however, he is not only a good mate, but a lover of classic lounge music of a bygone era. He and I can wax for hours comparing the merits of crooners Perry Como, Frank Sinatra and Andy Williams… and one day hope to mount our own cabaret show in tribute of performers like these and the eternally enjoyable standards they famously performed. Remember THAT next time you see a bunch of three-year olds singing along to Wiggles' hits such as *Hot Potato* and *Fruit Salad*! Since he and I were born in the same year, I had him answer a few questions for me… just to compare notes. Like me, he is the youngest member of a large brood (of seven kids) and laughs, "… being the last, I received preferential treatment for the good, from my mum, and preferential treatment for the bad, from my older siblings!"

NELSON: "Growing up, what was your perception of 50?"

ANTHONY: "Growing up, 50 may as well have been 500! Even in my 30s, I couldn't picture being here at 50!"

NELSON: "Did you have trouble adapting to the number? How did it affect you?"

ANTHONY: "In Australia, when you turn 50, the government doesn't send you a birthday card… they send you a 'bowel cancer test kit!' You also qualify for 'seniors insurance'. I guess, the government reminder of my mortality prompted me to rethink my lifestyle (especially my diet) and get super fit."

NELSON: "Does being a member of The Wiggles keep you young?"

ANTHONY: "Creatively it keeps me youthful, and I like challenging mine and others' opinions on things. I never want to be set in my ways. People sometimes say to me, 'Hey… you said you were in favour/against this or that', and I say, 'Well, I had a think about it, and changed my mind'."

NELSON: "What age-related changes have you noticed in yourself?"

ANTHONY: "My hair is almost completely grey. If I eat badly, the metabolism doesn't process the food as quickly as it used to. My long vision is shot. But apart from that, I am in good shape!"

NELSON: "So, what's the best thing about being your age?"

ANTHONY: "Not caring as much about what people think of me."

NELSON: "Are there any moments where you say, 'Oh, crikey… I'm an old fart!'"

ANTHONY: "Travelling around the world with our touring group, we have dancers/acrobats in their 20s/30s… and the music they listen to? Well, it makes me feel very old! Reality TV makes me feel old; I can't identify with it."

NELSON: "Here, here. Give me *Gilligans Island* any day! Any personal or professional role models who showed you how great it is to be 50 and beyond?"

ANTHONY: "Oh, for sure! Ranger Doug, from *Riders in the Sky*, still "doing it the cowboy way". And there is this dashing entertainment reporter on *Sunrise* who runs marathons. Mmmmmm… can't remember his name!"

NELSON: (blushing/rarely speechless)

RHONDA BURCHMORE (BORN 1960)

Another national treasure of Australia, multi-talented Rhonda has been a fixture of the stage and variety TV scene Down Under for almost as long as her legs! (to borrow a line from adult film star Julie Strain: "Six feet tall… and worth the climb!") She's delighted theater-goers with her powerful performances in musicals ranging from *Annie Get Your Gun*, *Mame*, and *Guys & Dolls* to *Mamma Mia*, *They're Playing Our Song* and her own successful one woman cabaret show. She and I (finally) met a few years ago in Melbourne when we were commissioned to do a musical meet-and-greet event to benefit flood victims. Leaving myself in her oh-so capable and well-manicured hands, we had an afternoon rehearsal in her Barbie-doll filled mansion, followed by a rollicking night performing standards and show tunes as if we'd been working together for years. Instant chemistry! Her sass and sex appeal belie her truly sweet and nurturing personality and anyone who gets to enjoy either her performance or her friendship (or in my case, both!) is in luck.

NELSON: "How did you develop your sense of style?"

RHONDA: "I grew up in very humble beginnings, but my mum Yvonne insisted we kids were always dressed immaculately. Mum was a great dressmaker and for years would buy the best quality fabrics to design outfits for my sister and me. I began performing on stage at an early age—and yes mum made all our incredibly glamorous outfits then—inspired by all the Hollywood movie musicals. So, I guess mum is responsible for teaching me about style and quality of dress."

NELSON: "You project an attitude that is confident and sexy, but not aloof or standoffish. Would you say 'what we see is what we get' when it comes to your image?"

RHONDA: "I guess my sense of confidence comes from performing for nearly 30 years. I've performed for everyone from Princess Diana to President Bill Clinton to Arabian Sheiks. I guess you gain confidence the more you do. That said, I still get nervous on some occasions."

NELSON: "Me, too. That just means we care. I remember an impressive

Barbie collection at your house. Was she a bit of an inspiration for you?"

RHONDA: (laughs) "I now have nearly 400 special edition Barbies in my collection, some of them worth a lot of money. The ones by designer Bob Mackie are my faves… and, yes, quite a bit of inspiration for my glam gowns comes from these dolls. I also adore the pop icon Barbies—the problem is: I take them all out of their boxes to look at them… a big 'no no' for true collectors!"

NELSON: "When you play a role, do you end up (consciously or subconsciously) adapting that character's style as your own?"

RHONDA: "When I perform a role I do try to inject a lot of myself into the characterization so that the work becomes unique. For instance, when I played in the original *Mamma Mia*, there was a lot of Rhonda in my character Tanya and some of that actually made it into the film version."

NELSON: "You seem glamorous, but what do you usually wear around the house?"

RHONDA: "I guess I try to be a bit glam when I go out in public or perform, but at home with friends and family, I'm most happy in tracker pants and tee shirt… bare feet and no make up."

NELSON: "Have you adjusted your style with age?"

RHONDA: "Yes. The dresses are getting longer and I believe a little more elegant and sophisticated. I love a good designer and buy pieces that will last. Armani suits and cashmere sweaters, and so on".

NELSON: "I love your *joie de vivre*!"

RHONDA: "Well, in the words of Auntie Mame: 'Life's a banquet and most poor suckers are starving to death!' I love life and try to make the most of every day."

RITA COSBY (BORN 1964)

She's another buddy of mine whose work I have long admired and then, when we finally met through mutual friends, I was happily surprised at how instantly we hit it off. Being mates with colleagues is a special treat in our business and she's appeared on my web series, while I frequently contribute to her popular weekday radio show. As a recipient of several Emmys and other distinguished service Awards (the state of New York even once declared a Rita Cosby Day for her 'extraordinary journalism and exemplary service on behalf of her community'). She is a special correspondent for the news program *Inside Edition* and a best-selling author. Her most recent book is *Quiet Hero* and even after all the high-profile, high-brow interviews she's conducted, she's still a warm and funny sweetheart.

NELSON: "What's the best thing about being a 'grown up' for you?"

RITA: "I don't have to use my fake ID anymore. In fact, when I get carded now, I give the bartender a hug!"

NELSON: "Is it what you expected, when you were young?"

RITA: "It's even better. I've exceeded my dreams and each day I still marvel at the new people I meet as well as the places I travel to for work and play. I learned at an early age that the 'work hard, play hard' formula is a good one."

NELSON: "Do you feel you've made any major sacrifices for the sake of your career?"

RITA: "I have no regrets, just massive sleep deprivation that I hope to make up for in my next lifetime."

NELSON: "What's the secret to your boundless energy and enthusiasm?"

RITA: "Do what you love and treat life as a great adventure. The minute you stop learning and growing, you need to find a new career… or a new husband."

NELSON: "Who were/are your role models for middle age?"

RITA: "Professionally, in television, growing up I admired greatly (and still do) Diane Sawyer, Lesley Stahl and Barbara Walters, who all look amazing for their ages and continue to chase stories across the globe. For me, age is a state of mind. There are people in their 20s who mentally are 'over the hill' because they are afraid to take chances and live life to its fullest. I hope I never grow up… like Peter Pan."

NELSON: "There seems to be a double standard between men and women when it comes to ageing. Do you ever experience that in the news biz?"

RITA: "Sadly, there are gender stereotypes, and you often see the old geezer guy with the hot young blonde on the show together. Luckily, I am blonde and can keep any male co-anchor on his toes! I do believe women often have to work harder, but I am also delighted to see many more women in TV news than when I started."

NELSON: "What are you looking forward to in the coming years, personally and/or professionally?"

RITA: "I have dreamt of taking a year-long world voyage, cruising to dozens of exotic, remote ports, sipping champagne and eating lobster. Then, I wake up and realize I have to wait a few decades before I can do that. After all, there are still many more celebrities and world leaders I have yet to interview. I guess my journey from Brooklyn to Bali to Belize... and beyond... remains on my bucket list."

MONICA HORAN (BORN 1963)

Best known (and beloved) by TV audiences as sweet and innocent Amy McDougall Barone on the long-running situation comedy *Everybody Loves Raymond*, I've been lucky enough to know Monica since we were teenagers back in Pennsylvania. I had started my college career and she was keen to audition to join our drama department at Hofstra University. Even back then, she was comedically talented in a Carol Burnett kind of way... a pretty girl who could manipulate her face like rubber or take a pratfall like a trained stuntwoman. I suggested we do a scene together from the farcical play *Bullshot Crummond*, which I had recently performed in a regional production. She was, of course, hilarious and became part of our campus family. Our core group of pals lived, loved, studied and partied together, which made for very memorable times and permanent close ties. She went on to marry one of the upper classmen, Phil Rosenthal (a *Raymond* co-creator and executive producer) in 1990, and they have had two beautiful kids together. It's always a delight to chat, email and (all too rarely) visit with my cherished old friend... who remains not only a gifted funny lady, but one of the kindest and most generous people I know. The passage of time only seems to make her more endearing.

NELSON: "At what age did you really feel you had come in to your own?"

MONICA: "50! For me, turning FIFTY marks a time of clarity and acceptance about myself, about others, about life. I have the sense that I know myself and feel a sense of purpose, knowing all that I know and have learned and experienced up to this point. Some things are profound, some are silly such as I don't have to cook. I need to feed my artistic sensibilities. I loved being an actor, but I haven't nurtured that identity since my 30s, even when working as an actor! During those years I identified as wife, mother, daughter, daughter-in-law, friend and philanthropist far more than I ever identified as 'actor'. Now with 23 years of marriage under our belts (my husband would say 'enough already'), the first child having graduated and gone to college, our foundation and philanthropic systems in place, great times as well as tragic times with friends, raising a child through their teen years, transitioning into the role of sometime caretaker for older parents, I feel as if I also have 'graduated'. I feel like I am 18 again. Since turning 50, I've started with a personal trainer (with a woman who started competitive figure skating at 50), writing, taking improvisation class and voice lessons—and thanks to the syndication of *Everybody Loves Raymond*, my parents and I don't have to take out college loans to do all that!

NELSON: "You have been one of those women who has successfully juggled home, husband, kids and career. What was the key to your finding balance?"

MONICA: "I would say there is no key and there is no balance, just the PURSUIT of balance—and that is based on personal priorities. The main thing is prioritizing, recognizing your choices and being satisfied with them. No one can do or have it ALL. And ALL is different for each of us. Whenever I start to feel that somebody looks like they have it all together, or when someone is telling me that I do, I remind myself that we only see each other in a 'snapshot'. We're all in the same boat when it comes to balance—we all have to work with what we've got, and work really hard, and accept that we will rarely achieve perfect balance while trying to do just that."

NELSON: "How has life gotten better for you after turning 50?"

MONICA: "I am HAPPILY through menopause and I find I'm not as reactive and histrionic as I have been in the past."

NELSON: "When we were in college, our folks were 50-something. How do you fathom that?"

MONICA: "My parents had fewer choices than I do! They were playing a whole different ball game at 50 and it wasn't nearly as fun. But I do love thinking about who my parents were when they were my age. It makes me understand who they were a little more."

NELSON: "If 50 is the new 40, what do you expect 50 will be like for your own kids?"

MONICA: "Now THERE'S something I can't fathom. They were so different from me as children, I can't imagine how different they will be from me at 50."

NELSON: "How does philanthropy fit into your life? I think that is a great way to keep grounded, keep perspective. Does it do that for you?"

MONICA: "The inclusion of arts in the core curriculum for public school is our main passion, but we are fortunate enough to regard philanthropy as part of our investment in the future for our kids. We tithe a portion and put it in a fund that becomes a portfolio for things we support in addition to arts education. That includes medical research, the environment, healthy city initiatives for Los Angeles, healthy food initiatives and veterans issues. I would advise people to start with what honestly speaks to them and what they find important… anything to repair the world."

NELSON: "You're one of the most naturally gifted comediennes I know… and always have been. I believe a sense of humor keeps you young. Do you agree?"

MONICA: "Awww, thanks, Nelson. That's my favorite thing to hear. A sense of humor not only keeps you young, it keeps you married, speaking to your family and helps you get along with just about anybody you come across."

NELSON: "You've been in a unique position to work with some of the great funny women over 50—Betty White, Georgia Engel (who played your Mom on *Raymond*), Doris Roberts, Katherine Helmond. Anybody who taught you something in particular?"

MONICA: "Georgia is a consummate actress with pure heart and impeccable instincts. She is so serious about comedy that I learned to focus, think and concentrate from her."

NELSON: "Can you believe from that roach-infested dormitory all those years ago that we have the amazing lives we have today!? Are we blessed or WHAT?"

MONICA: "SO BLESSED!!! And blessed further that, as I think back on that dump of a dorm, the studio sublet where FIVE of us slept like sardines on mattresses on the floor, the loft I lived in with four friends and the railroad-apartment that got broken into…I still have so many hilarious, sentimental and loving memories."

By now you have gathered from all these super celebrities and my own reflections on the components of fabulous living: for all the good things a person may have going for him/her self in this life, spirit may be the most important. That brings me to the next chapter...

CHECK YOUR ATTITUDE

Back in the 1980s, my friend Linda Dano hosted a daily women's talk show called *Attitudes*. Given the current proliferation of the all-female weekday gab fests on the airwaves, *Attitudes* seems like pretty standard fare nowadays but back then it was groundbreaking to have 'television for women' and Linda was a pro at getting to the heart of issues, all the while rocking her *Dynasty*-inspired shoulder pads, parachute pants and chunky jewelry. I'm sure plenty of research and focus groups went into the naming of the program, too. 'Attitudes' can imply haughty confidence, social conscientiousness or positivity. It's all up for individual interpretation.

Throughout these pages, I've written a lot about outlook and optimism… improving your life by improving your outlook. Happiness is infectious: if you're exuding 'happy', the people around you pick up on it and the feeling spreads. Of course, the same thing works with negativity, too, so you have to purposefully opt to see that glass as half full. And that can be daunting. Here's our opportunity to examine attitude.

The dictionary has several different definitions for attitude.
What's yours?

- *The arrangement of the parts of a body or figure:*
  posture.
- *A position assumed for a specific purpose.*
- *A mental position with regard to a fact or state.*
- *A feeling or emotion toward a fact or state.*
- *An organismic state of readiness to respond in a*
  characteristic way to a stimulus (as an object, concept,
  or situation).
- *A negative or hostile state of mind.*
- *A cool, cocky, defiant, or arrogant manner .*

I've gotten so used to being mistaken for someone younger than my actual age, that it doesn't surprise me anymore. But I am always flattered and never take it for granted. I once thought it must be due to my diligent moisturizing or bi-annual oxygen microdermabrasion treatments, but the more time that goes by, the more I realize the actual credit goes to my attitude. I pride myself on child-like exuberance and having an innate sense of excitement about life (Note, I did not say 'child-ish'). My gym trainer often remarks how he can't believe I'm much closer in age to his parents than I am to him.

So how can you unleash your inner child's attitude? I'd advise you to start by making some new friends who happen to be younger. I bet if you look around your workplace, school, church, health club or neighborhood, there are plenty of younger people whose friendship you would enjoy. As we get older, it's tempting to get set in our ways… even to the point of reclusiveness. We know what we like and what works for us, so consequently resist change or embracing new people and experiences. *Au contraire*, this is the time in our lives when we need to reach OUT, not withdraw IN.

My Mother and Dad have always been social creatures and have 'collected people' as they dance through their life together. Growing up, it seemed like there were always interesting new people of all ages coming over for dinner, or picking them up to go out on the town. Holiday meals always included 'orphans'… maybe a lonely oldster from the nursing home, but more often than not they were young: interns or student nurses from Dad's hospitals… university friends of my siblings… or just neighbors and acquaintances they'd befriended. Even now, their younger caretakers are all like our surrogate family members. Getting into their 80s, it would have been easy for them to remain insulated. Instead Mom is a borderline text addict and YouTube diehard, while Dad works on his computer for hours on end to crank out his Currency Club's monthly newsletter. They didn't teach themselves: they learned from their grand-kids and 'the geek squad' in the electronics store. It's okay to ask for help; most people love the feeling of being a teacher and having a talent or skill to pass on to others. Embrace technology, younger people, new trends. Keep up with current events and popular culture. Don't be left behind: get swept up in now!

Have you noticed how much air-time or print space in modern news is devoted to the entertainment genre? (Thank goodness, for me! Show-biz journalism has been my 'bread and butter' for many years.) We are a society, so there is an innate human need to know what everyone likes and dislikes. From cave paintings to the town crier to movie fan maga-zines and the advent of shows such as *Entertainment Tonight*, information matters. Of course, we have to keep our priorities straight. Like most, the TV show I have been appearing on daily since 1993, leads every hour with breaking news headlines. That is followed by a sports report… then the weather forecast, a financial/business update, a sprinkling of current affairs stories… and then show-business news, arguably the segment that brings the most interest and enthusiasm from the regular audience. Maybe because it's usually the most upbeat… or because there's a little something in it for everyone. The Kardashian clan may not be your cup of tea but who isn't a little bit fascinated by Brad and Angelina? Spend 20 minutes or so every day keeping up with the latest… whether that's via TV, internet, radio or print… and you'll be a more interesting and interested person.

Speaking of the Internet, let's look at social media. If you're not already taking advantage of interacting through Facebook, Twitter or Instagram, you're definitely missing out on some positive opportunities. Not that you should be glued to the ever-updating minutiae of it, but why wait for a wedding or funeral to connect with special people in your life? Magazine editor Tina Brown gave an interview explaining that she didn't use any of those social networking sites because she felt that certain of her life's relationships had a beginning, a middle and an end… and she wasn't compelled to be in touch with random classmates she knew as a child, or find out what one of her neighbors had for a snack. I think that's narrow minded: you get out of those experiences what you put in. Can you ever really have too many friends? It's not like you have to buy them all dinner.

Our elderly parents can often require as much patience as children, and usually don't provide the same satisfaction and delight that a child's progression and development give. Exercise as much tolerance as you can. They were patient with us, now it's our turn.

Anti-ageing is a term that was coined to help sell wrinkle creams, liposuction, smoothies and even medicines to help men's hair to grow. We've gotten used to anti-ageing as something desirable, perhaps even necessary, if we ever want to stand a chance of finding any peace after the age of 30. People even younger than that are feeling the prick of the botox needle, the puff of the inflated lips, burning off freckles and tweezing the odd stray white hair. We love anything anti-ageing!

I had a moment of clarity while browsing the aisles of a massive bookstore, with walls of books divided into every conceivable subject matter.

I asked an employee where I could find the books on ageing. She led me to the health section and indicated a fairly motley collection of paperbacks that didn't even take up an entire shelf. Most of those were titled, in one form or another anti-ageing. Why the heck are we 'anti' ageing? Why aren't we 'pro' ageing? As kids we couldn't wait to grow up… to get through school and begin our adult lives. Why were we so anxious to get over the hurdle of youth if the only thing waiting on the other side were endeavors to try and fool everyone—including ourselves—into believing we were still in the bloom of it?

Smart people and many cultures actually respect and revere the experience, knowledge and expertise its older citizens bring to society. For all the lip service Western civilization may pay to that notion, it doesn't often practice what it preaches.

Pushing forth positivity for pro-ageing should begin the moment your eyes open in the morning. Practice beginning each day by acknowledging as many upbeat things as you can.

* Gosh, that was an interesting dream.
* Boy, did I have a great sleep.
* This is the most comfortable bed in the world.
* Look at that weather… I can't wait to wear my (fill in the blank) today.
* Hooray, coffee time.

Have you ever stubbed your toe getting out of bed and thought, 'Well, that means this is going to be a crappy day?' Don't let any little stumbling block take down your entire day… ever. You have the power to change the entire course of your day, at any point, simply by adjusting your attitude.

When you flip that attitude people will automatically want to like you… be inspired by you and gravitate toward you. Their perception of you, however, is only a reflection of how you perceive yourself. And that begins with the face staring back at you in the mirror. Do you like what you see? I'm not talking about a new wrinkle or age spot. Flash a big smile at yourself and say 'Good morning, gorgeous'.

When we were kids, 'playing old' meant walking hunched over with a cane and saying in a squeaky voice, 'Eh? What's that, sonny? Speak up, I can't hear you.' Come on, you're nowhere close to that. Didn't you used to imagine what you'd look like as you got older? Now you're finding out! Chances are it's way better than you dared dream it would be.

Entire industries are built on 'how not to look older'. But who says there's anything wrong with looking older? Vanessa Redgrave and Clint Eastwood are two examples of famous folks who started out with (exceptional but traditional) youthful beauty and evolved over the decades to maintain their good looks and desirability, as well as their appeal thanks to personality, talent and attitude. Focus more on the fact that you are enjoying the privileges of reaching every new age. You deserve credit and respect for every year.

"Live fast, die young and leave a good-looking corpse", is a movie line usually (incorrectly) attributed to James Dean, who died tragically at the age of 24. It was actually uttered by actor John Derek in the 1949 film *Knock On Any Door*. After Dean, the poster child for 1950s teenage disillusionment, perished in a car wreck in 1955 the concept of associating old-age with unattractive looks flourished in popular culture... romanticized by his sad story. Not only is there no such thing as a good looking corpse, in my opinion, but who in their right mind would rather die young than enjoy life... even at the expense of a tight face and taut, lithe figure? Besides, Dean's on-screen attitude is nothing worth emulating unless you only want to attract the attention of mixed-up adolescents. By contrast, it was his true-life personality that made him such sought-after company: sensitive, romantic and a little bit silly.

For many years, on my mother's dressing table, alongside all the little bottles of perfumes and potions, amid her arsenal of face paint, false eyelashes, brushes and wands, was a screwdriver. And not the kind you drink. What was this little piece of hardware doing there? It turned out that she had one of those rotating mirrors; you know, the kind that reflects on one side, but on the flip side is a magnifying mirror to help you see every pore or stray hair up close. Well, as her face began to show the signs of age, she would occasionally get so frustrated with the reflection looking back at her that she'd give the glass a good swat. "I don't know how many times I knocked that poor thing apart," she told me. Finally, she had to keep the screwdriver handy for the times she broke the spinning mechanism. She has a good arm. Eventually, she came to terms with 'the Mom in the mirror', but that screwdriver stays there… just in case.

Wardrobe is an essential weapon in your arsenal of attitude. I don't mean 'costumes', either. Dressing too youthfully, trendy or overdoing it may succeed in getting you noticed, but for all the wrong reasons. Unless it's the Academy Awards or the Melbourne Cup, 'less is more' is a rule of thumb that works for even the classiest occasions. But even in every day life, you will carry yourself with more poise, confidence and commanding demeanor if you are sporting clothes that are clean, crisp and figure flattering. How many times have you seen older guys slouching around in old, ill-fitted clothes that offer up an unwanted glimpse of plumber's crack? A bedazzled tracksuit may be comfortable and easy to throw on for a grocery store, but why look like a great-granny when you don't have to? Whether it's a long flight overseas, a trip to the doctor's office or just a jaunt to the dry cleaners, make an effort to look good. People notice and remember. Growing up, we didn't just dress up for church or school photographs, we were always shined up unless we were going to a softball field. Sadly, for most people, those days are gone. But not only is it a sign of respect for others, knowing you look your best will make you stand up tall and strut your stuff.

I had a friend whose mother used to caustically tell her daughters to "suck in your stomachs, throw out your boobs and put on a little lipstick. When you look better, you feel better." She had a point, even if she didn't possess a way with words.

Like any proud parent, my Mother always loves it when I send her pictures of me with my friends, enjoying our adventures. As any loving and biased mom might comment, she recently asked me, after seeing a snapshot of me with a group of pals, "How are you going to handle it when you're no longer the best-looking person in the picture?" There was a trace of wistfulness in her voice, I suppose because for most of her life, her natural good looks had always stood out. Taking that into consideration, I thought for a moment and then replied, "Well, I'll just have to make sure I'm the most interesting looking!" It was the right answer for her... and I've been thinking ever since that it's the right answer for all of us. Stand out for your style and personality and looks will take a back seat, regardless. Don't settle for being a back-up act, be the headliner!

My dad's Aunt Miriam and Uncle Paul were married for an astounding 77 years and each lived to be 97 years of age. Talk about a lifetime commitment. I remember him being very tall and droll; she was tiny and giggly. They remained fiercely independent until their final days, traveling the world together and avidly photographing their adventures. What I remember most was their sense of style. They were always decked out in the most colorful 1970s styles... flamboyant riots of paisley and plaids. He was never without a handmade bow tie and she had a signature contemporary look. These were clearly senior citizens... but they were always *au courant* in both dress and manner. They provided great examples of having the right attitude. No wonder they enjoyed such long lives.

Thank goodness 'beauty is in the eye of the beholder'. It would certainly be boring if everyone's opinion of good looks was the same. Unfortunately, the mainstream media doesn't always realize that and we are force-fed carbon copies of Barbie and Ken as examples of what is attractive. If you don't fit that traditional stereotype, attitude really comes into play. Personality and carriage define beauty far more than luscious locks, long eyelashes and a svelte figure. Personalities such as Rebel Wilson, Sandra Bernhard and Ben Stiller redefined what contemporary audiences think of as 'sexy', and 'personality' just bursts out of stars such

as Melissa McCarthy, Seth Rogen, Zach Braff and Kristen Wiig, making
them darlings of fans around the world, even with their unconventional
looks. (By the same token, isn't it curious how society is always amazed
when 'beautiful people' display their comedic talents? Rose Byrne, Matt
Damon, Jennifer Aniston, Sandra Bullock and Ryan Reynolds are great
examples.)

Work with what you've got. Genetics and circumstance pretty much
deal you your hand... it's what you do with it that counts. Develop
your own individual sense of style. My running partner, Amy, posted
a very close up photo of us on social media... and our toothy grins
would have put the entire Osmond clan to shame. Many people posted
complimentary comments about our pearly whites but several expressed
jealousy. You already know where I stand on oral hygiene, but I also
happen to be fortunate in the dental department (no braces, no cavities).
Cosmetic dentistry is readily available but my response to those lamenting their own smiles is to say, "We all have physical traits we wish we
could change. Sure I'd love to be 5 inches taller, but it ain't gonna happen.
Embrace who you are... and others will, too!" Living in a culture of envy,
we are practically programmed to want to look like our ideals. Lauren
Hutton and Madonna made their gap-toothed smiles signature features.
Robert Downey Jr, Tom Cruise and Mark Wahlberg may not reach
the top shelf, but that doesn't diminish the height of their hunk-appeal.
Embrace your body type... it's all yours! Then dress to suit and flatter it
(don't 'costume' yourself. Annie Hall only works on Diane Keaton).

Best-selling author Lionel Shriver (don't be fooled by the name...
she is a woman), wrote a character in *The Post-Birthday World* who says
people who have always been good-looking "haven't a clue that how
they're treated—how much it has to do with their appearance. I even bet
that attractive people have a higher opinion of humanity. Since everybody's always nice to them, they think everybody's nice." Shriver herself
says "Socially, cosmetic transformation makes a big difference—an
appalling difference." I think that's an overstatement. But there is no

doubt that the more attractive your attitude is, the more attractive people will find you.

Find little ways to help improve your attitude, inside or out. Glenn has a regular spa night where he treats himself to a massage after a hard workout at the gym. I'll take a bowl of grapes and the crossword puzzle down to the park (leaving the phone at home) and indulge in some time on the bench away from life's other distractions. For you, perhaps it's a candlelit bubble bath… an old movie or sports event on TV… a trip to the museum. Think of your attitude as a battery that needs a routine charge. Maybe there are some other ways to treat yourselves now that you've reached an age where you have little to lose. My grandmother was in her 80s when she decided to have her ears pierced. Dad cleverly bought her a pair of diamond earring that Christmas and she was over the moon. And my sisters and nieces inherited her vast array of clip-on baubles. Did you always think about getting a tattoo? Could this be the right time? All those youngsters who inked themselves up years ago now have faded or blurred artwork that has sagged southward along with their skin. Think how fresh yours would be and the surprise your loved ones would have if you decided to give them a little glimpse. I started with my first tattoo in my 30s… carefully considering what it would be and where it could go that not only wouldn't interfere with my work, but was something I could tolerate on my body for a lifetime. Not only did I love my artist, but I enjoyed the experience of commemorating special passions with a tattooed tribute. I visited him six times over the next decade or so and I'm not certain I'm finished yet!

According to the world-renowned Mayo Clinic, physical benefits can be reaped from having a positive attitude. These include:

- *Increased life span*
- *Lower rates of depression*
- *Lower levels of distress*

- *Greater resistance to the common cold*
- *Better psychological and physical well-being*
- *Reduced risk of death from cardiovascular disease*
- *Better coping skills during hardships and times of stress*

Laughter, an essential component of a good attitude, comes more naturally to some people than others and not everyone is blessed with a good sense of humor. However, you can learn to laugh more. All it takes is a little patience, practice and perspective. If someone says something humorous, even if it doesn't really tickle you, try to respond with a chuckle. Learn a few good, clean jokes and tell them at the next dinner party you attend. The next time you see some children, why not ask them if they know any jokes? Chances are they do and would love the opportunity to tell some. Encourage them by laughing at the punchlines and praising them. You may be helping to cultivate the next Robin Williams or Margaret Cho!

I have to admit something: I hate hospitals. They give me the heebie-jeebies. Ironically, I have spent plenty of time in them and it never gets any easier for me. I have learned to cope with them, as I have with most of life's most difficult or unpleasant experiences, through humor. A hospital was my father's workplace. My brother experienced a crippling motorcycle accident that resulted in my visiting intensive care units and rehab centers almost daily throughout my teenage years. My mother's cardiac troubles cause her to wind up in hospitals far more than any of us would desire. So I have always reacted by being the 'class clown' whenever I'm forced to be there with them... and I imagine that when a day comes that I have to check in, I'll continue to put up a funny front to ward off any fear or anxiety.

The next time a scary or stressful situation comes up, take a deep breath and see if you can't find a way to see the silly side of it. Believe me, I dread going to the mailbox and finding a jury duty summons, tax notice or inflated credit card statement as much as the next guy, but

I'm always quick to crack wise about them when they appear. And they always do… it's a fact of life.

Those who tout the calming benefits of meditation also espouse controlled breathing techniques. It's not for me, but I don't scoff at it and fully acknowledge that it can certainly help quell anxiety and bring down an accelerated heart rate.

Because you can find absolutely anything in Manhattan, I found out about a high-priced Breathing Coach who, for $250–$350 per session is becoming well known in the city for helping nervous New Yorkers achieve natural highs, better sleep and halve their anti-anxiety meds. Hey, there will always be people willing to take your money in exchange for something you could just do on your own. So, before you move on to read the next paragraph, I want you to pause right now and take five giant, consecutive deep breaths. Inhale through your nose, exhale through your mouth. Go ahead. I'll wait for you.

Calmer? Good. Read on.

Want to feel better/happier? Find someone who needs cheering up or a helping hand. You may be surprised how profoundly it will brighten your day if you brighten someone else's.

Bad things happen. Sadness is a legitimate emotion. It would be unhealthy, inappropriate or manic to be happy all the time. We would never appreciate or achieve great moments in life without overcoming setbacks along the way. My mother, for example, has had a long lifetime of emotional challenges and, as she once told my friend Linda Dano, "I'm a closet crier. I hide my tears." That's her coping mechanism… it wouldn't work for everyone. Conversely, unless you're the star of your own reality show, no one wants you to wear your heart on your sleeve. At least my Mom found a way to vent her sad moments.

I think happiness boils down to resilience. When I get the blues—
which isn't often but when it hits... baby, they're the bluest of blues—I
am certainly my mother's son and prefer to be left alone. I let myself
wallow in it briefly, staying under the bed covers or indulging in some
fattening comfort foods or a tear-jerking old movie. Usually a few hours
or, at most, a day of that is sufficient for me to achieve an attitude
adjustment.

If it's a matter of the heart, that's tough too: I'm not used to feeling
lovelorn. But when those times occur, it's like the old adage of falling off
the horse... get up and climb back into the saddle. "There's no cure for
an old love like a new love", Mom says. No one wants to be the romantic
rebound, but a good rebound can really help you recover!

Are you sad over the loss of a loved one? Find an uplifting way to
remember and celebrate them. Turn your grief into something pro-active.
What would make them proud? Ask yourself and then go out there and
do it. One of the most uplifting showbiz stories of 2013 was that of *The
Simpsons* co-creator, Sam Simon. Diagnosed with terminal colon cancer
at age 58, he chose to spend his remaining time spreading the message
of charitable giving and dispersing the tens of millions of dollars received
every year from *Simpsons* revenue to worthy causes. Talk about making
every moment count.

*I posed the question to my Twitter followers: "When you
have a blue day, what is your trick for bouncing back?" I
received hundreds of responses, but some of the most user-
friendly, simple pleasures include:*
* *Go to the movies*
* *Bake a cake*
* *Watch a Sandra Bullock movie*
* *Meditate*
* *Get with friends and laugh*
* *Go shopping and buy yourself a present*

- *Take yourself out for a good coffee*
- *Take the dog to play in the park*
- *Prayer*
- *Cuddle the kids*
- *Swimming*
- *Have a mini dance party with toddlers*
- *Step back and count your blessings.*
- *Have a glass of very good wine (a glass, not a bottle!)*
- *Exercise*
- *Binge-view a season's worth of episodes of your favorite sitcom*
- *Listen to music*
- *Take a yoga class*
- *Play a game*
- *Make an ice cream sundae*
- *Go for a walk on the beach*
- *Organize a photo album with pics of happy times*
- *Tweet with friends*

Nothing can undermine your confidence like caving in to someone who gives you a guilt trip. It could be a partner, an employer, a neighbor... but the most common culprit seems to be a close relative such as a sibling or (cue the music sting... .Dum, dum, DUMMMMM!) your Mother. Whether it's blunt ("Do it for me?") or passive-aggressive ("Oh, that's all right... don't worry about me."), nothing wreaks havoc on the status quo like a well-placed guilt zinger. There may be no surer sign of emotional maturity than being able to spot and avoid their pitfalls. No matter how old we get, there is always the potential to give in... especially when it's launched by someone we love. Unless you can objectively identify something you've done wrong and haven't already rectified (unlikely), remember that a guilt trip is nothing but emotional blackmail. And if you're ever tempted to lay one on someone else, take a good long look in the mirror and talk yourself out of it. Achievement through manipulation results in ill-gotten gains.

> *Guilt trips prey on your insecurities. Strive to be your best and like yourself! Confidence and a healthy ego are your armor against attack.*

My own parents rarely resort to these tactics and, even then, I believe it was subconscious, not deliberate. Dad's angle was only ever performance based… getting good grades in school or, later, singing on demand at social gatherings. The latter made me feel like a trained monkey to be trotted out, even though I knew deep down it was merely his pride for my performing abilities. On one occasion, I really let it push my buttons when he tried to bribe me to sing at a fancy restaurant. I was struggling for money at the time and, as he peeled off currency and laid it out on the table, I became more and more frustrated and, frankly, insulted. Glenn was with me and, stupefied by what he was witnessing and memorably exclaimed, "I'll take it!. I'll sing!" (Glenn, bless his heart, can't carry a tune in a bucket.) Now I don't even remember if I ended up singing or not… I probably did. Heck, a job is a job. Eventually, I did have a calm, rational conversation with my father about not putting me on the spot like that… and he never did again. Mom's brief moments of manipulation were solely relegated to maternal matters… always wanting to make nice between family members. Blood may be thicker than water, but it doesn't necessarily guarantee harmony. As I matured and became more independent, I was able to nip those situations in the bud. Make your position clear, take responsibility for your actions, stand up for yourself and be a person you can be proud of… and no one can 'guilt' you into anything.

Of all the emotions, I think guilt has to be the worst. 'Guilt' a.k.a. 'culpability' for a crime or reprehensible act is one thing, but as a 'feeling', well… it's pretty much a waste of time. Sure, even the nicest, most moral person will occasionally make a gaffe that results in feelings of remorse or even shame. That's when one has to be an adult and make amends. I remember what a revelation it was when I learned the power of apology. Harsh words, a snooty text or surly voice message may merit atonement. Usually if you're grown up enough to make a sincere apology, the receiving party will be grown up and gracious enough to accept it. It's important to act quickly when it comes to mis-steps and regrets, so feelings of guilt don't linger or haunt you until you track down a good psychoanalyst.

Twice in her old age, my Mother surprised me by expressing remorse about what she perceived as 'failings' in her parenting. I have always believed that I have an exceptional, stupendous Mother who has loved me not only unconditionally, but enthusiastically. For as long as I can remember, we have had an honest and communicative relationship filled with candor and, blessedly, great humor. Not too long ago, we were in a taxi cab riding past Columbia University and I said, "I wonder why I never thought to go to college here." She got all misty eyed and said, "I'm sorry, honey. I just didn't know. I should have." Huh? She felt guilty because I didn't go to big NYC University? Since when? I vividly remember the arduous process of researching and applying for colleges and have always been happy with my choice of Hofstra University and the subsequent life path on which it led me.

Several months later, we were reminiscing about my adolescent obesity. Again, she apologized. "It was my fault. I just didn't realize. And when you were hungry, I couldn't say no to you." Never in my life did it ever occur to me to hold my mother accountable for my being fat. That's when I had to sit her down for a chat to make sure she felt absolved of any guilt. Guilt over something beyond your control is an all-around waste. Life is too short for misplaced regrets.

Get guilt out of your life. And if you recognize its existence in the life of someone you care about, help them get it out of theirs, too. It's as insidious as a disease.

Strive to be a forgiving person. When you get right down to it, what good does holding a grudge really bring to your life? You don't have to subject yourself to unpleasant or unkind people, but neither do you have to let them hold power over you by getting you emotionally worked up. Chances are, especially as we age, you won't change them. Steer clear whenever possible and you may just end up influencing or inspiring them to change on their own… simply by the act of 'taking the high road'.

If guilt is a bad boy, anger is his ugly older brother. I wish I understood why so many people are full of it. I'm not referring to race riots, war protests, holy wars, urban blight or anything of such grave and massive proportions. I mean the day-to-day, venomous ire we see reported on every TV newscast, being played out on streets in cities and towns all around the world. The pundits proclaim excuses such as 'disenfranchise- ment, societal pressure, economic disparity,' and 'pressure to conform or excel to capitalist standards'. Hogwash. I think, in most cases I witness, it all boils down to self-control.

Rage remains a rampant societal problem. On the highways, it's trucks versus cars. Cars versus motorcycles. Cyclists versus pedestrians. Off road, the phrase 'going postal' was coined after a mail carrier snapped and acted with violence. Even in everyday living, anger often seems to be simmering all around us. We witness in stunned amazement as the seem- ingly sanest, most well-heeled individuals instantly transform into harpies over a frozen computer screen, 'stolen' parking space, available dryer in the laundromat or treadmill at the health club, a perceived side-eye glance or slight or just a place in line. Their own insecurities or feelings of inferiority could manifest themselves through rage episodes simply because of jealousy. They can't stand seeing someone else they perceive as more attractive, happy, wealthy, successful… whatever. (Hence the expression, 'living well is the best revenge'.) Add a little alcohol to the mix and you have bar brawls, fist-fights and other assorted harassment… often turning into dangerous or deadly encounters.

Modern living seems to only exacerbate the problem. I've even gotten rage-filled texts and emails. Look at internet trolls and all the despicable deeds they do with their hate-filled postings. How many furious protesters at a demonstration do you suppose actually are there to argue an opposing point of view? Very few, I wager. They're just folks looking for an opportunity to be swept up in a movement of fury, to vent their own discontent at whatever personal demons have bubbled up to the surface. Don't engage with them. This is how mob mentality is born.

> *I applaud* **The Huffington Post***'s decision to ban anonymous commentary from their popular news website. Too often, hateful postings are defended as 'freedom of speech', and further protected by the veil of anonymity – which offers nothing constructive to the conversation. If you want real freedom, take ownership of your words. I'm against big government, but I do support a degree of regulation for the Internet.*

We all get upset. Anger is a normal human emotion. How we handle that emotion is what should separate us from the screaming, red-faced babies from which we have supposedly matured. Healthy adults do not have tantrums. To spiral out of control to the extent of throwing things, cursing others or other irrational behavior is a clear cry for help. If you tend to exhibit that kind of behavior, or love someone who does, you need to make some serious evaluation as to why. For me, I learned that, like most people, excessive alcohol can trigger poor decision-making. I watch that very closely and, when I drink, am conscientious to be a merry-maker… otherwise, it's taxi-time and off to bed for me. Do you have a 'trigger' you could be more aware of?

Being on the receiving end of someone else's wrath is never pleasant. It can be frightening. It can also incite you to become defensive and combative, yourself. Then, more than ever, you must exercise self-control and de-escalate the situation. If someone is losing it in your direction, no rational conversation you can offer will cool them down. They're looking for a fight. I'm not a big fan of 'turning the other cheek' with irrational people, but you can take satisfaction in knowing you are the better person if you ignore them and/or walk away from the situation altogether. Leave it to God, karma, fate or whatever you believe in to take care of them. You didn't turn them into a rage-aholic and you're not going to be the one to fix them.

Deflect how someone's rage makes you feel by commiserating with others. Odds are, someone else within earshot shares your reaction to the angry person. Chatting them up or sharing a sympathetic glance can really help keep you from compromising your own even disposition. Don't underestimate the power of a smile or a thumbs up. Consider this 'paying it forward'. Odds are, that person or someone observing you will remember your smart choice and remember to do the same the next time they're confronted with a similar situation.

> *'Paying it Forward', in addition to being a popular 2000 motion picture starring Kevin Spacey and Helen Hunt, has come to be common vernacular for repaying a good deed to others rather than to the original benefactor. Interestingly, its true origin lies in contract law pertaining to financial loans. As Wikipedia explains: a debtor can 'pay the debt forward' by lending it to a third party rather than paying it back to the original creditor.*

You may not believe it, but wearing bright, 'happy' colors can actually make a difference to the way other people respond to you. I have a certain yellow shirt that never fails to elicit upbeat responses from people (good thing yellow is my favorite color). Maybe when I'm wearing it, a would-be rager sees it and channels his emotions elsewhere. Consider that next time you're clothes shopping.

We've all been told to 'take five deep breaths' or 'stop and count to ten' as a method of keeping a lid on things. Not bad advice. Stepping away is even better. If you can't deal with a stressful situation, avoid it altogether until you can collect yourself. Certain people will always have a knack for pushing your buttons, so remember that you are probably never going to change their actions... what you can do is change your reactions.

When your inner two-year old wants to kick and scream, don't take it out on anyone else... even if you think they deserve it. How many times have you seen someone fly off the handle at the guy behind the counter in the doughnut shop or lady behind the window at the post office? Consider this: perhaps the reason for so much terrible customer service these days is because of all the terrible customers. I suggest you take yourself into the privacy of your bedroom and bury your face deep in a pillow. Punch the mattress underneath you if that helps, while you unleash the most blood-curdling scream into the bedding so that no one can hear you. If you have a swimming pool, you can do the same thing underwater. Just be sure not to inhale and get your lungs filled with water or it will be the last tantrum you ever throw. Chances are, you can find even healthier ways to deal with that kind of turmoil by engaging in calming activities.

> *"It takes 20 years to build a reputation, and 5 minutes to ruin it." Warren Buffet*

Having a sense of spirituality is useful (some would say essential) at any age, but probably never more so than when we really hit our stride in middle age. In addition to appreciating and giving thanks for our blessings, it is a comfort to have a foundation of faith on which we can rely during troubling times. My Grandmother used to 'tsk tsk' those she classified as 'C and E Christians' (only going to church at Christmas and Easter), but in 2003 when I started doing live telecasts to Australia every Sunday (my Sunday in the USA is Australia's Monday), I became an even more infrequent congregant. Sorry, Gram!

Reading inspirational books (Joel Osteen always leaves me feeling optimistic and reassured), keeping a gratitude journal and saying my prayers are ways I keep in touch with my spirituality, but I believe there is no better way to live an inspired life than by following the good old Golden Rule and 'do unto others, as you would have them do unto you'. From all my studies, that is pretty much rule #1 in any religion.

Let me be clear, none of this is easy business. It is rarely as simple as it sounds, especially for those of us with a taste for sarcasm and who appreciate the bitchy morsels of scandal (in my line of work, that is rampant!), but the more conscientiously you strive to practice virtue, the easier it gets. As time marches on, I become better at avoiding stressful, aggravating people and situations and when I can't, I err on the side of silence to avoid confrontations or unpleasantness. That doesn't mean you should be a pushover though… just be prudent when choosing your battles. Goodness isn't about the other person as much as it is about you. Don't wear your good deeds or sweet disposition on your sleeve. Otherwise, as we all saw when Reese Witherspoon was arrested ("Do you know my name?"), your halo could slip and choke you.

Religious buildings such as Westminster Abbey in London, Christ Church Cathedral in Dublin, The Riverside Church in NYC, St Thomas' in Hollywood, my hometown's Holy Trinity Church and the Quaker Meeting House where I was schooled as a youngster all affect me in different, positive ways. I also feel a connection with a higher power whenever I am in an idyllic spot out in nature, which is why running works in tandem with my spiritual nourishment. Powering my way down the rocky beaches of Galway, Ireland, around the winding cobblestone streets of Florence, Italy, along the dramatic coastlines of Wellington, New Zealand, through the vibrant falling leaves along the trails of the Catskill Mountains in New York, or just across my own Manhattan street on a spring morning provides nourishment for the soul.

Walking to work one afternoon, I ended up on a block I'd never walked before. I was struck by the magnificence of a seemingly ancient church with impressive black iron gates. The Church of the Transfiguration, also known as The Little Church Around the Corner, was built in 1849 and is a breathtaking example of early English neo-Gothic style, complete with a lovely manicured garden. Not surprisingly, it is a designated NYC landmark and listed in the National Register of Historic Places. While admiring it from the sidewalk, a dapper gentleman in purple bishop's garb greeted me. I recognized his accent as Australian, and so I was introduced to the church's vicar, the Reverend Andrew St John. He gave me a personal tour of the church's stunning interior, which includes two chapels. It didn't take long for us to become friends and I do pop in for a service whenever possible.

Andrew, a rather high-profile man in his field, always has time to answer questions as they pertain to matters of love and faith. He's conducting more and more same-sex marriages and reaching out for inter-faith relationships with Catholic, Protestant and Muslim communities. He even met Pope Francis the day after he was installed at the Vatican. How could I resist getting a few of his thoughts for this book?

NELSON: "Do you find people tend to embrace or eschew religion as they get older?"

ANDREW: "Some people are drawn to religion as they age but others become more cynical. It often depends on experience but also on the quality of their religious training."

NELSON: "What's the median age of the average church-goer that you see nowadays?"

ANDREW: "In NYC the median age appears to be lower than more settled suburban congregations. I would say ours is probably 50."

NELSON: "As we age, we tend to look back fondly on 'the good old days'. Are times more scary now than in the past?"

ANDREW: "I don't think times are more scary than the past (after all our parents and grandparents lived through two World Wars). Perhaps we know too much of what is happening because of the amount of media."

NELSON: "What can faith bring to middle-aged people specifically?"

ANDREW: "Faith can bring a sense of assurance regarding the future as well as a sense of community and continuity."

NELSON: "Biblical figures, such as Noah and Abraham, seemed to live well into their old age. Did the prophets have fuzzy math or did they have some longevity secret that was lost somewhere along the way?"

ANDREW: "I think the extraordinary ages of the patriarchs is more about their righteousness and their vocation than actual ages. Great ages go with great people. They are larger than life."

NELSON: "What have you found in your life that is wonderful about turning 50 and beyond?"

ANDREW: "What I have enjoyed most since turning 50 is being more relaxed about who I am and less fussed about what others think of me."

Regardless of your religious affiliations or spiritual tenets, believing in the power of goodness and striving to practice it in your daily life will do wonders for your attitude by bringing you self-assurance and peace.

IS YOUTH WASTED ON THE YOUNG?

We often hear the expression coined by George Bernard Shaw: 'youth is wasted on the young', and there's no surer sign that you're becoming an old fogey than when you say it yourself. It's hard to resist, though, when you see someone young making a mistake that you, in all your vast wisdom and experience, see so plainly as foolish and avoidable. Oh, if only you could go back in time and know then what you know now. Boy, would things sure be different. You'd never make missteps and you'd know all the traps to avoid.

Yeah, right.

Not only is 'woulda, shoulda, coulda' a colossal waste of time and energy (What's the point, anyway? You don't own a time machine), but going through all those perils and pitfalls is precisely what made you the smarter, older, wonderful version that is your current self. And please tell me, other than the halcyon memories of lazy summer vacations, carefree Christmases or romping around the playground with no stiff knees or back pain what the heck was so great about 'youth'? If you look back objectively, it was probably filled with indecision, insecurity and other assorted bits of awkwardness that are not worth the extra hair you remember having on your head (fellas) or perky position of your boobs and butt (ladies). Seriously: If your older self offered your younger self some sage advice, would that younger self really have paid any attention to it? Odds are… no way.

Certainly, I wish I hadn't totaled my new car on prom night, traumatizing my poor date Mary Catherine. Getting smacked in the face with a baseball bat in eighth grade was pretty lousy too. There are too many failed would-be romances to count. And I have all but blocked out my 23rd birthday altogether. But what's the point of imagining 'what if' when they are just the facts of my life? As Shakespeare so wisely wrote in *The Tempest*, "What's past is prologue."

No matter how wise, confident and grown up we become, there will be times in life where situations will cause us to revert immediately back to childhood. That's wonderful when it's the adrenaline rush of a new crush, the abandonment we feel on a roller-coaster ride, or the wonderment of seeing a spectacular sight such as Niagara Falls. What about when it's something not so great? Feeling like a wallflower at a party, doing a group exercise activity where you are the clumsiest component in an otherwise slick and agile team, or worst of all, encountering a bully in the workplace.

I spent nearly all of my 40s working alongside the kind of repugnant, socially inept bully that would seem a caricature in a comic strip. I assure you, however, there was nothing remotely amusing or comic about his behavior, but as a 'lifer' with the company, he was a fact of life for everyone who worked there. As is the case with most bullies, he selected his targets according to who he thought would put up the least fight, and in all those years, I can only remember blowing my lid on two occasions before I finally filed a formal complaint. Unfortunately, that fell on deaf ears and proved as futile as all my previous attempts at 'talking it out', ignoring him or trying to rise above the situation. Many of us know the uncomfortable frustration of having to deal with a bad seed on a daily basis, day in and day out. I found myself grateful for any kernel of kindness or civility he'd dole out… usually for the benefit of other people who might be in the vicinity. Determined not to let him ruin what was otherwise a dream job, I decided that if he was a necessary evil for my employment… I'd have to look for professional opportunities elsewhere. Finally biting the bullet, I made a difficult and costly change to move to another position and thereby all but eradicate him from my life. He's still around on the periphery of my work world, but minimally so… and I can now laugh and almost (I said 'almost') feel sorry for him that his own obvious unhappiness and dissatisfaction with himself makes him lash out at others. I'm sure he was the kind of kid who pulled the wings off fireflies (maybe he still does!), but now he's someone else's problem. Looking back on it, I may not have won the battle against his personality but I learned that not all battles can or need to be won. It's standing up for yourself that matters.

Just as dealing with the bullies I remember from my school days (yes, I mean you, Charlie, Wayne, Marc), rational behavior doesn't always work. All they're after is a reaction and a quick-fix feeling of superiority. There are times where you just have to bite the bullet, bide your time and wait it out until one of you moves on. Hopefully, you will be the better off for it when that time comes. I certainly am.

Guessing games are not my forte. I'm lousy at determining someone's age and generally base my impressions of people's calendar years on their maturity, not their looks. Because I happen to 'feel' 35 years old, I'm convinced that the folks around me with whom I most enjoy interacting must also be around that age. I'm always surprised when a new pal reveals their age and it's significantly off in one direction or the other. Consequently, my social circle has a broad age span ranging from early twenties right through and into the eighties (As you can imagine, my parties are an eclectic mix). As the old adage says, 'You're as young as you feel'. In my case, everyone around me is as young as I feel they are!

Most under 30s can't help but be lacking in some of the worldliness that they will acquire with time and travails, no matter how entertaining, enlightening, talented and professional they may be at the moment. (I also fully acknowledge that there are plenty of middle-aged folks who are perpetual Peter Pans; immature and ignorant. 'Childlike' can be an appealing quality... 'childish', not so much.) There are plenty of young people who are making the most of every moment by being responsible, civic-minded, outgoing professionals. Members of the military, philan-thropists, students... these will be the leaders of tomorrow and I have every confidence that the majority will be well equipped to look after us in our dotage.

In the interest of balance, I assembled some of my younger friends to weigh in with their thoughts on middle age. Are their responses different from what you'd expect?

CALLAN MCAULIFFE (born 1995) has been a working actor almost his entire, short life, transitioning from Australian TV to global film fame when hand picked by directors Rob Reiner and Steven Spielberg for plum roles in *Flipped* and *I Am Number Four*. Appearing as young Jay Gatsby in the Baz Luhrman-directed mega-hit *The Great Gatsby* launched him even further into the A-list realm, now working with the likes of Samuel L. Jackson, Sir Ben Kingsley and Djimon Honsou. Even with all the trap-pings of Hollywood, he remains a 'typical teenager' thanks to the watch-ful eye of his mom, Claudia, and his everyday penchant for activities such as playing music and video games.

VINNIE NGUYEN (born 1982) manges the satellite facility from where I broadcast daily. His boyish looks and enthusiasm belie his passion and expertise for the demands of live television production and coping with the stress of frazzled producers, demanding celebrities with their entou-rages, and late-breaking deadlines.

JACK TAME (born 1987), one of my reporting colleagues, is a lanky New Zealander with a cherubic, hairless face that makes him look even younger than he is, and a head of hair that any member of One Direction would envy. He can play and party like any other 20-something on the loose in a big wild city such as Manhattan, but when he is in work mode, he is a thorough professional with a canny sense of hard news credibility in addition to remarkable ad-lib skills. I foresee a great future for him on New Zealand airwaves and beyond.

HENRY ALLMAN (born 1996) is a sly young man who will grow up to be either the President of the United States or own and operate a chain of Vegas casinos. Maybe both! He currently attends Trinity School in Manhattan, where his father is headmaster. Henry is wise beyond his years, having formed philosophies and ideas about life that many people twice his age have yet to ponder, but still, amazingly, he's a pretty 'normal' teenager.

JOSEPH FENITY (born 1985) is a national correspondent for SiriusXM Satellite Radio, whom I met memorably in 2008. We were among the assembled throng of reporters gathered in the freezing cold outside of the SoHo apartment where Heath Ledger had been found dead. He's a clever and funny young man with a terrific journalistic flair.

LUKE WEBB (born 1993) recognized me on a subway car one afternoon on my way to the studio. (It's very flattering to be recognized for my work. As I get older, comments such as "You've been on that show forever!" or "I grew up watching you!" no longer sting. It's actually a tremendous honor to have been such a constant in people's everyday lives.) We became friends on Twitter and when I found out that he suffered an unexpected stroke, I immediately reached out. Even more unexpected was his innate sense of gratitude that the effects of his stroke weren't worse, and his resolve to persevere through the subsequent therapy to re-learn his walking and talking skills—even more important when he was due to walk his first-ever red carpet for the premiere of his film *Circle of Lies*. He's a wise and wonderful young man who recognizes that to "only live once doesn't mean to go out every weekend and get completely trashed. It means go out and make something of yourself."

ALEXIS (ALLIE) CHRISTINA BARNES (born 2001) is the young daughter of our studio engineer, Michael. We love when Allie tags along to work with her dad, because she is the prototype for what you'd want the 'All-American Girl' to be. She is sweet without being saccharine, smart without being precocious, funny without being intrusive, and all-round good company. She's a typical teen in many ways, enjoying shopping at the mall with friends, as well as pop-culture and music. She really stands out as being a well-adjusted, polite and pleasant person and I'm confident she'll sail through the rest of her school years remaining just that way, blossoming into an exceptional young woman—her father's pride and joy.

NELSON: "What do you think of as middle age?"

CALLAN: "I'd put it around 50. While I don't expect everybody will live to be a centenarian, it's nice to be optimistic, right?"

VINNIE: "45. I go with a lifespan of 90, so middle age is 45 to me."

JACK: "Age is a state of mind more than a state of body."

HENRY: "Someone who is married, has children, age range between 40 and 55."

JOSEPH: "In my mind, everyone's either 16, 30 or 90. I don't see any other age really. Young, 'regular', and then nursing home-ready."

LUKE: "I consider middle age to be when one rethinks life and says: Time for a change. Whether that be 30 or 60."

ALLIE: "30 or 40."

NELSON: "What age do you consider to be old? 50? 60? Other?"

CALLAN: "I wouldn't really describe anybody as old until the 70 mark. You're not old in my book until you're telling your grandkids war stories. Even if you were never in a war."

VINNIE: "60. When you can count the years to retirement on your hands, you're old."

JACK: "If 50 is the new 30, 60 is the new 25. It's not some reverse-ageing, Benjamin Button-type paradox, but rather a reflection upon the type of people you see traveling the world these days. Three-quarter pants, fanny packs and sensible shoes; the days of retirees confining themselves to azalea patches and lawn bowls has well and truly passed. That little sliver of latter middle-age, the 60+ crowd, is fitter, keener and more adventurous than ever before. Beating the backpacking routes of the world—Southeast Asia, the Americas and Europe, are tanned, poor, young backpackers in their early-to-mid-twenties, fresh from college life. And right on their heels, are their parents, embracing empty nests as a second chance to get out and experience life."

HENRY: "Old to me is 70 or older. My conception of old changed when I moved from Texas to New York because I came in contact with a lot of older men who became fathers in their sixties and still had lots of energy, and that was a normal, expected thing. In Texas you raise your kids when you're in your 30s and that's the norm.

JOSEPH: "80 and upwards."

LUKE: "I'd say you're pushing old at about 70."

ALLIE: "80 and up."

NELSON: "What's the average age of the people you hang out with?"

CALLAN: "It really varies, but I'd say it's mostly 18–25. I'm not a party animal, so they're usually people I meet on film sets… those people being adults."

VINNIE: "I'd say 32. I tend to hang out with people around my age."

JACK: "The majority of people I spend time with are of a similar age, but professionally and socially, I enjoy the company of older people easily as much. As you grow, you realise that age differences are increasingly insignificant. To think that an elementary school student would rarely consider speaking to a school mate just a year or two older! By your mid-twenties, most people I know have friends twice their age."

HENRY: "I hang out with people from age 9 to 70. I think that has a lot to do with my personality."

JOSEPH: "40."

LUKE: "16 to 30".

ALLIE: "11 to 14, not including my siblings."

NELSON: "At what age do you expect to have achieved your primary personal and professional goals?"

CALLAN: "I hope to do whatever it is I'm planning to do by 50 and be satisfied with what I've achieved by that age. Then I can stop worrying and just spend any money I've earned by gallivanting around the globe."

VINNIE: "55."

JACK: "By 40, I'd hope to have found a partner, begun a family, built a stable career and a achieved a degree of financial security."

HENRY: "50."

JOSEPH: "90!"

LUKE: "Before 40. But then I look at people such as actress Jacki Weaver who suddenly, at 63, found herself nominated for an Oscar, and then another one two years later. Her success and career is really only just beginning and really does prove that you're never too old to fulfil your dreams."

ALLIE: "25 to 30."

NELSON: "What do you suppose are the best and worst things of being 50+?"

CALLAN: "I'm not entirely sure what to expect. I suppose a common thing people would miss is the mobility they had at a younger age... running and jumping all over things. But I don't do that anyway, so I'm hoping the transition will be pretty seamless."

VINNIE: "Best? Respect, if you've earned it. Discounts... and being able to say and do what you want. Worst? Judgment by 'young' people, and worrying if you've saved enough for retirement."

JACK: "The thing that scares me about ageing, and of being 50+, is looking in the mirror and knowing full well that I'm past my physical best. Not in terms of looks, necessarily, but in terms of fitness and health. But I take solace from thinking that at that age, I'll have five decades of experiences to reflect upon. I'll be wiser, and better equipped to deal with the pathetic insecurities of youth."

HENRY: "Best: your children have, for the most part, grown up. You're in a stable career. You get to start enjoying what you've accomplished. You are secure and stable enough to accept change. My father moved my family from Texas to New York City when he was 52 years old. It has turned out to be a great thing for all of us. I don't think he could have done that in his 30s, he would have been too concerned with creating stability to leave a stable job. Worst: physical and mental difficulties start. Also, you know a lot more about the inevitability of death because you're over the hump and heading towards death."

JOSEPH: "I hear that for both genders random hair starts showing up where you never knew hair could or would grow. I'm not looking forward to that. Being old but not being able to get the senior citizen's discount yet. That would suck. At 50 you are old, but not old enough! The best part? When you know better, you do better!"

LUKE: "Best, life experience. And realizing that it's what you have that is important, not what you don't have. Worst would be regret. Looking back and wishing you had done all the things you wanted to do in life."

ALLIE: "Pro: You can stop working and move somewhere warm and/or tropical. Con: People call you old and stuff like that even though you're not that old."

NELSON: "Who would you cite as the coolest 50+ people? As nice as it would be, don't say Nelson Aspen!"

CALLAN: "Johnny Depp and David Attenborough."

VINNIE: "Johnny Depp, Ian McKellan, Bette Midler, Oprah, Ellen, Brad Pitt…"

JACK: "My 87-year-old grandma still writes academic papers. She travels the world. She exercises every day. Does she look as flash in a crop top and short shorts as she might have a few decades ago? Of course not. But she's not old."

HENRY: "(Manhattan-based philanthropist) Ann Tenenbaum. For all the money and the societal advantages she has, she has not lost her understanding of the important things in life, so she can relate to many different people of different ages and backgrounds."

JOSEPH: "Sean Penn because for his entire (public) life he has been an independent thinker, regardless of popular politics or Hollywood norms at the time."

LUKE: "The woman everyone wishes was their grandma, Betty White. She's a comedy genius. Kirk Douglas has some pretty hip fashions for his age, too! I love him and I love all his films. In fact, in hospital, I read his book *My Stroke of Luck* and it was a real saviour. I had shamelessly written him a fan letter a year before with a few DVD covers to be signed and, to my surprise, he sent them back autographed and even included a signed copy of his book."

ALLIE: "Dad, Mom… and too many musicians and TV stars to name."

These bright, young people are actually quite representative of popular thinking, in spite of current thinking that we have an entirely youth-obsessed culture. In late 2013, a Harris poll claimed that Americans overall considered the ideal age to be 50. Ten years ago, respondents claimed 41 as 'the perfect age'. Does society get better with age? It seems so. The same poll found that younger people coveted ages a bit older than their current ones, while those polled who were middle-aged and older were content in their current age bracket. For instance, those aged 18–36 thought the perfect age was 38. Those aged 37–48 selected 49 as ideal. The 49–67 voters opted exactly in the middle of their own group at 55. Those aged 68+ selected 67 as the best age to be. It also revealed a noteworthy gender trend: Men said 47 was the perfect age, while women chose 53. A Gallup poll happened to concur with the actual average retirement age of 61 as the best age at which to officially leave the work force, (with respondents 68+, that number was slightly higher at 64).

I'm lucky to have so many smart and interesting younger friends and colleagues. It all but eliminates the notion of a 'generation gap' in my life. However, it's very important for those of us over 50 to always remind ourselves never to underestimate or dismiss people on the basis that they are younger or less experienced. They may not remember Neil Armstrong's moon walk (or even Michael Jackson's, for that matter), nor may they possess what we'd consider the same social graces or niceties with which we were raised, but that is where our wisdom and skills can come into play to educate and inspire them.

I'll give you an example. So many times, when I regularly employ the use of 'ma'am' or 'sir' in addressing someone, they respond almost with a shiver. "Don't call me that. It sounds like I'm old!" I shake my head and explain that it is a sign of my respect for them. They should not only get used to it, they should similarly utilize it in their own encounters.

Some of my earliest memories are of my mother taking me to the local Woolworths for weekly shopping trips, the highlight always being a hamburger at the luncheon counter. It was a magical place where you could spend hours browsing sundry items ranging from clothing to small pets such as guinea pigs and canaries. The regular cashier, known only to me as 'Madame' because that's what Mom called her, was always friendly and chatty, and she kept up with my progress well into adulthood, through my mother, even after Woolworths shut. That's when and how I learned about courtesy and deference. Addressing adults of any age by 'ma'am' and 'sir' is something I have subsequently always done, and I always will. For anyone to feel uncomfortable being called by those terms is ridiculous. They are as important to good manners as 'please' and 'thank you'. (They also come in handy if you are blanking on someone's name!)

My friend Rick Richey is a master instructor for the National Academy of Sports Medicine, a personal trainer and massage therapist. He's also a husband and father of two little ones, Jazzlyn and Xavier. Like most new parents Rick and his wife have acquired many new friends since their kids entered school and, living in NYC, he admits that the age range of their friends can vary considerably. I asked him his thoughts on middle age. He went one better and included a mini-interview he did with his daughter.

"Middle age starts at year 40, and continues until you are officially old at 60 years," Rick believes. "The good news about 60 is that there are enough older people to keep telling you that you are still young. Sadly, there are too many younger people tilting the scales of perception on the old-o-meter to disagree. I asked my daughter her age, to which she responded 5. She then asked my age, so I told her that I was old. 'How old,' she asked? 35, I replied. 'That's not old,' she said. I was truly surprised at her answer. So, how old is old, Jazzy? 'I think 60,' she responded. I told her I thought that was a good answer."

I once asked Morgan Freeman, when he was age 76, to complete the sentence "Life begins at ___." He thought for a short moment and laughed, "Life begins at wherever I am!" That's the spirit!

CELEBRATING YOURSELF: HOW LIVING WELL IS THE BEST REVENGE

My brother, Reese, is an Episcopal priest. His calling and devotion were evident from an early age; he'd put on Sunday church services in the backyard the way other kids would put on plays or play cowboys and Indians. Talk about 'a calling!' We all played along because it got us out of having to go to actual services at Holy Trinity, and Mom's grape juice and crackers that were served during his services were tastier than the church's wine and wafers. He has had a long and distinguished career in the church, including a stint as an Air Force chaplain, and his complete and obvious faith in God and belief in an afterlife have made him one of the most self-assured, rational men I've ever known. It's no wonder that he is an expert in hospice and palliative care and end-of-life issues. There is certainly nothing depressing or 'old' about him, though—he sports a long, gray ponytail, rides a motorcycle and plays the guitar. He has found a way to celebrate every birthday (he's now in his 60s) with a child's sense of excitement, regardless of whatever problems are going on in his life. "Ageing is simply getting closer to God, day by day, year by year," he said to me shortly before I turned 50. "The closer we get, the more it begins to feel like minute by minute!"

"That sounds awful to me!" I exclaimed. "Like life is a time bomb."

He laughed and continued, "It's kind of like falling off a cliff. The ground seems to rush up at you the closer you get to it. But, unlike hitting the ground, we fall straight through into the arms of God. It's only terrifying if there's no one there to catch you."

Seriously: that's how he talks. And it never sounds preachy. You can't help but be impressed by someone whose utter faith in a higher power renders him completely fearless.

On a much lighter note, my mother simply says: "I love my birthday!" Even though hers falls close to (sometimes on) Mother's Day, she always takes advantage of having one day a year that is all her own and, after 364 other days when she is giving herself over to everybody else, we're happy to indulge her. Birthdays are indeed special… and we all deserve to celebrate them for the important anniversaries that they are.

When I was working in Italy (as a fitness instructor at a health spa), I learned the Italian custom that the birthday celebrant supplies the cake and champagne. I think that's a lovely thing to do. Encourage the people you enjoy the most to share in your own personal appreciation of your arrival on planet earth. I also make sure to send a 'thank you' note or bouquet of flowers to my folks. I wouldn't be here without 'em!

Why on earth would you ever lie about your age? Strut your stuff! Celebrate every day, not just your birthday.

I remember my 30th birthday being a boozy, bawdy night in Beverly Hills at my cousin's restaurant. My best pal, Glenn, flew in from NYC to surprise me and somewhere along the line I was singing with a jazz band. Everything else is a blur. My 40th was spent at Glenn's Hamptons home with a few friends and my parents. Unfortunately, I was still nursing my wounds from a recent break-up and there were 'tears before bedtime'. I was certain that being single and 40 meant I was destined to be lonely and miserable forever. How I wish I could go back and tell myself that, heck, life had barely begun. Now I just look at every failed relationship as a warm-up act for the main event. I don't know when the curtain will rise on that one, but it's shaping up to be one hell of a show.

So when 50 was looming on the horizon, I had to come up with something that would be joyful and significant, honoring the bounty of my friendships while I still had so many of the most important people in my 'life story' available to celebrate with me.

Glenn's new home in East Hampton is a spectacular property straight out of the series *Revenge* (which, incidentally, isn't even filmed in the real Hamptons). I don't get to spend enough time there, but when I do it's about the only place in the world where I can completely relax. As we spent an afternoon luxuriously floating in his pool, with hydrangeas in full bloom everywhere, it struck me that there was nowhere else I'd rather commemorate the beginning of my second half century than right there. Having never staged a wedding, family reunion or even a large-scale barbeque, I figured this would be the 'once in a lifetime' destination celebration to give friends from around the world a chance not only to help me celebrate, but to have a vacation for themselves in one of the world's most sought-after holiday spots.

Good, old-fashioned paper invitations went out after a 'save the date' email to my guest list. I included information on local transportation and lodging while Glenn and his partner, Tim, helped me begin the process of coordinating the planning of the party. I settled on a *Mad Men*-esque 1963 theme, encouraging retro attire and amassing a playlist of music from that era… heavy on the Herb Alpert, Andy Williams, Rosemary Clooney and Motown. The picture on the invitation was from my Baptism celebration, with my Mom in full 1963 regalia (eat your heart out, Tippi Hedren), cradling me in her arms while my brother grinned from the side.

Even with all the advanced notice and my incessant desire for pre-planning, the full throttle execution of details all came about relatively last minute. The great lesson of throwing a party, I keep reminding myself, is to enlist talented professionals who will make sure to get their jobs done. So while Chita was organizing the menu, Tim the music, photography and flowers, Jeff the landscaping and Glenn the overseer of logistics for everyone's travel to and fro (Hamptons Bureau of Tourism would be wise to hire him as a consultant!), I was left to stress only about having a good time and keeping an eye on the weather forecast. Having a running partner who happens to be our local NYC meteorologist, Amy Freeze—yes, that's her real name—helped alleviate some of that anxiety.

Taking charge of celebrating and enjoying your own milestones, I have learned, is a sign of maturity. There are times in life when it's totally appropriate to 'toot your own horn' and turning 50 was one for me. From all the alternately nasty and overly sentimental greetings cards, to our own misconceptions about a mere number, it can be easy to miss out on marking and reveling in the fact that achievements in living a happy, productive life are important. They are important to the individual as well as those who love him/her.

"There shall be an eternal summer in the grateful heart."
Celia Thaxter

As with any gathering, no matter how 'firm' the RSVP list, there will always be last-minute cancellations for legitimate reasons, or flakey friends. ("I have an ear infection… I got called in to work… I was invited to go to Vegas and play in a poker competition…) Forgive the former, but don't forget the latter. Just as you seasonally clean out your closets, so too should you routinely clean out your address book. One perk of growing older is not needing to be beholden to unreliable people. Surrounding yourself with folks you can count on is the way to go.

So after all the months of anticipation, the big weekend finally arrived and I'm happy to say that everything went off without a hitch.

> *Not everyone considered my party a 'must attend' event.*
> *One of the many 20-something guys that works at our*
> *satellite TV facility had other places to be that weekend and*
> *it dawned on me that, although I consider us all peers in the*
> *work environment, socially he viewed me as an old fogey.*
> *No hard feelings, though. After a night out with him at one*
> *of his favorite drinking establishments, I realized that a*
> *'generation gap' is not necessarily a bad thing. He went out*
> *cruising… I went home to bed!*

To get to the Hamptons is no easy feat, so I was dazzled by how many people managed to make it look easy, whether that was flying in from Australia, Palm Springs, North Carolina, Los Angeles or the NYC vicinity. Glenn made it easy with a shuttle service to and from all the local hotels and inns. For those who were making a weekend getaway of it, I wanted to offer more than just a spectacular party, so I commissioned a trainer to give anyone who wanted to play along, a fun boot camp on the beach in beautiful Amagansett, on the morning of the festivities. We all ran around in the sand, laughing and playing group exercise games and rode bicycles back to the house afterwards. Too often in our busy, grown-up lives, we forget to make time to play. I think it's vital and I'm fortunate to have so many loved ones who are good sports and join me in all the levity. (It doesn't even have to be anything structured: next time you're walking around the neighborhood, run through somebody's sprinklers or look for a faded hopscotch game and have a go! You think all those tough boxers are skipping rope just for the cardio?)

> *Fun fact. Hopscotch originated in Britain, during the early*
> *Roman empire. Originally used for military and agility*
> *training and more than 100 feet long, the hopscotch 'court'*

was run by foot-soldiers in full armour and field packs.
Children imitated them with smaller versions, added a
scoring system. The game of hopscotch was born.

The party was flawless, with even the smallest details perfectly executed. From the 'Beach Boys' attire of the servers (guys and gals, each one
more gorgeous than the next… Chita made sure to give me full casting
approval), to the signature cocktails Tim and his mixologist friend con-
cocted—and enjoyed researching. (Non-alcoholic 'mocktail' versions are
easy to adapt and we decanted them from glass barrels and served them
in big, ice-filled glasses.)

THE NIFTY FIFTY
* 2 parts ruby red grapefruit juice
* 1.5 parts reposado tequila
* 1 part St Germain
* Float or garnish with ruby red grapefruit slice

THE NELSON-TINI
* 2 parts watermelon lemonade with sliced, fresh cucumber
* 1 part vodka
* float or garnish with watermelon

Even the hydrangeas co-operated and burst into full bloom, allowing Tim
to make individual table settings with their floral glory tastefully spilling
out of simple white vases. The cocktail napkins were coordinated with
my blue-and-white color scheme and my Hosts surprised me with an
Andy Warhol-esque portrait of me to hang over the outdoor fireplace,
using one of my dramatic old headshots circa 1985, complete with my
mullet hairdo and bushy eyebrows (I don't think I figured out how to use
tweezers until about 1990). It was all so elegant, but completely play-
ful and unpretentious. Since my guests were all sizes, shapes, ages and

personalities, it was important that the party be welcoming to anyone and everyone.

Just as a performer should know their audience (Hello Jennifer Lopez, Hilary Swank and Jay-Z, are you listening? Don't get on stage for dictators and despots!) so too should a host know his guest list. You want everyone to feel at home, so circulating and getting everyone to relax and mingle is the secret of social success, whether it's an upscale do at the country club, or a pizza party in your living room.

As guests arrived and began to marvel at Glenn's magnificent home, the food and beverage service was promptly launched and the music cued. Everyone found a way to participate in the spirit of the occasion. Many of the guys wore fedoras or skinny ties, while the ladies went for mod mini skirts or diaphanous caftans. Gena Desclos looked resplendent in heavy eye make-up, wearing a long black gown with bangle jewelry… in honor of 1963s big blockbuster, *Cleopatra*. For myself I found the perfect madras jacket, which I matched with linen pants and topsiders.

> *"I turned 50 in 2013 and it was fantastic. The celebrations continued for weeks surrounding my special day. I had a lot to celebrate: 18 years previously, I was diagnosed with cancer. My life was thrown into a tailspin of tests, doctors, treatments and prognoses. In the years that followed, I wasn't sure if I would live to see 40 let alone 50. As it turned out, I was one of the lucky ones. Now, having arrived at the half-century mark, I may have to say no to a bowl of ice cream and yes to some extra eye cream, but I do it with joy… given the alternative." Gena Desclos*

Before sitting down to dinner, Glenn was kind enough to make an official toast and gave a funny speech, which, in spite of its humor, managed to move me, and most of the guests, to tears. In fact, I'm tearing up as I write this and suspect I always will when I remember it. (Does turning 50 turn a person into a cry-baby? I remember it happening to my Dad and I'll be darned if it hasn't started happening to me, too!) To have a friend that is as close as family is an amazing privilege and gift. Not only is Glenn that to me, but so too were so many of the faces of those gathered around me. Like George Bailey in *It's a Wonderful Life*, I felt like the richest man in town.

> *Here's an excerpt from sweet Glenn's speech. I can't wait to return the favor for his 50th in 2014: "Nelson Page Aspen Jr., whose nose, jawline, and last name are all authentic, and whose idea of being on time is being at least 15 minutes early, is really one of a kind. Nelson is the most upbeat person I know. He is smart, funny as shi*, hard working and always fun to be around. But most of all, and why I think we are all here today, is that he is a kind and loving friend, always the first to say 'I miss you' or 'I love you'. Always the first to call or email and make you laugh if you're having a bad day, and always, always there when you need him."*

Reuniting with special people from all phases of my life was wonderful to say the least. Even better was connecting them all with each other. "Oh, so you're Nelson's running coach, Scott... Oh, Melissa... I've seen you on TV so many times with Nelson over the years... Melanie, I've been hearing about your early days in the theater for years... So YOU'RE the notorious Cousin Keith!" Many hosts fret about their mixture of guests. Hey, we're all grown ups. Do the introductions and let everyone enjoy each other's company. Like the old saying goes, "Any friend of yours is a friend of mine!" And that's how it should be.

By now, everyone was relaxed and indulging in the luxurious fun of a summer party in this beautiful outdoor location. Night began to fall and the torches were lit and the music segued to the 1970s. Camera phones were snapping (we managed to recreate some hysterical moments from past shots) and laughter filled the air. At one point I counted 50 heads among the guests, how perfect and appropriate!

After dinner, my amazing friend Louan gave me my present in the form of a song she had written to mark the occasion. Everyone was dazzled by her creativity, wit and talent. I have known that woman since we were kids and we have both been through so much, together and separately. She is one-in-a-million. I always strive to make all my guests feel that way, even if it's someone I've never met, such as a date or escort of one of my friends. Heck, if they're in attendance at your intimate event, they are special. Find something positively unique about them and point it out. "Your eyes are gorgeous!" "What a good sport you are for playing along with all my crazy friends!" "Why haven't we met sooner?" "You have to try a 'Nelson-tini." Let's think up a name for your Signature Cocktail!"

> *"I've learned that people will forget what you said, people will forget what you did, but people will never forget how you made them feel." Maya Angelou, born 1928*

Then came the cake... my grandmother's famous chocolate recipe I remembered so well, expertly recreated in Chita's kitchen. There was no need to make a wish: I felt like I already had the world.

> *One guest did get stranded, having missed the bus back to NYC, so we found a spare room for her to crash. Being flexible and gracious are other must-have qualities for hosting any party.*

The next morning, for anyone still in the Hamptons who wanted to hang out, we had a 'bagels and Bloody Mary brunch'. It was the ideal way to carry on the party a little bit longer before saying our farewells. It was casual and comfortable in the kitchen and living room, and one by one my friends took their leave. There were plenty of tears, laughs and hugs.

TV star John Stamos and I obviously were on the same wave length. He turned 50 a month after me and had a rat-pack themed party to mark the occasion. He may have had Tom Jones perform at his bash, but I wouldn't have changed a thing about mine!

A playlist of the party tunes and a Dropbox for everyone's photos enables us to relive the special moments whenever we want and share it with others. Additionally, for a considerable time after the party, I got to stretch out the fun of turning 50 by getting 'rain check' dinners with those who had been unable to join us. It got me thinking: why shouldn't you let your birthday play out all year until the next one? I don't mean you should be indulging in cake and champagne every day, but making a significant and meaningful stab at fulfilling those 'milestone wishes' throughout the next 365 days. Resolutions aren't reserved strictly for January 1st.

While it might be impossible to ever duplicate such a special and successful occasion, I'm having fun considering possibilities to cook up for my 60th – if I can wait that long. I may just have to work out a way to disco out à la 'Studio 54' in 2017! In the meantime, Glenn and I are already brainstorming ways to help HIM turn 50 in a few months. So far, an upscale cycling tour through the countryside in the South of France or a trip Down Under seem to be winning the most votes.

A message from Glenn, "I met Nelson in 1984 when we both worked in Tommy Hilfiger's first clothing store in New York City. We instantly became very close friends, carefree, adventurous, silly, and always had a blast no matter what we were doing. Now all these years later, we have some wrinkles and life battle-scars but the laughter, loving friendship and loyalty to each other remains. And we're both thinner and in way better shape than we were back then!

Not too long after we met, Nelson decided to move to Los Angeles. I agreed to drive across the country with him, so, one early morning in the summer of 1986 we crawled into his tiny sub-compact car and headed west with a map and trunk full of his belongings. We sang, played silly word games and laughed until we cried every day while we drove. Lord knows how, but six days later we made it to LA, and our friendship was solidified forever.

Nelson moved back to New York only a few months later. I thought he had gotten Hollywood out of his system but alas, he did move back there in 1990, and that time it was for 20 years. It was difficult to see each other often and we did the best we could. Work and Nelson's family in Philadelphia brought him back to the east coast from time to time and I managed to get out to visit him a few times. What strikes me when I think back now is how often we spoke, sometimes several times a day. How the hell did we manage that with only landlines and answering machines?

Now that we live in the same city again we see each other as much as possible. Dinners with too much wine, weekend trips with too much wine, or meeting after work for some wine... Nelson and I both share a love of food (and did I mention wine?). We love to get together, either alone or with friends, and eat and drink our way through a menu. What could be more fun?

We also both have a passion for running... and we've both run many marathons (Nelson more than I). We got to run the same marathon only once, the New York City Marathon in 2011. That day Nelson got us all-access press passes which was a God-send. We ended up being able to lounge in the press tent before the race and got special treatment at the finish line, too. We made our way into VIP areas and private corporate tents… just because we could. Everywhere we go together is a party (even the time I was in the hospital with appendicitis!). My favorite part of the day, however, was at the starting line when all 25,000 runners were being corralled into position. I heard a group of Australians talking. I got their attention and asked if they knew who Nelson was. Of course they did, since he's a big star there, so instead of stretching or peeing in the bushes like everyone else, Nelson had to pose for pictures with the Aussie runners. He still scolds me for blowing his cover."

As callow youths, we rarely recognize the finite nature of life. With experience we must embrace time… **Carpe Diem** (seize the day). There's no telling if or when we will have moments like that again… so recognizing and cherishing them as they unfold is the secret to happy ageing.

Pull out your calendar. What is the next significant milestone you can celebrate? It may be time to get started on planning a party.

An important part of any social gathering? Good manners. You know by now whom you can trust to behave and add to the fun, rather than worry about who will act up and detract from it.

In the world of celebrity journalism, some celebrities exhibit more grace than others. From my own experience, I have been most impressed by Tom Cruise, Tobey Maguire, Zac Efron and Joseph Gordon Levitt—who will actually stand up to greet and shake hands, as proper gentlemen should. You'd be surprised how many use the 'I'm sick, let's not shake hands' excuse (such as Jake Gyllenhaal) but isn't that what hand-sanitizer is for? Angelina Jolie and Carey Mulligan benefitted from taking etiquette classes while preparing for their period films, *The Good Shepherd* and *The Great Gatsby*, respectively. Good manner are for everyone and make you feel good about yourself so you can, in turn, be more gracious to others. My biggest pet peeve in this department is lateness. An admittedly time-obsessed person working in a time-obsessed business, I am never more disappointed in a 'star' than when he or she disrespects the scores of people they inconvenience by chronic, unnecessary lateness… especially in an industry where time literally is money. Vin Diesel's horseplay and high-jinx on a junket for one of the *Fast & Furious* films wound up having the LA fire department shutting down the entire tour day, leaving the studio holding the debt… and all the assembled press without their interviews. The next day, to make matters worse, he showed up more than four hours late (sulking) and I was one of those poor suckers sweating it out on a hot outdoor concrete location for him to finally grace us with a few minutes of chat time. More recently, uber-talented Justin Timberlake, who generally has a reputation for being very considerate of his underlings, let a day of out-of-town interviews run so many hours over schedule that some journalists missed their interviews, airplane flights or both altogether—a huge expense and inconvenience for all concerned. It's kooky to think that the publicity machine that generates the fortune and fame for these people seems to so frequently distress them. Maybe they're in the wrong line of work. Suck it up, people! That's why it's called 'work', right? Fortunately, like so many other qualities and characteristics of us silly humans, time tends to make us more conscientious and compassionate. It's very rare for mature celebrities to behave in such a manner. Rihanna may leave her dressing room trashed for someone else to clean up, but you can bet that Reba McEntire never would!

No one knows manners better than my pal Patsy Rowe, author of **Business Etiquette,** *who manages to always be impeccable without ever coming over as haughty. I thought this was an excellent opportunity to ask her about good manners in a modern world, which apply not only to parties, but to all aspects of our daily lives!*

NELSON: "Where along the way did society lose good manners and why?"

PATSY: "There has been a sharp decline in manners over the past 20 years. I feel this is due to two factors: firstly, the influence of television where 'role models' behave badly and are laughed at, swear and are ignored, are violent and are admired; secondly, many families today are single mothers or mothers who go to work. In either case they arrive home at the end of the day to start work again: cook a meal, iron a shirt, cut lunches and help with homework… there is neither time nor energy left to even notice when manners are slipping let alone persist in teaching them. Interesting point: if you don't have good manners yourself, you can't pass them on!"

NELSON: "What celebrity, in your opinion, exemplifies good manners?"

PATSY: Everyone who comes into contact with Hugh Jackman comments on how courteous he is. Since two of the main factors in being courteous are consideration for the feelings of others and thoughtfulness it would seem Hugh covers every base."

NELSON: "Does etiquette mean/matter more as we age?"

PATSY: "Absolutely. And this is part of the problem too many young adults face when they enter the workforce. They may have rolled their eyes when mom went on about table manners or introducing people correctly, but when they're confronted with situations where they don't know the correct thing to do or say, they may well come across as being awkward or worse, standoffish and unfriendly. Manners are the oil that lubricate our daily lives so we glide through life smoothly, giving us confidence so that we make others feel at ease and view us in the best possible light and want to be friends with us, employ us or do business with us. Being well mannered is a win-win situation."

NELSON: "So how can we instill good manners in others without seeming pushy?"

PATSY: "The best way to teach is by example. Every day we're being judged in three ways: how we look, how we speak and how we behave. If our manners are good and we're polished and self-assured, we're judged favorably and often people will take a mental note of our popularity and copy, particularly children and teenagers. As adults in the workplace, we can read books or enrol in courses that cover the basics because, after all, having good manners simply means knowing what to do, when to do it and most importantly, how to do it."

NELSON: "How can one apply manners to social media? The Internet is rife with trolls and bullies!"

PATSY: "Never write anything you wouldn't say face to face. It's a world forum, so emails and texting can finish up on the other side of the world instantly. 'Sit' on an angry message. Write it to let off steam if it helps you to feel better but don't hit the 'send' button until you've cooled off. As far as sites such as Facebook are concerned, spiteful or derogatory remarks are cowardly and unacceptable. Remember the golden rule and 'Treat others the way you would like to be treated'… do this and you'll be a person of style, confidence and charm."

Don't put off 'til tomorrow what you can celebrate today. A letter from the President, a certificate from the Queen, or a mention on morning television seems like a small reward for living to be 100, so why wait to make an occasion festive? Kids seem to have all the fun with their birthday parties… teenagers of every culture are celebrated with big parties (bar mitzvah… confirmation… quinceañera…) and much is made of turning 18 or 21. After that, it seems like a big blow out only rolls around every decade. In Korea, there is a ritual called *hwangap*. Originally it was celebrated for a person's 60th birthday, but with prolonged life span, that has shifted to 70 (considering it's based on the zodiacal calendar, I assume there must be some fuzzy math there). You have to hand it to the Asian culture for respecting and revering its elder citizens.

File this under 'ghosts of birthdays past!' Did you miss out on a particular milestone birthday celebration? Prove that you can go back again and throw yourself a blow-out bash. Imagine having a 'sweet 16', 'sporty 40' or even a '29 again' themed party and the great reaction your friends will have. I guarantee that they'll want to be there to help join in the retro-fun.

What about celebrating for the sake of it? If you look at the calendar, there seems to be some kind of holiday every week, from National Pancake Day to Arbor Day. I read about someone who threw annual 'Pooh Parties' in honor of author A A Milne's birth. Some of the best get-togethers I ever had were planned for no 'good' reason at all. I bought a new piece of art, a lovely mid-century Tuscan oil painting, and couldn't wait to show it off, so I threw an 'art party' and displayed my humble collection of pieces, serving wine and cheese while a guitarist I hired strummed Italian classics in a corner.

I was so impressed with the musical skills I was able to find on that online site that I got it into my head to find a harpist. That alone became the impetus for my next bash: A gods and goddesses-themed garden party. While the toga-clad, laurel-wreathed harpist sat and strummed, my guests arrived in their heavenly attire that ranged from the sublime (Cleopatra, Ganesha) to the ridiculous (my buddy Marc came as a 'valley girl' and constantly said, "Oh my God"). Even with my elaborate Poseidon costume, complete with trident and assorted shells sewn onto my toga, the prize for most original had to go to Gena, who fashioned herself a dress made out of maps and called herself Atlas. We had a ball.

Once we reach middle age there are MORE reasons to hail than ever: A clean bill of health at your next physical, a raise at work, the last kid finally leaves home…. Songwriter Carol Connors has tea-parties for her cat-loving friends and they'd go all out with a feline-inspired dress code. You may think 'Oh, that could only happen in Hollywood,' but it is actually immensely amusing to sit around a table with Charlene Tilton, Rhonda Shear and Marilyn McCoo while they pour tea to purr-fection. Maybe a friend is nursing a broken heart after a divorce or bad break-up… throw them a surprise party just to show you love them. Is someone moving? Have a house 'cooling' instead of waiting for the 'house warming'. Put your mind to it and there are limitless possibilities.

When my springer spaniel turned 15, we had a barking good time with my friends who loved her and an assortment of her poochie pals who came for a play date enhanced with lots of canine-themed decorations and snacks. Anyone can have a New Year's Eve party… for years I hosted a traditional countdown to midnight in other time zones, so everyone could stop by for a champagne toast (and a bowl of my famous vegetarian chilli) and still be home in time to get a full night's sleep… but why not have a New Year's Day breakfast instead? A lucky and lovely way to kick off the new year. Perhaps you just repainted the living room or got some new furniture… show it off with an intimate cocktail party. Starting a book club will turns your celebrations cerebral and you can even theme your meetings around whatever literary works you're sharing. Imagine putting together a *Fifty Shades of Grey* luncheon!

> *Unless you're Shirley MacLaine, this is the only lifetime you're going to get. Be sure to honor and celebrate it as often and as festively as possible!*

These kinds of parties don't have to be expensive. You can make them as simple or elaborate as your whims and wages allow. The key for any successful occasion really boils down to putting together the right guest list. Who among your inner circle is the most social, sporting and good humored? If those are the people whom you invite, a simple pizza party and scrabble tournament will be a blast. Keep in mind that when you are an invited guest to any gathering, you have an obligation to help make it a success. Check your problems at the door and be an active social participant. That can range from helping to set the table or clear the dishes, keeping the conversation going, or just laughing at someone's less-than-hilarious jokes.

Unlike my globe-trotting granny, the more time passes, the less inclined I am to travel. (It's a good thing I live in NYC… it's like the whole world comes to me.) I can be a true Cancerian homebody… nester… hermit, if you will. I'd almost always rather have everyone come hang out at my place than schlep off somewhere else. And what's the key to being a good host? Don't just throw a party, go to it, too! You should always be prepared enough that you can relax and have just as much fun as your guests.

Not only a handy social skill, but a way to be a nicer person: if you're any place where disparate people have gathered, take an objective look around and pick out the person who is the 'wallflower'; in other words the loneliest or meekest soul you see. Offer to get them a beverage or simply strike up a chat… any opening line will do. (From "What brings you here?" to "Can you believe the weather we're having?") You might wind up meeting the most interesting person there or get some juicy tidbit of gossip… or, best case scenario, make a new friend. I moan a lot about the inconvenience and tedium of jury duty service, but the last time I served in a NYC courtroom, I ended up taking a lunch break with a young guy I'd probably never in a million years have met otherwise. We had so much fun conversing that, when our time was complete, we shared a taxi uptown and went out to dinner together. He does some kind of hi-tech job I'll never understand and his girlfriend is a scientist researching cures for different kinds of cancers. An absolute silver lining to civil service!

My parents have a core group of friends with whom they dine every Friday night at their local country club. The friends rarely see each other anytime/anywhere else, but those weekly gatherings are sacrosanct. If anyone has a birthday that week, it's celebrated and Mother and Dad always get the extra occasion of their wedding anniversary celebrated too. Marking achievements can be part of your routine without feeling routine.

While mothers and fathers get designated days of honor on the calendar, my Mom and I decided during my childhood to have an annual 'Nelson and Mom's Day' just for us. We randomly selected March 19, which isn't near anyone else's birthday. Throughout my youth, it was a day I was allowed to play hookey from school… or we'd have a special meal… or exchange little presents. Even now, we still send cards or gifts and either visit or have long telephone conversations. March 19th will always be OUR day. Why not start up a tradition like that with some of your friends or loved ones?

One milestone that we all eventually reach is death, but unless you're an excellent pre-planner, there isn't much say to be had when it comes to how the occasion should be marked. Most people, especially those with children and assets, include 'final arrangements' in their will and may even pre-pay for those expenses. But you can also give some thought to how you'd like your survivors to celebrate you. Do it while you're still healthy and full of life and it won't be as morbid as it may sound and at least you'll ensure it's carried out according to your wishes.

Ever wonder what your obituary may say about you? Here's an idea:

write it up now and make sure it includes everything you want it to say. Don't get maudlin about it. Sit down and write up an autobiography. You might actually find yourself enjoying the process of telling your story. Share it with someone close to you, in case there's anything you're forgetting and then type it up and save it with all your other important papers/ files for your loved ones. They will appreciate not having the burden when the times comes, as well as knowing that your history will be accurately saved for posterity. My dad's been having a hell of a good time tweaking his for years! At this rate, it's going to be a three-part mini-series!

The Irish hold 'wakes' for the departed and these often turn into a party of sorts for a community of family, friends and neighbors. Depending on the personalities of the parties involved, these ceremonies can get quite boisterous. My friend, Julia, lost her long battle against cancer but was quite adamant that she be remembered with a party and not a maudlin rite filled with tears and black attire. Instead, on what would have been their wedding anniversary, her widower threw the summertime beach party she had wanted… and her favorite Pinot Grigio was free-flowing as everyone remembered and toasted her *joie de vivre*.

Whatever you decide, make sure you put it in writing and let your next of kin in on the plan. While you're at it, consider being an organ donor if you haven't already… it's a wonderful act and as simple to indicate your wishes as adding it to your driver's license registration.

I started this book writing about the beginning of my life and unafraid to bring it to a close acknowledging that life will inevitably, one day end. I'm hoping that will be in the very distant future, but as you've read in these pages… it's the years in between that define our legacies. I'm honored to have been asked to put my experiences, impressions and musings down on paper not only in the hope that you will find them entertaining and inspiring, but also for me to be able to review and reminisce. Who knows? There may yet be another edition to come with all my future discoveries. After all, this is my prime time.

Nelson Aspen

50+ FUN AND GAMES

I've mentioned my penchant for trivia… a few personalized questions were thrown into Glenn's toast for me at my 50th birthday party, and, as a kid, answering questions correctly at the dinner table was how Dad calculated my weekly allowance. Everyone loves a good round of Jeopardy! or Trivial Pursuit, so I thought I'd put this quiz together to test your knowledge of middle-age pop culture (I told you I was a frustrated school teacher! I only wish I were with you in person to administer and grade your test results, ha ha). See how many you can answer correctly. You'll find the answers and how to score yourself accordingly at the end of the book. Good luck!

1 Who scored a massive hit record with Who's Sorry Now? and became the best-selling female recording artist to date?
2 And what female finally eclipsed her with the memorable album She's So Unusual?

3 Name the two children of John and Jackie Kennedy.

4 On what date was JFK assassinated and in what US city?

5 What was Richard Nixon's middle name?

6 And who was his first vice-president, who resigned?

7 Who was the only non-elected US President?

8 On *The Flintstones*, what was Fred's 'happy phrase'?

9 Who wed John Lennon and was blamed by many for breaking up The Beatles?

10 What was the name of the apartment building where Lennon last lived?

11 On *The Munsters*, what famous ghoul was Grampa supposed to be?

12 On *I Dream of Jeannie*, what body feature did censors not allow Barbara Eden to reveal?

13 What was the name of the dance craze made famous by Chubby Checker?

14 Who was the original "Tammy" in the movie series of films?

15 What Soho street was considered the center of Britain's fashion scene?

16 Who played "Fanny Brice" in both the Broadway and Hollywood versions of FUNNY GIRL?

17 Name Marilyn Monroe's final film.

18 What UK TV show featured the characters John Steed and Emma Peel?

19 On the *Batman* TV series, what was the name of the elderly aunt who lives at Wayne Manor?

20 What TV show was set on the Ponderosa Ranch?

21 Name the rock opera written and performed by The Who.

22 Who played James Bond after Sean Connery?

23 What US state was the setting for the TV series *Dynasty*?

24 Name the dog on *The Jetsons*.

25 Where was the NYC Marathon run until 1970?

26 How many gold medals were won by Mark Spitz in the 1972 Olym-

pics?

27 How many times did the New York Yankees win the World Series in the 1970s?

28 Who beat Babe Ruth's home run record in 1974?

29 What filmmaker was known as 'The Master of Disaster'?

30 Name Billy Joel's first album.

31 Who played TV's Wonder Woman?

32 On *The Sonny & Cher Show*, who appeared with the couple at the end of every episode?

33 Who was the housekeeper on *The Brady Bunch* and which actress played her?

34 What served as the family car on *The Partridge Family*?

35 In the *Peanuts* comics, who was Snoopy's sidekick?

36 Who was the original blonde on *Charlie's Angels*?

37 On what kind of TV show did Dustin Hoffman's Tootsie work?

38 On *Mork & Mindy*, from what planet did Robin Williams' character hail?

39 'Greed is Good' is a line from what film?

40 Name Jerry Seinfeld's postman neighbor.

41 What zip code became famous as a result of a TV show set in Beverly Hills?

42 How many Spice Girls were there?

43 What brand of underwear did Mark Wahlberg advertise?

44 In what year did Tiger Woods begins his professional golf career?

45 Name the figure skater who attacked Nancy Kerrigan, her competitor.

46 Name the late comic actress who was married to Gene Wilder.

47 What *All in the Family* spin-off series starred Bea Arthur?

48 Who owned the apartment complex on Melrose Place and what actress portrayed her?

49 When it went off the air in 1986, this soap opera was the long running one on TV. What was it?

50 Who advised, "Mr Gorbachev, tear down this wall"?

ANSWERS

1 Connie Francis

2 Cyndi Lauper

3 Caroline & JFK Jr. (John John)

4 November 22, 1963. Dallas, Texas

5 Milhous

6 Spiro T Agnew

7 Gerald Ford

8 Yabba Dabba Doo

9 Yoko Ono

10 NYC's The Dakota

11 Count Dracula

12 Her belly button

13 The Twist

14 Debbie Reynolds

15 Carnaby Street

16 Barbra Streisand

17 The Misfits

18 *The Avengers*

19 Aunt Harriet

20 Bonanza

21 Tommy

22 Roger Moore

23 Colorado

24 Astro

25 Central Park

26 Seven

27 Twice

28 Hank Aaron

29 Irwin Allen

30 The Stranger

31 Lynda Carter

32 Their daughter, Chastity

33 Alice Nelson was played by Ann B Davis

34 A multi-colored school bus

35 Woodstock the bird

36 Farrah Fawcett-Majors

37 A soap opera

38 Planet Ork

39 Wall Street

40 Newman

41 *90210*

42 Five

43 Calvin Klein

44 1996

45 Tonya Harding

46 Gilda Radner

47 Maude

48 Amanda Woodward, played by Heather Locklear

49 *Search for Tomorrow*

50 President Ronald Reagan

SCORING

41–50 correct answers. You are middle-aged and marvelous! Congratulations on your broad knowledge of pop culture events from the latter half of the 20th century. You deserve a glass of Boone's Farm Strawberry Hill wine.

31–40 correct answers. Not bad. But you might want to consider B Vitamins to help improve your memory. It seems you're a bit fuzzy on details from the past.

21–30 correct answers. You must have been partying too much in your youth. Were you paying much attention to the world around you?

11–20 correct answers. Are you sure you're middle aged?

0–10 correct answers. Step into the time machine. I'll meet you in 1960 and we'll go through this together.

ACKNOWLEDGMENTS

Everybody's individual journey into and through middle age will be as unique as a fingerprint, but I hope that by sharing my experiences (so far) they have been helpful and/or enlightening. Most of all, I hope they have entertained you regardless of your current age. After all, informing and entertaining are my true callings. If you tuck this book away on a shelf and pull it out again in a few years' time, you may re-read some passages and find yourself identifying with or challenging some of my musings as your own perspectives ripen on the vine. Ha… I bet that if I re-read it in a few years, I'll be similarly surprised by what I did or didn't know way back in 2014.

As time goes by, it seems to pick up pace. In our childhoods and teens, we anticipated all the freedoms we associated with adulthood. Even in our 20s and 30s (if we were smart), we were looking forward with antici- pation of the rewards ahead of us. No matter where, 'chronologically' the exact middle of our lives occur, one thing we must be sure to do is to live until we die. Time is a precious commodity and even the earliest risers, never have enough hours in the day. If there's something you want to accomplish, get started as soon as you put down this book. You have one, sacred life: Use it before you lose it.

If we are blessed enough to live many healthy years, it is our responsibility and privilege to squeeze the most out of them that we can. Please share your experiences with me on Twitter (@nelsonaspen) or via 'snail mail' letters to New Holland Publishing… and we'll continue on our trip through time together.

Every person who contributed their stories and is mentioned in these pages has my very deepest appreciation. They're all very special individuals.

Also special: My friends at New Holland including editor Simona Hill, and especially Linda Williams, who encouraged and supported the concept for this book. My managemet at Bravo Talent, Chris Giannopoulos and Alicia Dewhurst. The fellas at Pacific Television who get me on the air every day and keep me up to date on everything 20-year-old guys need to know. JAR, an unexpected and most cherished source of love.

In 2014, my friend of three decades, Louan Gideon, whom you met in these pages, succumbed to the return of cancer. She added so much to my life in so many ways and will always be a guardian angel for all of us who loved her.

ABOUT THE AUTHOR

Nelson Aspen (born 1963) began his career as a child actor and graduated to working on-and-off camera in daytime television in New York City. In 1990, he moved to Los Angeles and began reporting for various outlets while also expanding his expertise as a health and fitness professional. In 1991, while in the UK to instruct Princess Diana's personal training staff in new fitness trends, he was invited to appear on the national morning news program, *This Morning*. He has been working on international morning television and radio ever since as an entertainment journalist and TV presenter. It is quite accurate to say that millions of people have woken up with Nelson over the last two decades! (In fact, his most recent cabaret show was entitled *Wake Up With Nelson!*).

In addition to being extensively published in magazines and newspapers focusing on fitness and show-business, Nelson is a sought-after public speaker and master of ceremonies. He is the author of *Let's Dish Up a Dinner Party, Sacred Blood, Hollywood Insider: Exposed* and *Dinner at Nel-*

son's. In 2013, he launched his own web series, @ *Nelson's,* and continues to interview A-list celebrities, cover major showbiz and news events and file daily live reports to Australia's #1 morning show, *Sunrise.*

Having returned to full-time residency in Manhattan in 2012, Nelson has entered his 50s not only busier than ever, but at the peak of his prowess as one of the industry's leading, most trusted reporters and personalities. In 2014, he was recognized by the Publicists Guild of America with a nomination for International Media Journalist of the Year.

You may visit him at www.nelsonaspen.com